On Paper

ADDISON GALLERY OF AMERICAN ART   PHILLIPS ACADEMY   ANDOVER MASSACHUSETTS

On Paper

MASTERWORKS FROM THE ADDISON COLLECTION

This project has been made possible through the generous contributions of Cynthia Eaton Bing, Keith and Mary Kauppila, John and Louise MacMillan, Anthony M. Schulte, the Bernard and Louise Palitz Exhibitions Fund, and the Michael and Fiona Scharf Publications Fund.

Addison Gallery of American Art
Phillips Academy
180 Main Street
Andover, Massachusetts 01810
Tel. 978.749.4015
Fax 978.749.4025
www.addisongallery.org

ISBN: 1-879886-51-0

Library of Congress Control Number:
2002113370

Editor: Joseph N. Newland, Q.E.D.
Designer: Bill Anton | Service Station
Printer: Toppan Printing Co., Ltd., Japan

Cover and jacket images (left to right),
see pages:
Front
173, 303, 137, 282, 139, 102
Back
159, 191, 267, 213, 231, 163

Additional images on jacket flaps,
see pages:
Front flap
113, 129, 187, 149, 321, 76
Back flap
181, 313, 101, 127, 99

Foreword ADAM D. WEINBERG

P aper was invented in China some two thousand years ago. As an alternative to the weight of metal and stone and without the fragility of clay tablets, it provided a means for, literally, conveying information from one person to another. Paper was a transmission device that could be rolled or folded, discarded or reused. Unlike a text or an artwork that is permanently affixed to a surface and is in effect a "destination"—a stele, a relief, a mural—information and images on paper could and were readily transportable and transferable. Furthermore, the surface of paper accepts pigments and media in a fundamentally different way than other supports, giving pigment applied to paper unique characteristics. Artists are *drawn* to using paper for many reasons—its lightness, flexibility, affordability, mutability, and a vast array of physical variables.

This is the first Addison Gallery publication to examine exclusively the museum's finest unique works on paper. It reveals the range of our holdings: in size—from works measuring nearly eight feet long to ones roughly four inches square; in media—as diverse as graphite, charcoal, crayon, and chalk to ink, oil, acrylic, transparent and opaque watercolor; in support—ranging from wove paper, laid paper, and toned paper to rice paper, graph paper, tracing paper, and paper board; and in application— through means such as hand, brush, rubbing, tracing, transferring, mounting, and collaging.

This book is conceived to serve several functions. First, it is intended to make art accessible that is not regularly on view to the public. Because works on paper are fragile and their pigments often fugitive, they are on display infrequently. Moreover, since nearly one-third of the Addison's fourteen thousand objects are works on paper, it is impossible to have more than the tiniest percentage on view at any given time. Second, by selecting some of the very finest examples in the collection to represent a range of periods, styles, artists, and techniques, we are able to study them in detail, delight in their beauty, and take pride in the perspicacity of our curatorial predecessors. And third, we can provide "a primer" for the consideration of the purposes and artistic intentions that guide an artist's choice of this medium. Rather than present a conventional chronological view of two hundred years of American works on paper, we have chosen to organize this survey into four broad categories: the work as study: illustrating the ways in which artists use a work on paper as a tool for developing ideas, working out parts, or trying compositions; the work as record: illustrating record of place or event, as a medium for gathering information, or as the commitment of an experience to memory; the work as product: illustrating the work on paper as a fully realized artwork in which the medium of paper is chosen for its particular characteristics and its ability to make an independent artistic statement; and the work as concept: illustrating the work on paper as evidence of an artist's ideas and as a record of process and system. As with any curatorial construct, our assignment of objects to categories was somewhat subjective, yet we feel that this way of considering them will allow greater understanding of why and how these delicate, revealing objects were made.

Accordingly, the Addison invited four leading art historians to write short texts introducing each section. We are grateful to Carol Clark, Trevor Fairbrother, Faye Hirsch, and Linda Konheim Kramer for wholeheartedly embracing this speculative but energizing venture, and for the elegant and insightful execution of their writing assignments.

The selection of the works was made by Susan C. Faxon, Associate Director and Curator of Art before 1950. Guided first by the quality of the works and secondly by their ability to illuminate chronological, physical, and typological diversity, she also strove to reflect the character and depth of the Addison Gallery's holdings. Working with Jennifer Mergel, Addison Curatorial Fellow in 2001–3, Susan spent countless hours looking at and debating the merits of each work to be included. Paper conservator Leslie Paisley of the Williamstown Art Conservation Center gave assistance essential to this process by examining and assessing every object selected, often providing new and exact technical information as well as insights into the works' creation. The curator joins me in thanking Leslie for both her good counsel and her enthusiasm for this project.

The Addison Gallery gratefully acknowledges the many collectors, artists, and Phillips Academy alumni who have kept faith with the museum and demonstrated their commitment by donating many precious works. There are objects in this book that were given even before the museum building was completed in 1931, and others that were given as recently as last year with the desire to further fill out the drawing collection in time for this publication and an exhibition which provided a focus for its research. We also deeply appreciate the support of several individuals who, when approached about this project, recognized its critical short- and long-term importance to the museum. Keith and Mary Kauppila and John and Louise MacMillan deserve special mention for their early and generous financial commitments. We would also like to thank Anthony M. Schulte and Cynthia Eaton Bing for their support of this effort and their ongoing contributions to the Gallery. The research and presentation of our historical collection, and its ensuing publication, are supported through the Exhibitions Fund recently established by Bernard and Louise Palitz. The Michael and Fiona Scharf Publications Fund is critical to assuring that all of the Addison's books and catalogues are produced at the highest level. Additional acknowledgments are due Mike and Penny Winton, whose early support of the Addison's Curatorial Fellowship enabled much of the research presented here.

Above all, I would like to acknowledge Susan Faxon for her passion and perseverance. Because of her enthusiasm, what began as a modest catalogue has become a keystone collection publication for the museum. This book will join *Addison Gallery of American Art, 65 Years: A Selective Catalogue* of 1996 and the forthcoming catalogue of the Gallery's photography collection to become the foundation on which all future collection research at the Addison will be built.

Introduction DIRECTING A COLLECTION SUSAN C. FAXON

Drawing couples a directness of means with an ease of revision. This gives thought and feeling a direct access to visibility. The tools are simple…something to make a mark, an eraser, a sheet of paper. Each material has a particular quality, the choice of which gives a drawing its "color." Charcoal is dry and burnt, pastel is thick and luminous, conté crayon is crisp and translucent. Different papers are dense or light, resistant or absorbent, bright or dull. The flexibility of materials in combination is essential to the unique content of drawing.

Drawing can present conclusions. It can record the spontaneous appearance of a thought. It can contain the results of an investigation into the nature of relationships. Or, it can be the clear declaration of a complex idea.

Drawing is also a process of testing differences. In the process of questioning distinctions, the mind, eye, and hand sometimes shift in and out of synchronization. Speculation, or the suspension of decision, leads below the surface of order into the ambiguity of conflicting perceptions. Drawing becomes a meditation on the meaning of certainty. Erasures pile up. Containing the archeology of its own doubts, the work cuts across the conventions of finish. A tissue of overlaid impulses, the tangle of contradictions suddenly implodes into a drawing.

— Mel Bochner (1981)

I n his musing on the drawing as a tool for recording, learning, explaining, and thinking, Mel Bochner outlines the distinct roles and purposes of the work on paper, roles that have served as the organizing framework for this selection of objects from the Addison's collection. Our divisions—work as record, work as study, work as product, work as concept—are echoed in Bochner's words:

> Drawing can present conclusions. It can record the spontaneous appearance of a thought. It can contain the results of an investigation into the nature of relationships. Or, it can be the clear declaration of a complex idea.[1]

When Bochner wrote these words in 1981, the Addison's collection of works on paper amply proved the essential value of such works as illuminators of artists' ideas and intentions, or, to paraphrase Bochner, as containers of the "archeology" of an investigation. Forty-five years earlier, the first director of the Addison Gallery of American Art, Charles H. Sawyer, had recognized the work on paper as a record of artistic decisions. His report on the fifth anniversary of the opening of the museum described the special appeal of drawings and his dedication to their place in the collection:

> The most personal, the most direct approach to an artist's works is through the medium of his drawings. Through them, we can see more clearly the workings of his mind, study his intentions and examine his execution. The drawing, whether complete in itself or only a fragment of the completed work, is our first and last resort for a real understanding of the language of art itself. It is, therefore, especially appropriate for an educational institution to build its collections upon the foundation of good drawings.[2]

This essay traces the foundation of the collection of works on paper through the tenures of the museum's five directors, tracing, as it were, the archeology of directorial decision-making and the generational values that came into play over the years.

When the Addison Gallery of American Art opened its doors on the Phillips Academy campus in May 1931, it was the proud repository for a collection of over five hundred works of art deliberately and carefully limited to works of American manufacture. The founding donor, Phillips alumnus and trustee Thomas Cochran, had gathered a selection of works of the highest caliber, including masterpieces by Winslow Homer, Thomas Eakins, James M. Whistler, Maurice Prendergast, Abbott Thayer, John Singer Sargent, and John Twachtman. While the founding collection could be considered traditional in taste, the donor actually espoused an expansive collecting mission. As he wrote in his deed of gift,

> The word "art," as used in this letter, may be broadly interpreted by the Board
> of Trustees so as to include any American works of art and craftsmanship
> in addition to paintings, sculpture, and silver.[3]

The other works of art or craftsmanship encompassed pewter and glass, furniture and textiles, photographs and prints, and all varieties of works on paper—works in graphite, ink, transparent and opaque watercolor, charcoal, and pastel. Among them were drawings by Reginald Marsh, George Bellows, and Sargent; watercolors by George Inness and Charles Burchfield; pastels by Whistler and Mary Cassatt; three sketchbooks by John La Farge; as well as seven watercolors by Homer, thirteen watercolors by Arthur B. Davies, and six by Prendergast.

The initial group was an impressive one, but the growth of the collection was left to the vision of the museum's directors and generations of future donors. In spite of the extraordinary largesse of the original gift, the purchase fund was never enlarged, and almost immediately its buying power proved limited. In fact, in 1933, shortly after the museum's opening, director Charles Sawyer wrote, "One of the most serious problems of a small museum is to broaden the scope of its collections without sacrificing a standard of quality."[4]

Sawyer set out to craft a collecting policy that championed works on paper as the proper corollary to the paintings. He also embarked on a lively exhibition program that presented watercolors and drawings to the public. The popular success of *Water Colors by Twelve Americans* in 1933 was followed by an expanded version, *Water Colors by Contemporary Americans*, two years later; in between Sawyer kept up a steady diet of works on paper exhibitions, borrowed from Macbeth Galleries, the American Federation of Arts, and the College Art Association. He was convinced that this portion of the collection was ripe for development:

> It is the hope of the Art Committee that the collection of water colors and
> drawings will eventually be as representative as the collection of oil paintings.
> Additions to the latter collection are subject to the most careful study and

are selected with regard for the present high standard of quality. There is a splendid opportunity to form, at small expense, a fine collection of water colors and drawings which will represent every phase of American art.[5]

In 1935 the Addison acquired the largest number of watercolors and drawings yet, acquisitions that included works by Thomas Hart Benton, Guy Pène Du Bois, Eastman Johnson, Raphael Soyer, Preston Dickinson, and John Marin. In addition, Sawyer was able to add two sheets of sketches by Thomas Sully, three ink and crayon studies by Benjamin West, two sketchbooks by Albert Bierstadt, and four stellar drawings by John Singleton Copley. A year later, on the fifth anniversary of the opening of the Addison Gallery, Sawyer could say with pride, "While many gaps inevitably remain, this collection is already one of the most comprehensive in its field, and with revisions and additions which experience will suggest, should continue to grow both in quality and scope."[6]

Sawyer's fervent commitment to contemporary works on paper led him to initiate two significant exhibitions in 1938. The first, a survey of work by Charles and Maurice Prendergast organized with the close assistance of Charles, cemented the museum's relationship with the Prendergast estate, bringing many of the brothers' works on paper to the collection over the ensuing years. That year Sawyer also worked with John Sloan to mount the artist's first retrospective, which included, in addition to its thirty-three paintings, thirty drawings as well as eighty-three prints. There is no doubt that both the artist and director/curator felt that the works on paper were an essential and illuminating element in the presentation of the full scope of Sloan's oeuvre, and, following the exhibition, the Addison added a major Sloan painting and the graphite drawing *Nude on a Chaise Longue*.

At Sawyer's departure for the Worcester Art Museum in 1940, he could look back with tremendous satisfaction on the museum's first decade. Handed an extraordinary empty building and five hundred core objects, Sawyer had added life and energy. His contributions to the fledgling institution were grounded in his conviction that the art object has an ability to illuminate and enrich. He assured that the Addison would hold the work on paper as a "useful instrument for advancing our understanding of American art."[7]

Having assisted Sawyer and served as the museum's art instructor, Bartlett H. Hayes, Jr., took over the reins as the museum's second director. Where Sawyer's focus was founded on establishing the museum's tradition of connoisseurship, Hayes's belief in art's power to teach and his dedication to the museum's educational mission meant that he brought a highly didactic approach to the collecting, publishing, and exhibiting efforts. One of the great art educators of his generation, he embraced every avenue—print media, radio, TV, traveling exhibitions—to introduce concepts of contemporary art to both the students at Andover and national audiences.

His first major directorial enterprise, *The Architecture of a Painting: Edward Hopper's "Manhattan Bridge Loop,"* was an exhibition designed to illustrate the choices an artist makes in the construction of a painting through the display of preliminary studies on paper and direct quotes from the artist's experience. For the enterprise Hopper not only gave the Addison an extremely rare and candid explanation of his process but also donated two illuminating studies and a vintage photograph that remained after the exhibition.

The Hopper exhibition set the model for others organized by Hayes that explained difficult artistic issues and enhanced the collection as well. In 1948, Hayes worked closely with Hans Hofmann to mount the first major museum retrospective of the work of an Abstract Expressionist painter. Hayes's goal was to use Hofmann's oeuvre as a means of tracing his development as an artist, his influence as a teacher, and to show the progression toward abstraction in his long career. Given its avowed didactic purpose, this exhibition was careful to include a substantial number of the artist's drawings and studies, the first Hofmann exhibition to do so. From it the Addison purchased the four ink figure studies that had been the linchpins of the installation as well as two landscapes on paper.

Ten years later, as Hayes was organizing a definitive survey of one hundred years of American drawings, he recognized that the Addison's works on paper collection was "far more important than he had realized by comparison with other institutions."[8] *The American Line*, a project that included both a traveling show and an innovative publication of the same name, was based on the Addison collection, to which Hayes added, especially for the occasion, significant works on paper by artists such as Arthur Dove, Georgia O'Keeffe, Saul Steinberg, and Marsden Hartley.

Hayes's long tenure as director ended with his retirement in 1968; his assistant director of four years, Christopher C. Cook, stepped into the position and set yet another innovative direction for the museum and its collection. Cook, like Hayes, was a practicing artist, a profound thinker, a dedicated teacher, and a champion of the relevance of contemporary art to students and regional audiences alike. Cook, taking an expansive approach that reflected the open questioning of his time, embarked on an exhibition program designed to provoke new ways of thinking about art and the physical materials of art-making. Dedicated to the role of the museum in teaching, Cook worked with his colleagues in the Phillips Academy Art Department on exceptional exhibitions that explored sensory perceptions through nontraditional media: light sensation in *Projections: An Exhibit of Light Images*; physical stimulation in *Feelies: The Nature of Things Perceived Through Touch*; and auditory perception in *Noise: An Examination of the Aural Environment*.

He mounted yet another conceptual exhibition based on the medium of paper: *Tell Your Life in 25 Words: Real Art Data Project Installation* invited students, staff, and faculty at Bradford College to write their life stories on single sheets of paper that were then posted on the gallery walls. Marking his own conceptual approach to art, in 1970 he assembled a catalogue called *Possibles* that consisted of sheets of paper on which were inscribed exhibition ideas that might "possibly" be produced at the Addison. His recognition of paper as a particularly appropriate medium on which to record and share more ephemeral or conceptual ideas led to the acquisition of exemplary conceptual works, including Mel Bochner's *Via Santo Spirito* and Barry

Le Va's *Tangle Distribution*, and important alumni gifts, including an ambitious series of works in opaque watercolor, graphite, and dry pigment by Carroll Dunham, and Carl Andre's pivotal collaged book *Passport*.

When Cook gave up the directorship for full-time teaching in the Art Department in 1989, he convinced artist and alumnus Jock Reynolds to take over the position. Reynolds, whose personal artistic interests included minimalism, serialization, sequence, and process, began his tenure as the fourth Addison director with energetic commitment to excellence in the museum's education programs, exhibition projects, and a collecting policy that upheld the value of the work on paper. He engineered the acquisition of four Blanche Lazzell drawings and two Charles Sheeler opaque water-color studies related to his Andover residency; he encouraged the acquisition of two illuminating studies made by Stuart Davis that related to the Addison's masterwork *Red Cart*; and he negotiated the gift of alumnus George Tooker's entire drawing archive.

A prodigious acquirer not only of art but of people, Reynolds engaged numerous previously uninterested alumni in support of the museum's efforts. In the implemen-tation of the Addison Art Drive, he brought to the collection objects by major contemporary artists such as Jasper Johns, John Chamberlain, Robert Frank, and Ad Reinhardt, among many others. Art Drive acquisitions of works on paper included formative works by Mark Rothko, Jackson Pollock, Stephen Greene, and Sol LeWitt and drawings by Carl Andre, Robert Grosvenor, Lawrence Weiner, and Michelle Stuart. In honor of Reynold's championing of the museum and encouragement of alumni involvement, alumnus Michael Scharf donated Joseph Cornell's collage *Homage to Brancusi*.

Adam D. Weinberg, who took over the directorship in 1998, merged his predecessors' dedication to the museum's teaching mission, its engagement with contemporary artists, and its exhibition and publication of the best of American art with his own reverence for the object as the salient statement of an artist's idea and process into a directorial vision of energy and excellence.

Weinberg's most innovative exhibition projects brought artists into direct contact with students and the museum. His ambitious exhibition *Sitelines* of 2002 invited nine nationally known artists to campus to work with students in the development of their site-specific installations. Created during his residency at the museum, Jason Middlebrook's eponymous drawing *Site Lines* was given to the collection to commemorate the exhibition's dynamic spirit. José Bedia's magnificent work on—and of—paper, *Islote Inaccesible, Lejano, Solo*, was donated by alumnus John Axelrod in acknowledgement of the artist's residency at the Addison the previous year.

Beyond his additions to the collection of works by Arthur Dove, Richard Pousette-Dart, Louise Nevelson, and Robert Mangold, Weinberg recognized the ability of the work on paper to delight, intrigue, energize, and challenge, and sought out drawings, watercolors, and collages by Terry Winters, Milton Avery, Norman Bluhm, and Jane Hammond, all of which make their debut in this publication. Proving that a collection is enriched not only by the single object but also by the accumulated presence of an artist's effort, Weinberg negotiated the acquisition of a group of works on paper by Sol LeWitt, part of a substantial gift that has now made the Addison's holdings of works by this pivotal twentieth-century artist one of the most important in the country.

Throughout its history, the Addison's unusual character and quality has rested in its unwavering dedication to the power of the object to teach, enrich, and engage students and the public alike. It has been steadfast in its affirmation of the importance of close and productive relationships between artists and students within the museum. As each of its five directors has made his mark on the institution, it has been in recognition of the opportunities and challenges the museum owes its audiences through the presentation of the best in American art.

The holdings of works on paper, like the entire body of the collection, have been nurtured by each director to meet the goals of founding donor Thomas Cochran to enrich lives "by helping to cultivate and foster…love of the beautiful." Whether they were produced as singular statements, as steps toward learning to see, as developments of ideas, or as records of a concept, works on paper have immediacy, tenderness, and vulnerability. They are revelatory. In Mel Bochner's words, they give "thought and feeling a direct access to visibility." In Charles Sawyer's words, "The drawing [indeed, the work on paper], whether complete in itself or only a fragment of a competed work, is our first and last resort for a real understanding of the language of art itself."

18

Notes

1. The epigraph to this essay is from Mel Bochner, *Mel Bochner: Twenty-Five Drawings, 1973–1980* (n.p, 1981), p. 5.

2. Charles H. Sawyer, *The Bulletin of the Addison Gallery of American Art*, 1936, p. 3.

3. Trustees of Phillips Academy, *Terms of Trusts and Other Records* (Andover: Phillips Academy, 1932), pp. 177–78.

4. Charles H. Sawyer, *Annual Report, Addison Gallery of American Art*, 1 October 1933, Addison Gallery Archives.

5. Charles H. Sawyer, *Annual Report, Addison Gallery of American Art*, 1 October 1935, Addison Gallery Archives.

6. Sawyer, *Bulletin*, 1936, p. 3.

7. Ibid., p. 11.

8. Summary of the Addison Gallery Art Committee Meeting held at the apartment of Mrs. Bliss Parkinson, 27 January 1959.

NOTE TO THE READER

The Addison Gallery's collection contained 2,541 works on paper as of 31 October 2003. This portion of the collection includes drawings, pastels, charcoals, oils, and watercolors on paper supports: that is, all works on paper except photographs and prints. This publication highlights almost one hundred fifty works chosen to represent the most significant aspects of the works on paper collection.

For the purposes of this publication we have organized the artworks into four general themes, each introduced by an essay, followed by the group of works assigned to that section. Within each section items are generally ordered chronologically by date.

Because this publication concentrates on works on paper, detailed descriptions of the supports have been composed; these follow the guide for classifying and describing paper published in *The Print Council of America Paper Sample Book: A Practical Guide to the Description of Paper* by Elizabeth Lunning and Roy Perkinson (1996).

The titles are those given to the artwork by the artist when known. In some cases, previously published titles and dates have been changed to reflect current research. Measurements are given in inches; height precedes width. Unless otherwise noted, measurements refer to sheet size. Inscriptions are quoted verbatim. Abbreviations for inscription locations read top to bottom, left to right, combining the first letters of "upper, center, lower" and "left, center, right." For example, u.l. signifies "upper left."

ENTRIES

SUSAN C. FAXON, **SCF**, *Associate Director and Curator of Art before 1950*

ALLISON N. KEMMERER, **ANK**, *Curator of Photography and of Art after 1950*

KLAUS KERTESS, **KK**, *Independent Curator and Author*

MAURA LYONS, **ML**, *Boston University Graduate Intern 1991–92*

JENNIFER MERGEL, **JM**, *Curatorial Fellow 2001–3*

SUSAN J. MONTGOMERY, **SJM**, *Independent Curator*

GILLIAN G. SPENCER, **GGS**, *Boston University Graduate Intern 2002–3*

ADAM D. WEINBERG, **ADW**, *Director 1999–2003*

The work as a **record** FROM VISION TO HAND FAYE HIRSCH

...I, a watchman, all-heeding and unheeded.

— Nathaniel Hawthorne, "Sights from a Steeple"

Although we know that, before photography, drawing was the primary and most immediate means by which artists could make a visual record of their world, it is difficult today to imagine how indispensable drawing once was to picturing nature and the people who inhabited it. We have come to take for granted that we can make records of any visual phenomenon, even those, like bacteria or quasars, invisible to unaided sight. Thanks to photography and electronic media, we are bombarded with visual records in such profusion that their particularities, not to mention their social significance or emotional resonance, are easily lost on us. Such images may be seized upon merely because they are sensational in some way, aberrations in the sheer spectacle of a physical world that, as it grows ever more visible, recedes into deepening shadows of disregard.

Even after the invention and diffusion of photography, of course, artists turned to paper to render in ink, pencil, charcoal, and watercolor what they saw and, increasingly, what they felt. That sensate link between vision and the hand has never been fully relinquished, and among the many drawings in the Addison Gallery collection there are those in which a relationship between the two is immediately apparent. We feel, in George Luks's crayon drawings of the playful bears, great cats wary or sleeping, and placid deer that he saw one May afternoon in 1904 at the Bronx Zoo,[1] that the artist was recording not only animal mood and gesture in a few swift and amusing strokes, but also his own near-animal pleasure in drawing them. We sense that it *felt* good to be the unheeded observer in a world that would otherwise move along indifferently. Reginald Marsh presents the case more explicitly in his random sketches of scantily clad bathers at Coney Island, preserved at the Addison Gallery in some leaves from a sketchbook.[2] But there are records of all sorts among the Addison drawings—of newly discovered landscapes, identified or anonymous persons, situations, and events. All these drawings are inflected by degrees of skill and subjectivity; some are quite precise and observant, while others are more concerned with the state of mind that arose from contact with the objective world, or with the desire to achieve its idealized distillation.

Artists are still compelled to draw what they see, to make a record; indeed, the presumption persists that an artist who cannot draw in this way is not really an artist. Jasper Johns is said to have lamented his (self-described) inability to do so, as if it matters in the end. Today, though, making drawn records is more a choice born of inner compulsion than of external necessity; photography tipped the scales. Gone are the days when artists like George Catlin or Thomas Moran accompanied expeditions and geological surveys, drafting a visual record of the sites and the people encountered. Such records were not always virtuoso, and sometimes look like the hired work they were. When the artist and playwright William Dunlap recorded the manmade fortifications and natural wonders of New York State around 1815, he did so with an appealing yet sometimes awkward factuality that gives us little sense of the excitement with which he might have viewed them. This was his job. Though he had been a successful playwright, the nearly fifty watercolors in the precious visual record that Dunlap made while assistant paymaster-general of the New York State Militia are notably lacking in drama. Niagara Falls, tumbling through the background of Dunlap's view "from the bank above the Stone house (an old distillery)," as he dutifully annotated on the drawing, is almost an afterthought in a landscape just as consumed by a gnarled foreground tree and the steep decline to the gorge. By contrast, when the artist John Trumbull drew the Cohoes Falls, also carefully inscribed ("12 miles from Albany on the Mohawk River 27th Sept 1791"), he reveals this natural phenomenon from a knoll suggestively capped by dead and scraggly trees. We can't help but wonder if the trees were really there, or if Trumbull added them as Romantic embellishment.

We feel the will to precision deployed by hands more agile and enthusiastic than Dunlap's in other Addison Gallery drawings, for example of the village and cathedral of Chartres or of innumerable sailboats made by Carlton Theodore Chapman in sketchbooks from the late 1880s; or in the contemporaneous view by Moran of *The Mountain Range on the West Side of San Luis Valley above San Francisco* (1883), incompletely colored but a telling example of the kind of freshly observed information the artist tapped for his more imaginatively contrived paintings. A delicate fastidiousness marks Edwin Whitefield's earlier *View of Portsmouth, N.H.*, with every roof and spire in that New Hampshire riverside town minutely depicted. We know little of the artists who made drawings like the portrait *Charles Woodworth* by Manley Nehemiah Whipple, with its spare delineation of a child's distinctive profile, or the primly seated, soberly dressed *Hannah Ingersoll*, a watercolor by Henry Walton, but we sense just as great a care being expended on what the artists must have considered the accuracy of their depiction.

Yet between Chapman, Whitefield, and Moran, on the one hand, and Whipple and Walton, on the other, stands a great divide in which academic training and membership in artistic circles, as well as familiarity with a long tradition of European art, must be figured. John Singer Sargent is all too aware of European art in drawings like his five studies after murals, in which he records not the natural world but the tradition that informs his own practice. In the Addison drawings, copied in his youth from the ceiling decoration of the Palais Garnier Opera House, music-making putti in graphite and ink are cavorting in spandrels labeled for Barbari, Britannia, Hispania, Italia, and Persia. As John La Farge wrote in 1908, "The habit of the studio has so acted on modern art that the greater mass of even extraordinary successes are pictures of pictures and not pictures of Nature."[3] The exquisite *Boulder and Trees* by Marsden Hartley may have been observed from the rocky landscape of southern France, but it is as much a tribute to Hartley's hero, Paul Cézanne, who might have chosen just such a juxtaposition of simple forms, the dematerialized boulder barely grounding the counterpoised trees above, and the entire scene swept bare by diagonal patches of abstract faceting.[4]

Drawing presents, as for Moran, an opportunity that does not exist in more monumental formats, where issues of marketability, patronage, and artistic legacy restrain spontaneous execution. A remarkable example of this may be found in the pages of the scrapbooks of sketches by John La Farge, an otherwise highly self-conscious artist whose work here presents the "homogeneous artless simplicity" that James Yarnall has found in other La Farge sketches.[5] In the Addison sketchbooks we see sprays of flowers, a big brooding rock near Newport, vignettes of the South Seas, even a song lyric musically notated. La Farge may have had his eye on the future in some of these sketches, actually writing the names of colors in landscapes where he perhaps lacked the time, materials, or inclination to actually fill them in, so he could remember them later. But the future was not to be realized in any monumental versions of these vignettes, which exist as a precious record not only of what La Farge saw, but of his wide-ranging intellect, his travels, and a nimble side to his hand that is often eclipsed in his larger commissions.

Among these drawings are many in which it is clear that the artists sought to infuse their "records" with sensibility, to provide visual glosses on the observed world in order to make more of what would always be its subjective experience. While the landscape depicted in William Morris Hunt's *The Wooded Knoll* may well have existed, the artist's choice to render it dark and melancholy, with brooding woods and turbulent sky, transforms it into an imaginary place where we might well find the haunted grave of Hawthorne's Roger Malvin. How much more specific and concrete, by contrast, are Robert Swain Gifford's nonetheless lonely *Barneys Joy Willows* and George Inness's luminous *June*. Each is closely tied to the artist's sensibility and formal interests but just as securely to a specific, identifiable place. Winslow Homer depicts sailors awaiting *The Last Boat In* in one of his drawings of the Life Brigade House in Cullercoats, near Tynemouth, England, where he was staying in 1881;[6] but in concentrating the darkest area in the huddled and hunkered forms of the featureless men, he creates of them a dark and anxious knot. In obliterating details, the artist remains faithful to the mood of the event, creating a record of the recurring life-and-death preoccupations of this little fishing village. So, too, Isabel Bishop catches an intimate moment that suggests a wider narrative in her *Make-Up*, with its modern woman from the 1930s bent intently over her mirror as she applies her lipstick. This woman could almost be preparing for the sort of meeting between a man and a woman on the street shown in *Encounter No. 2*, a 1940 painting by Bishop also in the Addison collection.

"The physical eye," wrote Hans Hofmann, "sees only the shell and the semblance; the inner eye, however, sees to the core and grasps the opposing forces and the coherence of things."[7] At a certain point the record that is being made matters less in its objective truth than in its deeper implications as art in its most intimate form. We do not doubt for a moment that, in Hofmann's remarkable ink nudes made between 1932 and 1935, the artist was after something more than merely an objective record of what he saw. "Form discloses itself to us as a living thing in its surface tensions," he wrote;[8] and one feels the truth of that statement in his depiction of these women, rendered in a fascinating variety of bold forms—a claw for a hand, a target for a breast—and set into a space made more alive by the inclusion of stretches of solid black ink that are as diverse in shape as the body parts, or perhaps more pertinently, as forms similar to those found in the artist's untitled 1947 watercolor abstraction, also reproduced in this book. The impulse to record has spawned many such modest drawings, made by artists in a private moment and often for personal reasons. And often in personal places—sketchbooks, for example, which were never meant to be viewed in anything as formal as a collection catalogue. While more premeditated and finished works may also stand as records, it is in the mercurial sketch that we find the most poignant evidence of the irreducible relationship between the artist and the world.

24   **Notes**

1. *George B. Luks: Bronx Park, May 8, 1904. Thirty-three Drawings of Animals in the Bronx Zoo* (Andover: Addison Gallery of American Art, Phillips Academy, 1990).

2. In another large and finished Marsh drawing at the Addison, *Crowded Day at Coney*, the artist goes to fantastical extremes to portray writhing figures along the edge of the shore and cavorting in the water. Though Weegee's photographs of Coney Island prove that Marsh was not inventing the crush of bodies, he clearly took artistic license when he set them in motion.

3. In *The Higher Life in Art* (1908), quoted by James L. Yarnall, "Nature and Art in the Painting of John La Farge," in *John La Farge* (Pittsburgh: Carnegie Museum of Art; Washington, D.C.: National Museum of American Art, Smithsonian Institution; New York: Abbeville Press, 1987), p. 81.

4. Gail R. Scott, *Marsden Hartley* (New York: Abbeville Press, 1988), pp. 76–77.

5. Yarnall, "Nature and Art," p. 85.

6. Franklin Kelly, "A Process of Change," in *Winslow Homer* (Washington, D.C.: National Gallery of Art; New Haven: Yale University Press, 1996), p. 208.

7. Hans Hofmann, *Search for the Real and Other Essays*, ed. Sara[h] T. Weeks and Bartlett H. Hayes, Jr. (first published by the Addison Gallery of American Art, 1948; rev. ed., Cambridge: M.I.T. Press, 1994), p. 62.

8. Ibid., p. 67.

The work as a **record** PORTFOLIO

BORN
6 June 1756
Lebanon, Connecticut

DIED
10 November 1843
New York, New York

John Trumbull drew this tiny landscape study of the banks of the Cohoes Falls in upstate New York in 1791. The landscape is inscribed with great specificity on the reverse: "The Cohoes Falls- / 12 miles from Albany / on the Mohawk River / 27th Sept 1791 / Jn Trumbull."

Two years earlier, in 1789, the Harvard-educated artist and patriot, son of the governor of Connecticut and veteran of the Revolutionary conflict, had returned from England. His purpose was to raise money for his grand cycle of paintings commemorating events of the American Revolution, as well as to make portraits of American statesmen to be incorporated into future paintings. In the ensuing four years, a period that the Trumbull scholar Theodore Sizer called one of "feverish activity and promise," the artist traveled up and down the East Coast.[1] It was undoubtedly during one of these trips that Trumbull found himself at the Cohoes Falls and made the Addison's sketch, one of only a handful of landscapes the artist created, all executed prior to his return to Europe in 1808.[2]

The Addison's sketch exhibits an unusual confluence of on-the-spot observation and artistic convention. The artist carefully recorded the dramatic waterfall drop and the surrounding terrain, then ordered the factual elements according to traditional picturesque practices—the shaded foreground that mediates the drama of the water, the two trees that frame the scene, the distant horizon line, and billowing cloud forms. As dramatic counterpoint, Trumbull placed the broken tree, a device common to works by him and other American and English artists, in the center of the composition to emphasize the asymmetry and variety typical of the picturesque landscape.[3]

SCF

26 John Trumbull

THE COHOES FALLS — 12 MILES FROM
ALBANY ON THE MOHAWK RIVER,
1791

Iron gall ink and watercolor on blued white,
thick, moderately textured (1) laid paper
mounted on board

2 15/16 x 4 11/16

Signed in ink on verso c.: Jn Trumbull

Inscribed in ink on verso c.:
The Cohoes Falls- / 12 Miles from Albany /
on the Mohawk River / 27th Sept 1791

Museum purchase

1940.27

THE NOTES FOR THIS SECTION BEGIN ON PAGE 84

BORN
18 February 1766
Perth Amboy, New Jersey

DIED
18 September 1839
New York, New York

William Dunlap variously occupied himself as a professional painter and miniaturist, chronicler of the state of the arts and theater, businessman, magazine publisher, playwright, theater manager, and, in 1815–16, as assistant paymaster-general of the New York State Militia. In the last-named capacity Dunlap traveled from Long Island to upstate New York to make payments to veterans of the War of 1812, and he made watercolor sketches of the scenery he encountered. Of the forty-nine watercolors known from this trip, the Addison owns twenty.[1]

In the biographical section of his ambitious history of the arts in America of 1834, Dunlap described that "a habit of early rising and pedestrian exercise gave me time and opportunity to visit and make drawings of spots within several miles of the place at which I was to labour in my vocation of paymaster during the remainder of the day."[2] An inveterate diarist, Dunlap committed daily notes to the back or margins of many of his modest watercolors. Taken together they form an engaging travelogue—a glimpse into the process of settlement, change, and growth in early-nineteenth-century America. Part of the naïve charm of his watercolor *View of Niagara...*, made in September 1815 during Dunlap's four days at Niagara Falls, can be attributed to the fact that it was, in the artist's words, "carefully coloured in the open air" as he perched on a portable three-legged stool.[3]

S C F

28 William Dunlap

VIEW OF NIAGARA FROM
THE BANK ABOVE THE STONE HOUSE
(AN OLD DISTILLERY), 1815

Watercolor and graphite on beige (1), medium weight (2), slightly textured (1) wove paper

9 x 11

Unsigned

Inscribed in graphite u.l.: yellow;
c.: light green; in ink on verso u.l.: View [? illegible] 8:1815 from the Bank above the Stone house (an old distillery)

Gift of Heathcote M. Woolsey

1939.13

TOP TO BOTTOM

*Barracks at Black Rock by Redoubt,
with a Distant View of Fort Erie*, 1815
Watercolor and graphite on cream (3),
medium weight (2), moderately textured (1)
laid paper
5 13/16 x 9 9/16
Unsigned
Gift of Judge John M. Woolsey
Addison Gallery of American Art, 1983.8

Ticonderoga, c. 1816
Watercolor and graphite on beige (1),
medium weight (2), slightly textured (1)
wove paper
8 13/16 x 11 1/8
Unsigned
Gift of Heathcote M. Woolsey
Addison Gallery of American Art, 1939.14

BORN
19 June 1783
Horncastle, Lincolnshire, England

DIED
5 November 1872
Philadelphia, Pennsylvania

Thomas Sully was one of America's most prolific and popular portrait painters. Over his long career, he painted some twenty-six hundred portraits as well as hundreds of history and genre pictures.[1] Born in England, Sully came to America as a child with his parents and siblings. He lived in South Carolina, Virginia, New York, and Connecticut before finally settling in Philadelphia in 1807. He continued to travel frequently, seeking commissions for portraits, and was often away from home for months at a time. In the 1830s and 1840s, he made at least eighteen business trips up and down the East Coast and spent nine months in England. The Addison's sketches could have been made on any of those trips, or in Philadelphia, where Sully maintained a thriving business.

These four studies represent the earliest stage in Sully's portraiture process, general designs for poses and props.[2] The quick little drawings would have been made at the first meeting with the sitter. Thus, these sweet but generic faces were never meant to be likenesses and are, therefore, very difficult to identify. It was not until the client approved the general design that Sully proceeded with very accurate pencil drawings, usually at a second sitting. If he was working in his own studio, Sully developed a kind of interim portrait in chalk on a prepared canvas, which served as a full-size model for the final oil painting. (He skipped this intermediary step if he was on the road and began working directly on the final picture.) At the third sitting, Sully introduced color and corrected any inaccuracies in the likeness. He required as many as six sittings in all, and sometimes dressed a mannequin to refine details of clothing and jewelry.

SJM

30   Thomas Sully

STUDIES OF YOUNG WOMEN,
mid-1830s–mid-1840s

Chalk, ink wash, and ink on beige (2),
medium weight (2), slightly textured (2)
laid paper

8 7/8 x 11 9/16

Unsigned

Museum purchase

1938.6

BORN
25 August 1804
Ballston, New York

DIED
1865
Cassopolis, Michigan

The popularity of painted portraits in America increased in the first half of the nineteenth century as the country began to prosper and more people desired and could afford artistic renderings of themselves and their family members. The creators of most such portraits were itinerant artists, generally untrained young men who traveled from town to town for their commissions. Henry Walton was living in the Finger Lakes region of New York State when he painted this portrait of Hannah Ingersoll. Born in Ballston, New York, in 1804, Walton moved to Michigan in 1830, returned to New York in 1836, and for the remainder of his life traveled between Michigan, New York, and California.[1] He painted portraits and landscapes throughout his travels, capturing people and places in the self-taught style of American folk artists.

Walton's small watercolor portrait of Hannah Ingersoll displays several of the characteristics of American folk-art portraits. She sits soberly, dressed in her best clothes, and her form is created through strong contour lines with minimal use of shading.[2] Where she lived and what her life was like is unknown, but her image shows a quiet, dignified, well-dressed young woman. A brightly colored shawl lightens her somber but elaborate black dress, and her slender hands hold a white handkerchief. A triple-strand necklace and formal, elegant hairstyle complete her adornment, and she looks out of the portrait with a calm gaze. Walton included her name in capital letters below the figure, where he also signed and dated the picture. Originally a captured likeness of a living person, the portrait now functions as a record of the existence of Hannah Ingersoll, the art of Henry Walton, and the intersection of their lives.

GGS

32

Henry Walton

HANNAH INGERSOLL, 1836

Watercolor and ink on beige (1), moderately thick, smooth wove paper

8 1/2 x 6 3/16

Signed in ink l.c.: HANNAH INGERSOLL. / Drawn by H Walton 1836.

Museum purchase

1961.4

HANNAH INGERSOLL.
Drawn by H Walton 1836.

33

BORN
17 April 1814
Whiting, Vermont

DIED
August 1843
Rossville, Ohio

Manley Nehemiah Whipple represented the eighth generation of a family that had emigrated from Essex, England, to Ipswich, Massachusetts, in the 1630s. One of his kinsmen, William Whipple of Portsmouth, signed the Declaration of Independence. During the Revolution, his own grandfather relocated to Vermont, where Manley was born in 1814. Virtually nothing is known of Manley Whipple's life. By 1843, when he died at the age of 29, leaving a wife and infant daughter, he was living in Rossville, Ohio, near Cincinnati.[1] He advertised in the local newspaper on 9 February 1843: "M.N. Whipple would respectfully inform the citizens of Rossville and vicinity that he is prepared to execute Portrait or Bust likenesses in a style to please the people, and prices to suit the times."[2]

Only a handful of Whipple portraits are known to exist. All are profiles with very fine facial features and conventionalized hair and clothing. The Addison's drawing of a young boy identified as Charles Woodworth has a delicate portrait of an even younger child on the verso. The defining line of the Woodworth profile is a confident, fluid stroke, suggesting that perhaps Whipple projected the silhouette of his sitter onto paper and traced the outline. The precise nature of each idiosyncratic detail—the modeling of the nose and lips, the delicacy of individual eyelashes—shows a remarkably keen eye and skillful hand for an apparently untrained artist. In contrast, Whipple's depiction of Woodworth's hair and clothing is surprisingly clumsy. Still, the overall effect of his portraits is charmingly straight-forward and earnest.

SJM

34 Manley Nehemiah Whipple

CHARLES WOODWORTH, 1841

Graphite and chalk on beige (2), moderately thick, smooth wove paper

9 7/8 x 8

Unsigned

On verso: profile portrait; inscribed on verso l.c.: Charles Woodworth drawn by/ Manley N. Whipple / April 1841

Museum purchase

1940.7

BORN
31 March 1835
New York, New York

DIED
14 November 1910
Providence, Rhode Island

John La Farge was an artist, a writer and critic, an extraordinary conversationalist, an inveterate traveler—he was cosmopolitan in taste and scope, and "something of the universal genius," in the words of his biographer.[1] The art historian Henry Adams has called La Farge's work "almost encyclopedic in its variety," encompassing as it did painting, illustrations, mural paintings, watercolors, as well as decoration, sculpture, architecture, and stained glass.[2]

This omnivorousness is evident in his myriad sketchbooks, such as the small volume of about 1863 owned by the Addison. At the time that these pages were being filled, La Farge was living in Newport, with a young wife and his first son; he and his friend the artist John Chandler Bancroft had, as he said, "plunged into the great questions of light and color,"[3] and he had been commissioned to create a Crucifixion triptych by a New York church. All of these elements in La Farge's life and career are represented in this little sketchbook. With a delicate line he captured the round babyness of his son; on the next page he lovingly studied his protruding lip and tiny nose. On another sheet, he covered the barest outline of a landscape with copious notations of color. On yet another is a shallow bowl with flower forms defined in rich tones of black charcoal. And, perhaps in preparation for his mural commission, the artist has filled pages with sketches of religious images—the Crucifixion, putti and doves, Daniel wrestling with a lion, trumpeting angels.

This sketchbook attests to the essential role that drawing played in La Farge's artistic life. As he told his biographer, "I drew and painted because it was so tempting, always drawing or painting in the way of study of some special side of the things we see."[4]

SCF

36 John La Farge

Sketchbook, 1863

Graphite and charcoal on 123 bound sheets of cream (2), medium weight (1), smooth wove paper

3 1/2 x 5 13/16 x 3/4

Signed in graphite on sheet 1 c.:
John La Farge

Inscribed in graphite on sheet 1 c.:
Oct 2d / 63_ / La Farge House / Broadway / NY

Museum purchase

1931.104.1–123

LEFT TO RIGHT
Page 34 [View of ocean through branches on side of tree]
Charcoal and graphite on paper
1931.104.34

Page 109 [Tree]
Graphite on paper
1931.104.109

BORN
22 September 1816
East Lulworth, Dorset, England

DIED
25 December 1892
Dedham, Massachusetts

Edwin Whitefield, who lived for several years in Reading, Massachusetts, was a prolific topographical artist who produced hundreds of views of cities and towns and individual historic houses, from Massachusetts to Minnesota and across southern Canada.[1] During the summer of 1873 he was in Portsmouth, New Hampshire. *The Portsmouth Journal* announced on 14 June: "two very perfect sketches of this city have been drawn by Prof. E. Whitefield who is now very successfully teaching drawing from nature in this city. One of the views is from the north side of the North pond and the other from the south side of the South pond. They are to be lithographed and the pictures will be for sale by the Fourth of July." In the Addison's drawing Whitefield recorded his on-site observations of Portsmouth's growing industrial district on the North Millpond. The largest building is the five-story textile mill built for the Portsmouth Steam Factory

in 1846. An extensive network of railroad tracks, freight yards, car sheds, and a semi-circular engine house runs behind the factories along the shoreline.[2] Whitefield later worked his sketch into a finished drawing, replacing the delicate rowboats with a more substantial foreground.[3]

Reproductions of both views were ready for sale during the popular reunion known as the Return of the Sons of Portsmouth that July. On 5 July Whitefield advertised in the local newspaper:

> Whitefield's Portsmouth Views.
> These are two handsome pictures, a copy of which every Son of Portsmouth should take back with him, a memento of his birthplace. They are very truthful and beautiful representations of our city, and will be appreciated as charming pictures, independent of their being Views of Portsmouth as she appeared July 4th, 1873.[4]

SJM

38

Edwin Whitefield

VIEW OF PORTSMOUTH, N.H., 1873

Ink, iron gall ink, ink wash, graphite, and opaque watercolor on two joined sheets of beige (1), moderately thick, smooth wove paper

7 x 20

Inscribed in graphite u.r.: The village of Elliot / across the river / Go to Prospect Hil, Newington / or Dows Hill / on the old stage road to Knights Ferry / about 4 miles from Portsmouth / A very fine view / Go in the aftern.; in graphite on verso l.c.: Dr. Hayes or Jeffries / M.W. + F. / 10 o'clock / Eye Infirmary / Cor Charles + Cambridge

Museum purchase

1969.20

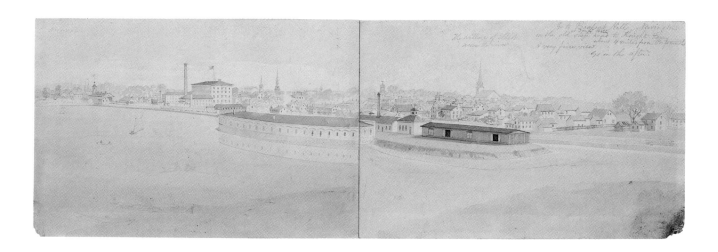

BORN
1 May 1825
Newburgh, New York

DIED
3 August 1894
Bridge-of-Allan, Scotland

Although they never became a major part of his oeuvre, George Inness left behind a small group of impressive watercolor sketches. Most, and probably including *June*, were executed in Italy during the course of his third European sojourn of 1870–75. This sketch depicts a panoramic view across a countryside that extends to the dim outline of a mountain in the distance. Two small figures stroll along a path in the foreground, which is defined by a group of billowing trees to the right. Inness demonstrates his mastery of the watercolor technique through the glowing tones of the sketch, and by his sparing use of opaque watercolor to suggest the path as well as the heavy atmosphere of the sky. The simple massing of forms in *June*, perfectly suited to Inness's choice of scale and medium, resembles the abstracted landscapes that characterize his late style of the 1890s.

The Inness scholar Michael Quick has suggested that *June* may be related to two oil paintings: *Landscape near Perugia* (c. 1873; private collection) and *The Olives* (1873; Toledo Museum of Art). All three share a common vista and compositional structure. In fact, the watercolor may have served as a study for the larger works.[1]

Inness's watercolors were rarely exhibited and remained in the artist's possession during his lifetime. A number of them, including this one, passed to the artist's daughter, Helen Inness Hartley, after his death and did not reach the attention of the public until the sale of Mrs. Hartley's collection in 1927.

M L

40

George Inness

JUNE, c. 1873

Transparent and opaque watercolor and graphite on blue, thick, smooth wove paper

7 3/16 x 12 1/2

Signed in graphite l.r.: G. Inness;
l.l.: G. Inness; on verso u.l.: Geo. Inness

Gift of anonymous donor

1928.45

G. Inness.

G. Inness

BORN
12 January 1856
Florence, Italy

DIED
15 April 1925
London, England

After an itinerant childhood migrating with his family through Italy and southern Europe, the American expatriate John Singer Sargent arrived in Paris in May 1874. Just eighteen years old, he was already a talented draftsman whose diligent work was encouraged by such masters as James McNeill Whistler.[1] With his sights set on mastering oil painting, Sargent immediately applied to the well-regarded atelier of the French portraitist Carolus-Duran, who, in reviewing Sargent's early work, judged that he had "much to be unlearned… but promise above the ordinary."[2]

After his mornings in Carolus's atelier and before afternoons at the École des Beaux Arts for further practice, Sargent was in the habit of sketching from the figurative master-works in Paris's museums and art houses. Since his family had settled close to the Palais Garnier Opera House at the time that it opened in January 1875,[3] it is not surprising that the neo-Baroque building's grand foyer caught his eye. There, inset in the ceiling, were over thirty tableaux by the French academic painter Paul Baudry illustrating the mythical history of music's power and including ten medallions of cherubs with instruments representing ancient and modern nations.[4] Five of the young Sargent's faithful copies of these medallions are at the Addison.[5] Represented are: Barbary's trumpet, triangle, and tarabouka; Great Britain's bagpipe and Irish harp; Spain's castanets, mandolin, and Basque tambourine; Italy's violin and tamburello; and Persia's cymbals, symphonia, and Pandora.[6] Whether Sargent copied these works for personal pleasure or as an assignment from Carolus-Duran,[7] they are a revealing prelude to his late-career passion for his own mural projects commissioned for the Boston Public Library, the Museum of Fine Arts, Boston, and Harvard University.

JM

John Singer Sargent

42

LEFT TO RIGHT
STUDY AFTER MURAL OF BARBARI,
c. 1875

Graphite and ink on beige (2),
medium weight (1), moderately textured (3)
wove paper
4 7/8 x 3 7/8
Unsigned
Inscribed in ink u.r.: BARBARI; in graphite
l.l.: J.S. 207c
Gift of Miss Emily Sargent and her sister,
Mrs. Francis Ormond
1932.7.1

STUDY AFTER MURAL OF BRITANNIA,
c. 1875

Graphite and ink on beige (2),
medium weight (1), moderately textured (3)
wove paper
4 7/8 x 3 9/16
Unsigned
Inscribed in ink u.r.: BRITA; in graphite
l.l.: J.S. 207a
Gift of Miss Emily Sargent and her sister,
Mrs. Francis Ormond
1932.7.2

STUDY AFTER MURAL OF HISPANIA,
c. 1875

Graphite and ink on beige (2),
medium weight (1), moderately textured (3)
wove paper
5 3/8 x 3 7/8
Unsigned
Inscribed in ink u.r.: HISPAN; in graphite
l.l.: J.S. 207b
Gift of Miss Emily Sargent and her sister,
Mrs. Francis Ormond
1932.7.4

STUDY AFTER MURAL OF ITALIA,
c. 1875

Graphite and ink on beige (2),
medium weight (1), moderately textured (3)
wove paper
4 7/8 x 3 13/16
Unsigned
Inscribed in ink u.r.: ITALIA; in graphite
l.l.: J.S. 207
Gift of Miss Emily Sargent and her sister,
Mrs. Francis Ormond
1932.7.5

STUDY AFTER MURAL OF PERSIA,
c. 1875

Graphite and ink on beige (2),
medium weight (1), moderately textured (3)
wove paper
5 3/8 x 3 15/16
Unsigned
Inscribed in ink u.r.: PERSIA; in ink l.l.: NNIA ;
in graphite l.l.: J.S. 207e
Gift of Miss Emily Sargent and her sister,
Mrs. Francis Ormond
1932.7.3

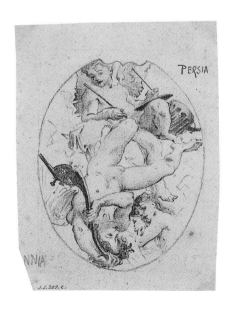

BORN
27 September 1840
Landau, Bavaria

DIED
7 December 1902
Guayaquil, Ecuador

Thomas Nast is widely recognized as America's first great political cartoonist. The wood engravings produced during his employment at *Harper's Weekly* from 1861 to 1884 brought him national renown, and his political views had a profound influence on the country. All three U.S. presidential candidates that Nast supported while working at *Harper's Weekly* (Lincoln, Grant, and Cleveland) won their elections. Among the artist's most famous contributions to American culture are the symbols of the Republican Elephant and the Democratic Donkey, the figure of Uncle Sam, and the representation of Santa Claus as a jovial, rotund, and slightly mischievous old man.[1]

The Tammany Tiger, another famous Nast symbol, embodied the corruption of New York City politician William Marcy "Boss" Tweed. The tiger emblem followed Tweed from his job as foreman of New York's Big Six Fire Company to his post in City Hall, where he was head of the politicians who became known as the Tweed Ring. Tweed appointed his supporters to prominent positions in city government and awarded lucrative contracts to companies who would provide financial kickbacks. In 1870, Nast launched a two-year campaign of political cartoons that resulted in the overthrow of the Tweed Ring and, eventually, the imprisonment of Boss Tweed.[2]

The Tammany Tiger, open-mouthed and roaring in this drawing, became symbolic of Tweed's voracious greed. Tweed himself was painfully aware of the power of Nast's work, and through a third party unsuccessfully attempted to bribe him with an offer of a half-million dollars to study art abroad. Of Nast's damaging cartoons, Tweed said: "Stop them damned pictures. I don't care what the papers write about me. My constituents can't read. But, damn it, they can see pictures."[3]

GGS

44

Thomas Nast

TAMMANY TIGER, c. 1870

Ink, graphite, and chalk on beige (1), moderately thick, rough (1) wove paper

14 15/16 x 22

Unsigned

Museum purchase

1938.69

BORN
31 March 1824
Brattleboro, Vermont

DIED
8 September 1879
Appledore, Isles of Shoals, New Hampshire

The path curves softly and emerges from the quiet dark of the wooded interior into a world of air and light. William Morris Hunt created the hazy atmosphere of this drawing with loose, expressive strokes of charcoal that indicate rather than outline his forms. His darkest darks define the trunks and branches of the trees, while patches of untouched paper highlight the brightest points of sky beyond. The suggestion of a lone figure, standing on the promontory bridging earth and sky, creates an impression of both intimacy and isolation. The figure is at once embraced by nature, held close in the shadows of the trees, and captive to its sublime power, faced by the infinite reach of the sky.

Hunt traveled to Europe in the early 1850s for his artistic training and was greatly influenced by his two French teachers,

Thomas Couture and Jean-François Millet. In Couture's studio, Hunt learned to conceive of his works as a whole, to create forms out of masses, and to use light to define those forms.[1] Millet and the painters of the Barbizon School also promoted the creation of forms through the use of light and color, but emphasized the importance of direct observation of the effects of light in the natural world.[2]

After his training in France, Hunt returned to America and settled in Boston, where he became the premier portrait painter for nearly two decades. In 1876 he built a studio in Magnolia, Massachusetts, and traveled along the North Shore area to draw forest and coastal scenes *en plein air*.[3] *The Wooded Knoll* likely belongs to the group of works Hunt produced during his time at Magnolia, and as a late work captures the skill, style, and spirit of a lifetime.

GGS

46 ## William Morris Hunt

THE WOODED KNOLL, c. 1876–77

Charcoal on beige (1), medium weight (2), moderately textured (2) laid paper

8 3/4 x 11 1/2

Signed in charcoal l.r.: WMH [in monogram]

Museum purchase

1934.48

47

BORN
23 December 1840
Naushon Island, Massachusetts

DIED
15 January 1905
New York, New York

The velvety black tones of charcoal laid across the soft, thick, beige paper of Robert Swain Gifford's *Barneys Joy Willows* create a monochromatic work with great evocative power. Sure lines capture the bending, wind-blown trees on a Massachusetts beach called Barneys Joy, near where the New York–based painter, etcher, and teacher was born and raised.

Drawn to the moody romantic character of the French Barbizon painters he had encountered during his extensive European travels in the 1860s and '70s, Gifford eschewed the meticulousness he had learned under the tutelage of the New Bedford artists Albert Van Beest and William Bradford for broad sweeping vistas in close-toned compositions.[1]

Finding respite from the New York art scene of which he was an active part, Gifford returned each summer to the fishing village of Nonquit, where he painted and drew the familiar southern Massachusetts coastline. In this drawing of a beach close to his summer residence, the artist has chosen a melancholy moment in which the sky is overcast. The distant outline of the shore is framed by the trunks and intertwined canopies of the silhouetted willows that are the dominant actors in the drama of wind, sea, cloud formation, and vegetation. As his contemporary George Sheldon wrote the same year as this drawing was made, Gifford's landscapes are "full of mystery and of meaning; the meanest flower that blows can, when he has placed it on the canvas, give thoughts that often lie too deep for tears. Mr. Gifford will paint a barren moor under a leaden sky so that it shall almost palpitate with emotion."[2]

SCF

48

Robert Swain Gifford

BARNEYS JOY WILLOWS, 1879

Charcoal on beige (2), moderately thick, moderately textured (3) wove paper

16 3/16 x 22 1/4

Signed in charcoal l.l.: R Swain Gifford / Aug-79

Inscribed in charcoal on verso u.l.: ho D.

Gift of Robert G. McIntyre

1941.40

BORN
24 February 1836
Boston, Massachusetts

DIED
29 September 1910
Prout's Neck, Scarboro, Maine

The career of Winslow Homer, one of America's most revered nineteenth-century painters, was transformed by a twenty-month stay in the small English coastal town of Cullercoats in 1881–82. In the 1870s, while sustaining himself as an illustrator for popular magazines, Homer eagerly mastered the craft of painting in oils and watercolors, capturing scenes of American life in the rural South, the shores of Massachusetts, and the rolling countryside of upstate New York. His trip to England and his experiences with the rugged life of the fishing village marked a distinct shift in his work. The fishermen and women, as Helen Cooper has pointed out, were "symbols of life lived close to nature—serious, concise, and true."[1] Perhaps prompted by the noble and sturdy inhabitants, and his growing surety as a watercolorist, Homer's English compositions became broader, his figures more substantial, his subjects more serious, his technique more ambitious.[2]

The perils of the life of the sea were ever present in this seaside village, and *The Last Boat In* relates to one such event—the grounding of the barque *Iron Crown* in 1881. In this drawing Homer caught a group of oilskin-clad men at the base of the town's Life Brigade House following the progress of a rescue boat moving toward shore.[3] The immediacy of the viewpoint, the economy of line and form, the close balance of the dark charcoal tones against the beige of the paper, all contribute to the intensity of the captured moment. Homer later used such sketches and drawings to translate the event into several large watercolors, such as *Wreck of the Iron Crown* (1881; collection of Carleton Mitchell, on extended loan to The Baltimore Museum of Art).

S C F

50

Winslow Homer

THE LAST BOAT IN, c. 1881

Charcoal on beige (1), moderately thick, slightly textured (1) wove paper

8 7/16 x 12 3/16

Signed in charcoal l.l.: HOMER

Museum purchase

1934.39

BORN
12 January 1837
Bolton, Lancashire, England

DIED
26 August 1926
Santa Barbara, California

Thomas Moran is said to have embodied "the expansionistic, scientific, patriotic, and romantic late nineteenth-century mind."[1] A member of eight expeditions through the American Far West in the 1870s and 1880s, he celebrated the astonishing natural phenomena of North America. He documented rock formations, geysers, sulfur springs, canyons, and cataracts, but he was not a true topographical artist. Moran was awed by the wild landscape before him, yet he gave it no moral weight. He considered truth to be impressionistic rather than topographic. "I place no value upon literal transcripts from Nature," he reportedly told one critic. "My general scope is not realistic, all my tendencies are toward idealization.... Topography in art is valueless... while I desired to tell truly of Nature, I did not wish to realize the scene literally, but to preserve and to convey its true impression."[2]

Moran made his reputation with images of the Yellowstone River Valley, paintings powerful enough to help convince Congress to establish the first national park in 1872. Over the next twenty years he recorded sites in Wyoming, Idaho, Nevada, Utah, Colorado, New Mexico, and Arizona. In 1883, Moran set out for Mexico via Cuba. He landed at Vera Cruz on 3 February and traveled inland. A month later, about two hundred miles northwest of Mexico City, he stopped above the village of San Francisco to sketch the San Luis Valley[3] of central Mexico and the mountains beyond. Moran skillfully established the bones of the landscape in pencil, leaving some of them exposed, and used washes to create depth, detail, and atmosphere in the resulting study, now considered "one of his best watercolors of this or any season."[4]

SJM

52

Thomas Moran

THE MOUNTAIN RANGE ON THE WEST SIDE OF SAN LUIS VALLEY ABOVE SAN FRANCISCO, 1883

Watercolor and graphite on beige (1), moderately thick, smooth wove paper

10 x 14 1/4

Signed in graphite l.r.: T.M.

Inscribed in graphite l.r.: The Mountain Range on the West Side of the San Louis Valley / above San Francisco. March 1st 1883

Museum purchase

1953.6

The Mountain Ranges on the West side of the San Louis Valley above San Francisco. March 1st 1853

Carlton Chapman was born and raised in the Midwest but spent summers in his uncle's Maine boatyard, where he developed his love of the sea. When he was in his early twenties he moved to New York to study at the Art Students League and the National Academy of Design. Like many young American artists of his generation, Chapman then traveled and studied abroad. The sketchbooks he used to record these summer travels were purchased from his widow in 1939. In them, some vignettes are fairly complete. Other images are packed together on a single page without regard to scale. All are the snapshot observations of a trained eye.

In July 1886 Chapman hastily sketched the crowd gathered around a beached sailboat in Holland. Details of the wooden boat and its rigging are all noted. The posture and clothing of figures—down to their wooden shoes—are captured in a few strokes.

In 1939 Mrs. Chapman confided to Charles Sawyer, director of the Addison, "I know Carlton would like his sketchbooks to be useful in the New England environment from which he sprang and to which he remained so ardently attached."[1] That affection is also reflected in an 1889 ink drawing of a bearded seaman in watch cap and jacket. Below is a more careful study of the man's right hand gripping his oar. Chapman took this sketchbook to France, where he stopped in the medieval Brittany village of Vitré and recorded the exterior pulpit of the Church of Notre Dame.

Chapman was best known as a maritime painter. He covered the Spanish American War for *Harper's Weekly* as a "special artist."[2] His work was widely published as illustrations in maritime histories and was well received in international exhibitions from the early 1890s until his death in 1925.

SJM

54

Carlton Theodore Chapman

Sketchbook, 1886

Graphite, ink, and watercolor on 77 bound sheets of beige (1), medium weight (2), smooth wove paper

5 7/8 x 9 1/8 x 11/16

Signed in ink on verso of front cover u.r.: July 14 1886; c.: Carlton T. Chapman / Katwi[j]k van Zee / Holl / Groot[B]ad Hotel

Museum purchase

1940.11.1–77

LEFT TO RIGHT
Page 18 [July 14, 86, sailboat KW3 ashore with crew and passengers]
Page 19 [July 29, 86, three sketches— view along shore]
Graphite on paper
1940.11.18 and 1940.11.19

Page 24 [July 21–86, anchored sailboat with people along shore]
Graphite on paper
1940.11.24

Carlton Theodore Chapman
Sketchbook, 1889–90

Ink, ink wash, graphite, transparent and
opaque watercolor, and collage on 134 bound
sheets of beige (1), medium weight (1),
smooth wove paper

6 13/16 x 9 x 7/8

Signed in graphite on verso of front cover
u.r.: CHAPMAN, C.T.

Museum purchase

1940.10.1–134

Page 65 [Man in hat with beard, oar in hands;
detail of hand]
Ink and ink wash on paper
1940.10.65

Page 113 [Chaire extérieure, église Notre
Dame]
Ink on paper
Inscribed u.r.: CHAIRE EXTÉRIEURE, ÉGLISE
NOTRE DAME, VITRÉ 12 JUIN 1889; l.c.:
Buttress and gargoyle from Notre Dame—
French Flamboyant Church of XV–XVI
Centurys
1940.10.113

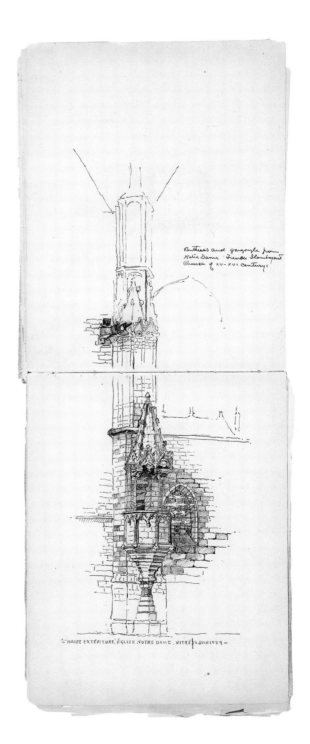

BORN
12 January 1856
Florence, Italy

DIED
15 April 1925
London, England

Just fifteen years after his early studies in Paris, John Singer Sargent, then one of the most sought-after portraitists in both American and European social circles, was awarded a major mural commission for the Boston Public Library, for which he boldly chose the theme of the Triumph of Religion.[1]

Embarking in 1890 on what would become thirty-five years of participation in Boston's mural renaissance,[2] Sargent began the project with hundreds of preparatory drawings. By 1891, established in a large studio in England, he delved into sketching the male nude to work out the intricate and expansive compositions of figures for his grand mural canvases, a practice he maintained for all such commissions.[3]

The range of drawings produced in these sessions reveals Sargent's deliberate use of the medium and attention to his subject. In *Nudes in Action*, the repetition of the moving figure in shifting angles, poses, and scales suggests that the work may be a record of the kind of quick warm-up exercise Sargent often employed to test his eye and hand with difficult twisted and foreshortened poses.[4] Once a definitive pose for a composition was chosen, however, he would focus in on details to refine the form to be painted in the finished mural. The attention paid to the folds in *Drapery* and the facial expression in each of the *Three Heads* (pp. 60, 61) indicate that the artist may have used these works to perfect some elusive aspect of a final composition.[5]

Collectively, Sargent's mural studies serve as a valuable record of his mature working method, his diligent commitment to his commissions, and his deep respect for mural painting as a tradition deserving of great craftsmanship and care.

JM

John Singer Sargent

58

NUDES IN ACTION, c. 1890/1925

Charcoal on gray, moderately thick, moderately textured (1) laid paper

18 11/16 x 24 13/16

Unsigned

Inscribed in graphite l.r.: (153)

Gift of Miss Emily Sargent and her sister, Mrs. Francis Ormond

1932.12

John Singer Sargent
THREE HEADS, c. 1890/1925

Charcoal on beige (2), moderately thick,
moderately textured (1), Michallet laid paper

24 1/2 x 18 1/2

Unsigned

Inscribed in charcoal l.r.: Olympio Fusco /
63A Aspenlea Road / Hammersmith;
in graphite l.l.: 6.158

Gift of Miss Emily Sargent and her sister,
Mrs. Francis Ormond

1932.14

60   FAR RIGHT
DRAPERY, c. 1890/1925

Charcoal on blue, moderately thick,
slightly textured (2), Ingres wove paper

24 1/2 x 19

Unsigned

Inscribed in graphite l.l.: 6.99;
on verso l.l.: S.6.99

Gift of Miss Emily Sargent and her sister,
Mrs. Francis Ormond

1932.9

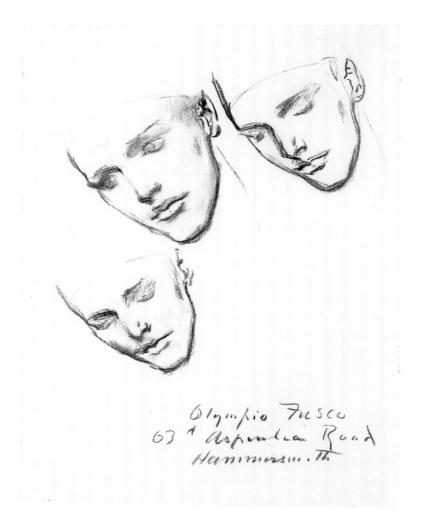

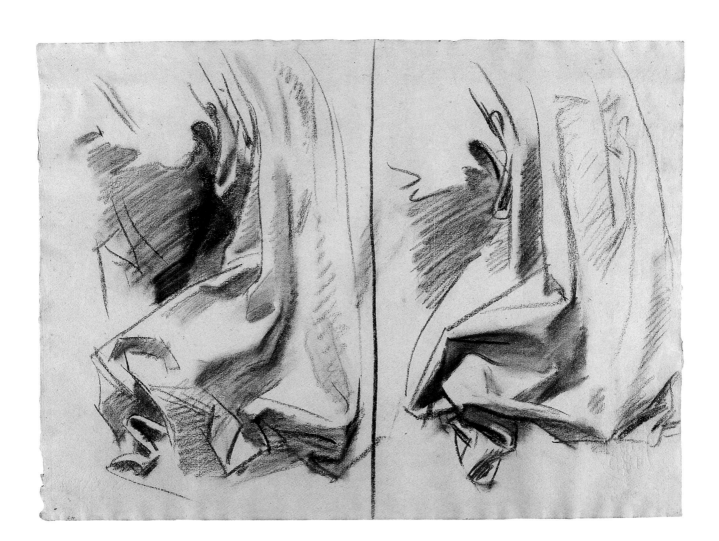

BORN
13 August 1867
Williamsport, Pennsylvania

DIED
29 October 1933
New York, New York

As a young newspaper illustrator, George Luks learned to record the essential details of an event with a few brief strokes. Reportedly, he was never without his sketchbook.[1] These four drawings of animals at the Bronx Zoo— part of a group of thirty-three sketches— were all made in a single day, 8 May 1904. With quick, efficient line Luks captured the essence of his subjects, from a tiger's powerful grace to the fragile timidity of fawns. These drawings reveal an empathetic heart behind the reporter's eye, just around the time that Luks was giving up newspaper work to devote himself full time to painting. Best known for his unapologetic portraits of the urban poor, Luks depicted children in particular with a sense of irrepressible optimism, innocent of what others saw as squalor in their lives. Here, he recorded in the same simple, unaffected way the almost human qualities of playful young bears, unaware of their captivity.

George Luks gave all of the Bronx Zoo drawings to his friend Edward Wales Root, an editorial writer for the *New York Sun*, who first met Luks and other members of The Eight just before their landmark exhibition in 1908.[2] Under their influence, Root became an art teacher and astute collector of early-twentieth-century American art. He lent several of the zoo drawings, including *Tiger*, *Bear + Cubs – Cubs*, and *Fawns*, to the Armory Show in 1913.[3] Root was a generous patron of the Addison Gallery from 1940 until his death in 1956, when he bequeathed twenty works of art to the collection, including paintings by Charles Burchfield, Arthur Dove, and Edward Hopper.[4] In 1958 his widow, Grace C. Root, donated the Bronx Zoo drawings to the Addison.

SJM

George B. Luks

BEAR + CUB – CUBS, 1904

Crayon on brown, medium weight (1), smooth wove paper mounted on board

9 15/16 x 7

Unsigned

Gift of Mrs. Edward Wales Root

1958.20

TOP TO BOTTOM
FAWNS, 1904

Crayon on brown, medium weight (1),
smooth wove paper mounted on board

7 x 9 15/16

Unsigned

Gift of Mrs. Edward Wales Root

1958.26

LIONESS, 1904

Crayon on brown, medium weight (1),
smooth wove paper mounted on board

7 x 9 15/16

Unsigned

Gift of Mrs. Edward Wales Root

1958.35

TIGER, 1904

Crayon on brown, medium weight (1),
smooth wove paper mounted on board

7 x 9 15/16

Unsigned

Gift of Mrs. Edward Wales Root

1958.33

BORN
15 November 1859
Goose Island, Chicago, Illinois

DIED
19 January 1937
New York, New York

An artist well connected with such American Renaissance painters as Abbott Thayer and George de Forest Brush, Alexander Shilling was known for his facility as a draftsman, printer, and painter.[1] After moving from his native Chicago to Manhattan in 1885, his life centered around his studio work and the camaraderie of fellow members of the New York Etching Club, New York Water Color Society, and Salmagundi Club. Fully devoted to his love of the landscape, especially the Dutch and Belgian countryside of his mother's homeland, Shilling traveled to Europe more than fifteen times between 1888 and 1935 to gather imagery in his sketchbooks, which he would later translate into oil and watercolor paintings in his Eighth Avenue studio.

These sketchbook drawings from one such trip to Holland, in autumn of 1907, deftly capture the signature geography and architecture of the Zeeland coastal town of Veere, a favorite destination of Shilling's before he served in the First World War. A delicate yet deliberate construction of hatched layers, Shilling's drawing method betrays his predilection for etching and engraving techniques that require such simple and direct conception, vision, and execution. Produced on the spot, spontaneously, rapidly, and unerringly, these sketches are as much records of his process as of place.

J M

64 Alexander Shilling

Sketchbook, 1907

Graphite and ink on 39 bound sheets of beige (1) and gray-blue, moderately thick, smooth wove paper

9 13/16 x 13 3/4 x 9/16

Unsigned

Inscribed in graphite on cover u.c.: Oct 20th to November 30th 07

Gift of Robert G. McIntyre

1940.4.1–39

LEFT TO RIGHT, TOP TO BOTTOM
Page 8 [Nov. 8/07, winding river and land]
Graphite on paper
1940.4.8

Page 21 [Nov. 11/07, pollarded tree]
Graphite on paper
1940.4.21

Page 27 [Nov. 13/07, four trees]
Graphite on paper
1940.4.27

Page 33 [Nov. 28/07, village road with buildings]
Graphite on paper
1940.4.33

BORN
28 February 1887
Eurburick-Kovno, Lithuania

DIED
15 November 1966
Bath, Maine

William Zorach's artistic life was continually informed and enriched by the natural world, to which his connection was revived yearly when he and his wife, Marguerite, retreated from New York to spend summers in the countryside. As he wrote in his autobiography, in these summer forays he would rediscover "the richness of invention in nature."[1]

This delicate drawing of fractured rock and falling water was prompted by a significant trip to California in the summer of 1920. After visiting family, the Zorachs camped in Yosemite National Park, an area familiar to Marguerite from her childhood in California. Both Marguerite and William drew and painted in this landscape. William was captivated by the mountain terrain and climbed into the mountains with Ansel Adams, who was destined to be Yosemite's most reverential photographer, but at that time was an eighteen-year-old boy serving as custodian of the Sierra Club headquarters in Yosemite.[2] Adams recounted that on their hiking trip, "Bill sketched madly whenever we stopped for a breath."[3]

Zorach translated the joy of his Yosemite experience into countless drawings and watercolors, and a number of oils. The crayon drawing owned by the Addison captures not only the majestic height of Yosemite Falls but also the pulsating beat of falling water in short shimmering marks barely framed by the energized play of thick and thin lines and planes. In the spirit and animation of the drawing, the artist reflects the emotional exuberance of this natural wonder.

SCF

66 ## William Zorach

YOSEMITE FALLS, 1920

Crayon on white, moderately thick, smooth wove paper

20 1/4 x 13 1/2

Signed in graphite l.r.: William Zorach 1920

Inscribed in graphite l.l.: Yosemite Falls

Museum purchase

1961.51

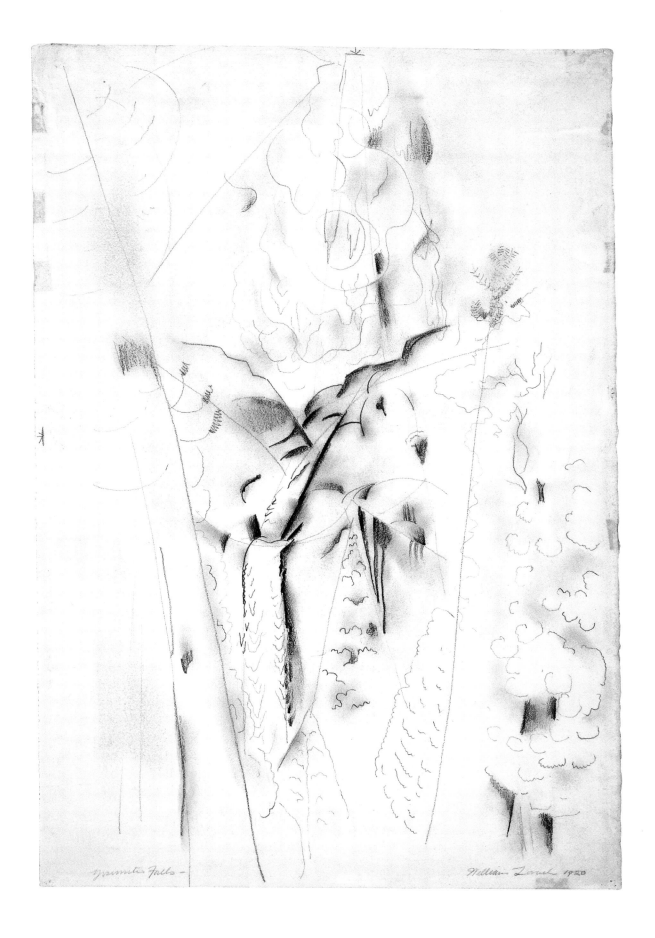

Yosemite Falls —   William Zorach 1920

67

BORN
4 January 1877
Lewiston, Maine

DIED
2 September 1943
Ellsworth, Maine

In 1911 Alfred Stieglitz sent Marsden Hartley two reproductions of paintings by Paul Cézanne. Hartley enthusiastically responded: "They come indeed like the purest light after a dark season—and refresh the eye, the mind, indeed, the soul."[1] Influenced by many of the avant-garde artists who exhibited at Stieglitz's "291" gallery, Hartley was also drawn to Cézanne, whose work and ideas became a lasting source of instruction, inspiration, and renewal.

In 1926, after spending several years in Europe experimenting with different styles and subjects, Hartley settled in Cézanne's native region of Aix-en-Provence in search of new direction. While at Aix, Hartley eschewed the emphasis on inner vision and subjectivity that had characterized his previous work for an art more rooted in the observable facts of nature. Literally and figuratively following in the French painter's footsteps, Hartley immersed himself in the Provencal landscape and created works incorporating both Cézanne's ideas and vocabulary.[2] Working directly from nature, he made oils, watercolors, pencil drawings, silverpoints, and lithographs of many of the motifs found in Cézanne's paintings.

Boulder and Trees is one of the numerous studies the artist made of rocks and trees in the forests near Chateau Noir. Emulating what the art historian Gail Scott has described as Cézanne's "genius for selection and penetration,"[3] Hartley eliminated extraneous detail to get at the essence of his subject. Stripped down to passages of delicately drawn parallel lines and patterned contours, the drawing is less a likeness of nature than a depiction of the design that lies beneath nature. Hartley's spare lines and simple forms transcend the particular to touch upon the universal. Conveying the motion, volume, and interconnectedness of forms, this drawing captures the very heartbeat of nature.

ANK

68 Marsden Hartley

BOULDER AND TREES, 1927

Graphite on beige (1), moderately thick, moderately textured (2) wove paper

14 11/16 x 11 3/4

Signed in graphite l.c.: Marsden Hartley / 27

Museum purchase

1959.16

BORN
29 June 1885
Chicago, Illinois

DIED
22 April 1956
Mer, Loire-et-Cher, France

Profile Head of a Girl exists as a testament to the sensitive, delicate aspect of the art of John Storrs, who is best known for his geometric and often abstract sculptural work. The drawing, executed with a controlled but gentle hand, displays in its few expressive lines the sophistication of its creator. Storrs received extensive training in art at numerous American art schools and under the guidance of Auguste Rodin in Paris.[1] The naturalism of his early sculptural work soon evolved toward abstraction: basic geometric forms illustrated the artist's interest in Cubism and Futurism, while his sleek, streamlined aesthetic is now heralded as a precursor to the Art Deco movement.[2]

In 1926 Storrs began drawing in silverpoint, a medium he would use to sketch his sculptures, capture the fragile faces of contemplative women, and memorialize the anguish of prisoners in the German camp where he was interned during World War II. Storrs created his naturalistic silverpoint drawings on a smooth, coated paper that caught fragments of silver as the drawing instrument passed along the surface. Silverpoint creates a thin, delicate line and requires a surety and steadiness of hand, as mistakes cannot be corrected without detection.[3]

Storrs's *Profile Head of a Girl* exhibits his skillful draftsmanship and his ability to capture a moment—here, one of contemplative beauty. Of his silverpoint drawings, Storrs said, "The glide of the silver needle over the prepared paper is easier than even the softest pencil, and that very smoothness invites a subtler, more flexible line. The resulting drawing is evanescent—it gives you the feeling it is about to vanish away. This delicacy helps [create] an illusion of a quick jotting down of a vivid impression of a moment."[4]

GGS

70 # John Bradley Storrs

PROFILE HEAD OF A GIRL, 1928

Metalpoint on light gray, moderately thick, very smooth coated paper

13 1/8 x 10 1/8

Signed in metalpoint l.r.: STORRS / 29-10-28-V

Gift of Richard S. Davis

1949.10

BORN
2 August 1871
Lock Haven, Pennsylvania

DIED
7 September 1951
Hanover, New Hampshire

"Lines can mean form, depth, shadow, and light…. The good line does more than describe the outside edge, it contains the form."[1] John Sloan explicated his theories on the making and meaning of art in his book *Gist of Art*, published in 1939, the year after his first major retrospective exhibition was presented at the Addison Gallery of American Art. Best known as a member of the Ashcan School, Sloan produced work in both print and paint media that captured the energy and life of the city and its inhabitants. By the 1930s, however, his work had changed from the social realism for which he had become renowned to a style characterized by crosshatched figures, likely derived from the linear quality of his contemporary etchings.[2]

Nude on a Chaise Longue, purchased by the museum from the 1938 retrospective, illustrates the search for more sculptural forms that dominated Sloan's work in the thirties. Strong, simple lines form the contours of the figure and lead the eye from the tip of her big toe in the foreground through the S-curve of her legs, up her torso and over her sloping shoulders, to her head that rests on the pillow in the background. The crosshatches both define her form, lending shape to the swell of her thigh and breasts, and reject it by calling attention to the surface of the paper. We see the figure at once alive and physically present in three-dimensional space and as an obvious creation of the artist, a form composed of a series of intersecting lines. According to Sloan, the signifying of form through texture led to a "realization" of the figure, which "comes when you make something more real to the mind than it is in nature."[3]

GGS

72

John Sloan

NUDE ON CHAISE LONGUE, 1932

Graphite on beige (1), medium weight (1), smooth wove paper

12 1/16 x 15 1/2

Signed in graphite l.r.: John Sloan

Museum purchase

1938.68

BORN
21 March 1880
Weissenburg, Bavaria

DIED
17 February 1966
New York, New York

After moving to the United States in 1930, Hans Hofmann began reshaping the American art scene, mostly unacknowledged, until 1948, when the Addison Gallery organized his first museum retrospective, *Hans Hofmann: Painter and Teacher*.[1] Celebrating the evolution of his influential Abstract Expressionist work in both the studio and classroom, this historic exhibition debuted a selection of Hofmann's formative drawings, including these four.[2] In his exhibition text, Addison director Bartlett H. Hayes asserts their significance for Hofmann's mature style: "Hofmann's figure drawings illustrate a progression…from early studies of natura-listic shapes to a powerful development of planes and volumes in space."[3] Comparing *Reclining Figure*—in which dark areas represent shadows beneath objects to form "realistic" patterns—with the seminal image *Figure Drawing* (p. 76), he notes the breakthrough: "natural light sources are disregarded for the sake of imparting a pictorial vitality to

the two-dimensional composition. The contrast of light and dark areas then becomes the coordinating element of the picture."[4]

Like the exercises he assigned his students, such drawings freed Hofmann to explore his conviction that "things exist only in relation"—the model to the room, the solid to the void, light to shadow, white page to black ink.[5] Produced by the thousands from 1932 to 1935, a period of rapid stylistic transition for Hofmann, the drawings limbered his hand and eye to simplify and reduce natural forms to an abstractness that prepared him for the spontaneous arabesques of bold form and contrasting "push and pull" in his later painting.[6] Recognizing how clearly they delineate this transition when sequenced, Hayes acquired these four drawings as the perfect record of Hofmann's develop-ment as an abstract artist and an illustration of the synthesis of his teaching theory.[7]

JM

74

Hans Hofmann

RECLINING FIGURE, c. 1932–35

Ink and ink wash on cream (2),
medium weight (1), smooth bond paper

8 9/16 x 11 1/16

Unsigned

Museum purchase

1948.14.3

BOTTOM
SEATED FIGURE, c. 1932–35

Ink and ink wash on cream (2),
medium weight (1), smooth bond paper

8 x 11

Unsigned

Museum purchase

1948.14.1

76   Hans Hofmann
      FIGURE DRAWING, c. 1932–35

      Ink on cream (2), medium weight (2),
      smooth wove paper
      10 15/16 x 8 7/16
      Unsigned
      Museum purchase
      1948.14.4

FIGURE, c. 1932–35

Ink and ink wash on cream (2),
medium weight (2), smooth wove paper

10 15/16 x 8 1/2

Unsigned

Museum purchase

1948.14.2

BORN
19 March 1882
Paris, France

DIED
19 October 1935
New York, New York

The artist Marsden Hartley described Gaston Lachaise as an "indomitable pagan who saw the entire universe in the form of a woman."[1] Lachaise received his formal art training in France, the country of his birth, but it was the American Isabel Nagle who inspired him to move to the United States at the age of twenty-three. She became his muse, his model, and eventually his wife, and much of his work is a testament to her presence in his life.[2] A modernist before the movement was popular, Lachaise had a small but elite audience, and through the aid of Arthur B. Davies, one of his sculptures appeared in the pivotal 1913 Armory Show.

Figure Walking to the Left exemplifies Lachaise's unique vision: a woman created by the explosive impact of Rodin's heroic figures and Brancusi's simplification of form, with a character stemming from the personal, erotic fantasy of the artist.[3] The exaggeration of the female form makes the model both solid and buoyant, her heavy breasts bouncing, while walking coquettishly away from us on her tiptoes. She invites us into her world with a flirtatious look over her shoulder, dominating the space of the paper and commanding our attention. Lachaise drew his inspiration from the monumental figures of French academic art but also from prehistoric sculpture.[4] The woman of this drawing was formed with a limited number of lines and yet embodies womanhood: she is both sensuous and comforting, Eve and Mother Earth. "Finally and first," said e. e. cummings of the figures of Lachaise, "what human or inhuman aspect beckons as intensely as the vast creature, weightless but resolute, in whom we experience not flesh and not form but idea; dreamlike, authentically impossible?"[5]

GGS

78 Gaston Lachaise

FIGURE WALKING TO THE LEFT,
c. 1934

Graphite on beige (1), medium weight (2),
smooth wove paper
24 1/8 x 19 1/16
Signed in graphite l.r.: GLachaise
Gift of John B. Pierce, Jr. (PA 1941)
1968.5

BORN
10 December 1900
Naples, Italy

DIED
10 May 1964
Malibu, California

Toward the end of his life, Rico Lebrun wrote about his creative process:

> I find it best to work from objects and the figure literally, then to continue in the same stride, working away from model or object but still fresh from the contact with them. But it is not until the drawing assumes the look of a protest against the fetters of dictation from the object, and breathes a definite air of controlled deliverance, that I feel perfectly at home and totally involved. I keep telling myself that the line should finally look as if traced with a full sense of life, not traced *from* life.[1]

He could have been speaking specifically about his ink drawing *Dancers*. At various times in his career, Lebrun engaged some very difficult subjects—the Crucifixion, Dante's *Inferno*, the Holocaust—often on a very large scale. But in this small drawing, Lebrun expresses only the sheer joy, the utter abandon of dancers surrendering to music. The drawing is about motion. The artist's quick strokes emphasize the dancers' race across the unseen stage. Anatomical details of hands and feet are lost to speed. There is something of Pablo Picasso's classical period in the transparent dress and facial features of the female dancer. Her partner, significantly older than she, pursues her with "a full sense of life."

Lebrun was born in Naples, where Italian and Spanish cultures merged and Picasso and Francisco Goya permeated the imagination of young art students. After attending the local art school, Lebrun worked in a stained glass factory. In 1924 he was sent to America to oversee an installation and decided to stay. He became a successful commercial artist in New York before turning his full attention to painting in the 1930s.[2]

SJM

80

Rico Lebrun

DANCERS, 1940

Ink on beige (1), medium weight (1), smooth wove paper

10 7/8 x 13 1/4

Signed in ink l.r.: Rico Lebrun / 1940

Museum purchase

1945.7

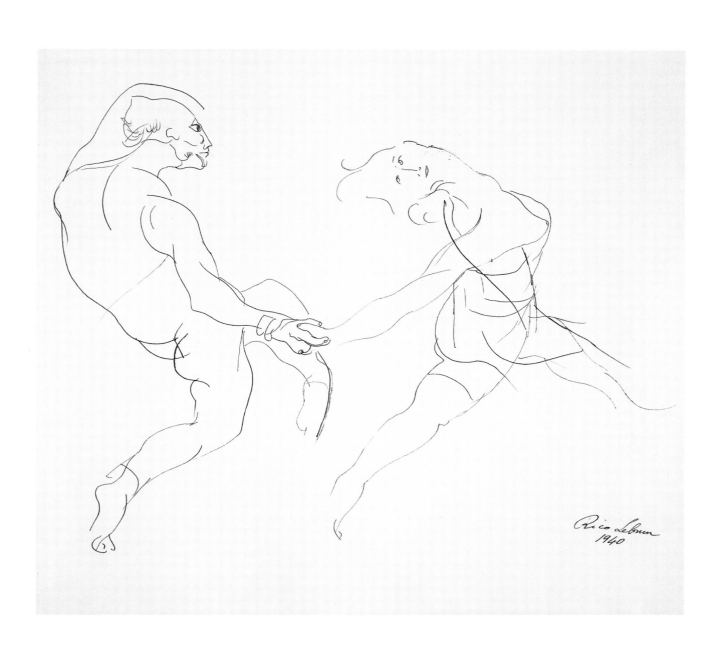

BORN
3 March 1902
Cincinnati, Ohio

DIED
19 February 1988
Riverdale, New York

For more than forty years, Isabel Bishop observed the hustle and bustle of New York City's Union Square. Office workers and bums, shop girls, waitresses, and students all remained types for her, not individuals. In the 1930s she focused on working girls at lunchtime, trying to convey a sense of their social mobility:

> It's a moment in their lives when they are really in motion, because they, of course, are looking for husbands and, at the same time, they're earning their living.... The time that I try to catch them, that I'm interested in trying to present, is when they are in their lunch hour, the hour of respite, when both these things seem to me to be communicated—that is, their double purpose. I feel, in a moment during the day when they have stopped but, in a sense, the work day is continuing.[1]

Bishop paid close attention to gestures and body language—the way young women habitually flex their feet to relieve the strain of walking in fashionably high heels, for example. After making preliminary sketches in the square, Bishop would invite her subject to her studio to replicate the pose that had caught her attention.[2] In *Make-Up*, a waitress checks her face in her compact. With characteristic virtuosity, Bishop simultaneously animated the figure and expressed her idea of mobility in life. The nervous energy of this woman's back, the merest suggestion of her right hand, and the delicate lines defining her feet convince us that she will move on at any moment.

The untitled drawing below is probably of Rosalynd, a girl whose face appears frequently in Bishop's work of the 1930s.

SJM

82 Isabel Bishop

MAKE-UP, c. 1935–36

Ink, ink wash, and graphite on cream (3), moderately thick, smooth Strathmore wove paper

11 1/2 x 6

Signed in graphite c.r.: Isabel Bishop

Inscribed in graphite l.r.: mat 4 1/2 / 4 1/2 / 5

Museum purchase

1936.42

JOHN TRUMBULL, THE COHOES FALLS

1. Theodore Sizer, *The Works of Colonel John Trumbull* (New Haven: Yale University Press, 1967), p. 7.
2. For discussion of Trumbull's landscape paintings, see Bryan Wolf, "Revolution in the Landscape: John Trumbull and Picturesque Painting," in Helen A. Cooper, *John Trumbull: The Hand and Spirit of a Painter* (New Haven: Yale University Art Gallery, 1982), pp. 206–15.
3. The Addison's study is illustrated and discussed in Cooper, p. 218.

WILLIAM DUNLAP, NIAGARA FROM THE BANK ABOVE THE STONE HOUSE; BARRACKS AT BLACK ROCK; and TICONDEROGA

1. A list of the known watercolors is included in William Dunlap, *Diary of William Dunlap, 1766–1839*, 3 vols. (New York: The New York Historical Society, 1931), 1:xxiii–xxv.
2. William Dunlap, *History of the Rise and Progress of the Arts of Design in the United States*, 2 vols. (New York: George P. Scott and Co., 1834), 1:275.
3. Ibid.

THOMAS SULLY, STUDIES OF YOUNG WOMEN

1. For the most complete review of Sully's career, see Monroe H. Fabian, *Mr. Sully, Portrait Painter: The Works of Thomas Sully (1783–1872)* (Washington, D.C.: Smithsonian Institution Press, 1983).
2. Ibid., pp. 19–20.

HENRY WALTON, HANNAH INGERSOLL

1. Leigh Rehner Jones, *Artist of Ithaca: Henry Walton and His Odyssey* (Ithaca: Herbert F. Johnson Museum of Art, Cornell University, 1988/89), pp. 5–10.
2. John and Katherine Ebert, *American Folk Painters* (New York: Charles Scribner's Sons, 1975), p. 40.

MANLEY NEHEMIAH WHIPPLE, CHARLES WOODWORTH

1. Genealogical information as well as several Whipple drawings are posted on the Whipple family Website, 23 October 2001, <www.Whipple.org> (13 April 2003).
2. Mary Sayre Haverstock, Jeannette Mahoney Vance, and Brian L. Meggitt, eds., *Artists in Ohio, 1787–1900* (Kent, Ohio: The Kent State University Press, 2000), p. 931.

JOHN LA FARGE, Sketchbook

1. Royal Cortissoz, *John La Farge: A Memoir and a Study* (1911; reprint, New York: Da Capo Press, 1971), p. 262.
2. Henry Adams, "The Mind of John La Farge," in *John La Farge* (Pittsburgh: Carnegie Museum of Art; Washington, D.C.: National Museum of American Art, Smithsonian Institution; New York: Abbeville Press, 1987), p. 14.
3. Quoted in Cortissoz, p. 121.
4. Ibid., p. 120.

EDWIN WHITEFIELD, VIEW OF PORTSMOUTH, N.H.

1. For a thorough review of Whitefield's work, see Bettina A. Norton, *Edwin Whitefield: Nineteenth-Century North American Scenery* (Barre, Mass.: Barre Publishing, 1977).
2. Richard M. Candee, *Building Portsmouth: The Neighborhoods & Architecture of New Hampshire's Oldest City* (Portsmouth, N.H.: Portsmouth Advocates, 1992), pp. 146–50.
3. Whitefield's pencil and wash drawing of "The View from Mount Vernon Street looking across the South Millpond" is in the M. and M. Karolik Collection of the Museum of Fine Arts, Boston. The whereabouts of the finished version of the Addison's drawing of the North Millpond is unknown. Whitefield's margin notes are unrelated to this Portsmouth scene. They refer to a hill in nearby Newington which offered a "very fine view" of Eliot, Maine, across the Piscataqua River.
4. *The Portsmouth Journal*, 5 July 1873. The Portsmouth views and five other Massachusetts towns drawn in 1876 were reproduced as sepia photographs rather than Whitefield's customary lithographs (Norton, p. 53). The advertisement in the 4 July 1873 *Portsmouth Chronicle* indicated that the photographs were available in two sizes. The Strawbery Banke Museum, Portsmouth, New Hampshire, owns photographs of both views. The Addison is grateful to Rodney Rowland and Richard M. Candee for their expertise in Portsmouth history and their assistance with research on Edwin Whitefield's work.

GEORGE INNESS, JUNE

1. Michael Quick to Maura Lyons, 21 February 1992, Addison Gallery Archives.

JOHN SINGER SARGENT, Mural Studies

1. See Charles Merrill Mount, *John Singer Sargent: A Biography* (New York: W.W. Norton, 1955), p. 29.
2. Ibid., p. 32.
3. "Palais Garnier: Opera House and Masterpiece," <www.opera-de-paris.fr/> (8 April 2003).
4. See Edmond About, *Notice sur les peintures décoratives du grand foyer de L'Opéra par Paul Baudry de L'Institut* (Paris: Guérinet, 1876), pls. 25–33. For the discovery of (and reference to) this source material, thanks are due to research curator Alvin L. Clark, Jr., and assistant curator Miriam Stewart of the Department of Drawings, Fogg Art Museum, Harvard University.
5. Originally drawn on a single sheet, the images were sectioned into five separate works before being given to the Addison by Miss Emily Sargent and her sister, Mrs. Francis Ormond, in 1932.
6. See About.
7. In a letter to the author dated 5 February 2003, Miriam Stewart suggests that these studies may be related to Carolus-Duran's work on the Palais du Luxembourg, which would attribute them a later date. In the winter of 1877, Carolus was at work on a ceiling decoration for the Palais du Luxembourg and had engaged Sargent's assistance on commissions by this time (see Mount, pp. 46–47).

THOMAS NAST, TAMMANY TIGER

1. Thomas Nast St. Hill, *Thomas Nast: Cartoons and Illustrations* (New York: Dover, 1974), pp. 1–2.
2. Ibid., pp. 17–19.
3. Jim Zwick, "Political Cartoons of Thomas Nast," *Political Cartoons and Cartoonists*, ed. Jim Zwick, 1995, <www.boondocksnet.com/gallery/nast_intro.html> (18 April 2003).

WILLIAM MORRIS HUNT, THE WOODED KNOLL

1. Marchal E. Landgren and Sharman Wallace McGurn, *The Late Landscapes of William Morris Hunt* (College Park, Md.: University of Maryland Department of Art, 1975–76), pp. 13–14.
2. Ibid., pp. 17, 21.
3. Helen M. Knowlton, *The Art Life of William Morris Hunt* (Boston: Little, Brown, 1899), p. 116.

84　Notes

ROBERT SWAIN GIFFORD, BARNEYS JOY WILLOWS

1. "Robert Swain Gifford," *AskART*,
   <www.askart.com/Biography.asp> (13 May 2003).
2. Quoted in Natalie Spassky et al., *American Paintings in the Metropolitan Museum of Art, Vol. II; A Catalogue of Works by Artists Born between 1816 and 1845* (New York: The Metropolitan Museum of Art, 1985), pp. 549–51.

WINSLOW HOMER, THE LAST BOAT IN

1. Helen A. Cooper, *Winslow Homer Watercolors* (Washington, D.C.: National Gallery of Art; New Haven: Yale University Press, 1986), p. 98.
2. Nicolai Cikovsky, Jr., and Franklin Kelly, *Winslow Homer* (Washington, D.C.: National Gallery of Art; New Haven: Yale University Press, 1995), pp. 180–82.
3. Ibid., pp. 204–11.

THOMAS MORAN, THE MOUNTAIN RANGE

1. Carol Clark, *Thomas Moran: Watercolors of the American West* (Austin: University of Texas Press, 1980), p. 21.
2. Quoted from G.W. Sheldon, *American Painters* (1881), in ibid., p. 30 n. 32.
3. Moran mistakenly spelled it "San Louis Valley."
4. Clark, p. 59.

CARLTON THEODORE CHAPMAN, Sketchbooks

1. Aurelie R. Chapman to Charles Sawyer, 11 November 1939, Addison Gallery Archives.
2. *Harper's Weekly*, 7 May 1898, p. 450.

JOHN SINGER SARGENT, NUDES; THREE HEADS; and DRAPERY

1. Charles Merrill Mount, *John Singer Sargent: A Biography* (New York: W.W. Norton, 1955), p. 187.
2. See Carol Troyen, *Sargent's Murals in the Museum of Fine Arts, Boston* (Boston: Museum of Fine Arts, 1999), pp. 9–10, for a list of Boston-area mural projects by Sargent and others.
3. See Patricia Hills, "A Portfolio of Drawings," in her *John Singer Sargent* (New York: Whitney Museum of American Art and Harry N. Abrams, 1986), p. 266.
4. Ibid., see pp. 266–69.
5. Miriam Stewart to Jen Mergel, 29 January 2003, suggests that the poses in *Nudes in Action* may be related to the mural friezes of athletic scenes in the stairwell of the Museum of Fine Arts, Boston, and that the heavy dark paper of *Drapery* is similar to that used for studies for the Boston Public Library murals. (One section of the library project installed in 1919 depicts Christ folded up under the draped garments of a seated female figure who personifies the Church.) See "BPL-John Singer Sargent-Church," <www.bpl.org/guides/sargentmurals.htm> (22 April 2003).

GEORGE B. LUKS, Zoo Sketches

1. *George Luks: An Artistic Legacy* (New York: Owen Gallery, 1997), p. 15.
2. Joseph S. Trovato, *Edward W. Root: Collector and Teacher* (Clinton, N.Y.: Fred L. Emerson Gallery, Hamilton College, 1982), p. 43.
3. Grace C. Root, handwritten notes, c. 1957, Edward Wales Root Papers, Archives of American Art, Roll 2376. Quoted by permission of the Board of Trustees, Munson-Williams-Proctor Arts Institute, Utica, NY.
4. Susan C. Faxon "Portraits of Patronage: The History of the Addison Gallery's Collection and Its Donors," in *Addison*

Gallery of American Art, 65 Years: A Selective Catalogue (Andover: Addison Gallery of American Art, 1996), pp. 55–58.

ALEXANDER SHILLING, Sketchbook

1. Alec J. Hammerslough, "The Annals of an Artist," in *The Book of Alexander Shilling* (New York: Paisley Press, 1937), pp. 52–60, 68–69, is the source of all biographical information given here.

WILLIAM ZORACH, YOSEMITE FALLS

1. Quoted in Jessica Nichols, *Marguerite & William Zorach: Harmonies and Contrast* (Portland, Maine: Portland Museum of Art, 2001), p. 37.
2. James Alinder, ed., *Ansel Adams, 1902–1984* (Carmel, Calif.: The Friends of Photography, 1984), p. 25.
3. Ansel Adams with Mary Street Alinder, *Ansel Adams: An Autobiography* (New York: Little, Brown, 1985), pp. 61–63.

MARSDEN HARTLEY, BOULDER AND TREES

1. Jeanne Hokin, *Pinnacles and Pyramids: The Art of Marsden Hartley* (Albuquerque: University of New Mexico Press, 1993), p. 30.
2. Barbara Haskell, *Marsden Hartley* (New York: Whitney Museum of American Art and New York University Press, 1980), p. 75.
3. Gail R. Scott, *Marsden Hartley* (New York: Abbeville Press, 1988), p. 34.

JOHN BRADLEY STORRS, PROFILE HEAD OF A GIRL

1. Noel Frackman, *John Storrs* (New York: Whitney Museum of Art, 1986), pp. 12–13.
2. *John Storrs (1885–1956): A Retrospective Exhibition of Sculpture* (Chicago: Museum of Contemporary Art, 1976), p. 6.
3. Bruce Weber, *The Fine Line: Drawing with Silver in America* (West Palm Beach, Fla.: Norton Gallery & School of Art, 1985), pp. 19–20.
4. Ibid., p. 21.

JOHN SLOAN, NUDE ON CHAISE LONGUE

1. John Sloan, *Gist of Art* (New York: American Artists Group, 1939), p. 57.
2. David W. Scott and E. John Bullard, *John Sloan, 1871–1951* (Boston: Boston Book & Art, [1971]), p. 31.
3. Sloan, p. 60.

HANS HOFMANN, Figure Drawings

1. See Cynthia Goodman, "Hans Hofmann: A Master in Search of the 'Real,'" in Cynthia Goodman, *Hans Hofmann* (New York: Whitney Museum of American Art; Munich: Prestel, 1990), p. 58: the Addison exhibition was the first one-person show given to any of the Abstract Expressionists.
2. See the exhibition's publication, Hans Hofmann, *Search for the Real and Other Essays*, Sara T. Weeks and Bartlett H. Hayes, Jr., eds. (Andover: Addison Gallery of American Art, 1948), p. 75: an illustration of the installation shows all four drawings, labeled as "figure drawings, New York, 1932–35" and hung in the sequence (l–r): *Reclining Figure, Seated Figure, Figure Drawing, Figure*, which is followed here; Barbara Rose, *Hans Hofmann Drawings: 1930–1944* (New York: André Emmerich Gallery, 1976), n.p.: Rose notes that the exhibition included "many inks of the thirties and early forties, which were entirely unknown to the public."
3. Hayes, in Hofmann, p. 24.
4. Ibid., p. 25.

5. See Goodman, p. 34: Hofmann is quoted by a student who recalls his vanguard teaching theory: "The idea that forms exist in relation was not part of the formal art instruction in the typical school of the time. I never had it before Hofmann and I don't think a great many people did either."
6. See Rose, n.p.
7. The drawings were purchased for the collection on 4 March 1948 following the exhibition's closing. For more on Hayes's interest in presenting Hofmann's evolution, see Jock Reynolds, "The End Depends on the Beginning: Some Reflections on Teaching," in Susan C. Faxon et al., *Addison Gallery of American Art, 65 Years: A Selective Catalogue* (Andover: Addison Gallery of American Art, 1996), pp. 244–45.

GASTON LACHAISE, FIGURE WALKING TO THE LEFT

1. Hilton Kramer, *The Sculpture of Gaston Lachaise* (New York: Eakins Press, 1967), p. 27.
2. Ibid., p. 10.
3. Ibid., p. 12.
4. Ibid.
5. Ibid., p. 26.

RICO LEBRUN, DANCERS

1. Rico Lebrun, *Drawings* (Berkeley and Los Angeles: University of California Press, 1961), p. 30.
2. Ibid., p. 9.

ISABEL BISHOP, MAKE-UP

1. Isabel Bishop interviewed by Louis M. Starr, September 1957, quoted in Helen Yglesias, *Isabel Bishop* (New York: Rizzoli, 1988), p. 66.
2. Linda Weintraub, "Isabel Bishop—First Impressions," in Yglesias, p. 147.

85

The work as a **study** EVIDENCE OF THE CREATIVE PROCESS   LINDA KONHEIM KRAMER

Many works on paper in the collection of the Addison Gallery of American Art are studies that artists made to explore visual ideas. They are the artist's notes, used as tools for developing concepts, trying out compositions, or examining specific details. In the same way that the first drafts of a manuscript expose the writer's decision-making process, a drawn study may reveal any one of the stages in the realization of a project, from the initial inspiration to the final composition. As a record of the artist's thoughts about a subject or a composition, the study provides valuable evidence of the creative process.

The earliest studies in the Addison collection are those that John Singleton Copley made to develop details for the contemporary battle scenes and biblical stories that he painted in England in the late eighteenth century. The beautiful drawing in chalk on blue paper, apparently from life, is of a helmsman in the painting of *The Siege of Gibraltar*, 1783–91 (Guildhall Art Gallery, London), who appears in the finished work as a tiny figure that can barely be made out amidst the commotion of the battle. Other such studies were undoubtedly prepared for many of the figures in this action-packed composition, as many similar drawings by Copley are known. In another chalk drawing on blue paper in this collection, he examines the alert head and prancing forelegs of a horse for the dramatic biblical scene of 1798, *Saul Reproved by Samuel* (Museum of Fine Arts, Boston). Copley did not, however, always draw on nature for inspiration. For his 1783 painting of another modern battle, *The Death of Major Peirson, 6 January 1781* (Tate Gallery, London), Copley seems to have taken the pose of the central figure from that of Patroclus's dead body in his 1774–75 chalk and charcoal drawing *The Battle over Patroclus's Body*. Perhaps this was to acknowledge the parallel between their heroic deaths.[1]

About the same time, Mather Brown, another American history painter living in England, achieved public recognition for his three oils depicting Lord Cornwallis's victory over Tipu, the sultan of Mysore, in 1792. Although Brown never went to India, the subject matter of these paintings was reportedly based on the real details of the event supplied to him by an eyewitness.[2] In this case, the Addison's sensitive and delicately detailed black and red chalk drawing fully renders the entire composition for the first painting of the series, *Tipu Sahib Taking Leave of His Children* (location unknown). Brown depicts a touching family scene as the sultan's two boys prepare to depart from home in 1790 to deliver the peace treaty to Cornwallis and become his hostages.

Preliminary studies from nature often possess a spontaneity and immediacy that is not carried into the final presentation. For example, the charm and spirit of the crested titmouse and the golden crested wren that John James Audubon captured in watercolor sketches painted in their natural habitats—in 1810 and 1820, respectively—were not transmitted to the engravings that illustrate the double-elephant-folio volumes of *Birds of America*. Attention to formal design and factual accuracy prevailed in the large watercolors that Audubon developed from these studies and from which the plates were faithfully engraved.

The poetically evocative graphite drawing of Mount Vernon, one of a number of views that William Trost Richards drew directly at the site during a week in October of 1854, was also a preliminary study for an engraving. Richards had been sent to Virginia by the Philadelphia Art Union to prepare studies for a painting of Mount Vernon from which a print was to be engraved for distribution to its subscribers. A more conventional portrait of the house than the Addison's atmospheric landscape study was chosen for the 1855 painting (Newark Museum), but the engraving project was abandoned when the Art Union disbanded in 1855.[3]

Unlike Richards's spending one week at Mount Vernon, Eastman Johnson worked in a Nantucket meadow for years as he struggled to resolve the composition for his large, multifigure painting *The Cranberry Harvest* of 1880 (Timken Museum of Art, San Diego).[4] The Addison's small watercolor and graphite sketch, *Berry Picking*, was one of the many preparatory studies that the artist made between 1875 and 1880. Although the purpose of this sketch was primarily to note the poses, activities, and clothing of the berry pickers, with minimal means it captures concisely their layout and the sunlit coastal atmosphere of the final painting. In this quickly recorded sketch, according to Theodore Stebbins, "the artist—perhaps for the first time—[was] sensing the pictorial potential of these sun drenched workers in the fields."[5]

Quite the opposite is Johnson's polished and meticulously crafted 1856 charcoal and chalk, bust-length portrait of James Cochran Dobbin, the Secretary of the Navy, modeled after the successful "crayon" portraits of Washington dignitaries that Johnson made in the 1840s. It could have served as a final work, as had his earlier such portraits on paper, but he went on to use this one as a study for a three-quarter-length oil portrait of Dobbin. Johnson made the drawing soon after he returned to America from his studies in Europe, and he may have decided to make the oil version to demonstrate the new skills he had acquired abroad.

John Singer Sargent's splendid drawing of the head and torso of a man is one of the hundreds of works on paper he executed in preparation for murals commissioned in 1921 for the stairway of the Museum of Fine Arts in Boston.[6] The study from a model of a man pulling a mighty bow establishes the pose for the figure of the leaping centaur Chiron teaching the young Achilles to use a bow and arrow. The expressive and dynamic character of the drawing was abandoned in favor of a two-dimensional, formal aesthetic in the decorative ceiling panels of the trials of classical heroes and demigods.[7]

The desire to construct representational compositions according to formal design principles seems to have caused other artists in the early twentieth century to make full compositional drafts in preliminary drawings before realizing them in another medium. The triangular composition that George Bellows invented for his drawing of a raging drunk being restrained by two women is based on Jay Hambidge's theory of dynamic symmetry. Every detail, down to the use of lithographic crayon to approximate the finished print, is completely worked out. Perhaps because of the theoretical construction of the composition Bellows needed to see exactly what it would look like before reversing it for transfer to the stone. The lithograph was used to illustrate an article supporting prohibition in the May 1924 issue of *Good Housekeeping*.

Several American artists who had returned from Europe in the 1930s and '40s found the task of applying Italian Renaissance styles and practices to American subject matter daunting enough to require that they prepare finished studies for their paintings and prints. Paul Cadmus's fully realized ink and graphite drawing entitled *Study for "Horseplay"* (c. 1935) recalls the manner of Italian Renaissance drawings. Even though the figure looks like one of the male nudes in Luca Signorelli's frescoes at Orvieto that had attracted the artist's attention in Italy,[8] this satiric drawing focuses on the back view of a nude man in a New York locker room. Cadmus used this drawing, with some variations, for an etching and for a painting in oil and egg tempera.

George Tooker's pencil and wash study on toned paper called *Study for "Market,"* executed in 1949, soon after he came home from Italy, depicts an open-air market on Bleeker Street in New York City, rendered in the solid architectonic style of the figures of fifteenth-century Italian masters such as Piero della Francesca. Tooker's drawing, like those made by the Renaissance fresco painters, is squared for transfer, in this case to a somewhat smaller painting that the artist executed in the labor-intensive Renaissance medium of egg tempera.

Another group of twentieth-century American modernists is represented in the collection by drawings or sketches of real scenes in which they saw forms and arrangements that conformed to the kind of abstraction they were seeking in their paintings. Preston Dickinson's small oil on board study, of about 1923, is a cityscape of factory rooftops in which he has focused on the interplay between the triangular shapes of the pointed roofs, the rectangular forms of the tall buildings, and the rounded water tanks and air vents, all in accord with the theories of Cubism that he learned when he was a student in Paris. Though the geometric forms of the buildings are emphasized in the study, the scene is grounded in reality through the careful detailing of every object as well as the shading and tonal variations that enrich and enliven the surface. The final, somewhat larger, oil on canvas is very closely related to this study, although the subject matter has been somewhat simplified, the active surfaces smoothed to areas of flatter color, and the edges hardened.

Notes

1. In Homer's *Iliad*, Patroclus was killed as he led the Greeks to victory over the Trojans, and in 1781, Major Peirson was mortally wounded after repulsing a French attack on the island of Jersey.

2. "Lord Cornwallis Receiving the Sons of Tipu as Hostages," *The Tiger and the Thistle: Tipu Sultan and the Scots of India*, National Gallery of Scotland, Edinburgh (2000), <http://www.nationalgalleries.org.uk/tipu/tipu325.htm> (15 August 2002).

3. Linda S. Ferber, *William Trost Richards: American Landscape & Marine Painter, 1833–1905* (Brooklyn: The Brooklyn Museum, 1973), pp. 48–51.

4. Teresa A. Carbone, "The Genius of the Hour: Eastman Johnson in New York, 1860–1880," in *Eastman Johnson: Painting America* (New York: The Brooklyn Museum in association with Rizzoli International, 1973), pp. 87, 98.

5. Theodore E. Stebbins, Jr., with John Caldwell and Carol Troyen, *American Master Drawings and Watercolors: A History of Works on Paper from Colonial Times to the Present* (New York: Harper & Row, 1976), p. 186.

6. See Carol Troyen, *Sargent's Murals in the Museum of Fine Arts, Boston* (Boston: Museum of Fine Arts, 1999), pp. 21–22, for details of the commission.

7. For the relation of these drawings to the murals in the Boston Museum, see letters from Thomas Fox (architect for the Museum of Fine Arts' rotunda decoration) to Charles Sawyer, 31 December 1931 and 3 March 1932, Addison Gallery Archives.

8. Justin Spring, "Paul Cadmus: Drawing from the Heart," in *Paul Cadmus: 90 Years of Drawing* (New York: D.C. Moore Gallery, 1998), pp. 4, 6.

9. Edward Hopper to Charles Sawyer, 19 October 1939, Addison Gallery Archives.

10. Stuart Davis, 29 September 1932, quoted in *Stuart Davis: Motifs and Versions* (New York: Salander-O'Reilly Galleries, 1988), n.p. (opp. fig. 21).

11. William C. Agee, "Stuart Davis," in *Addison Gallery of American Art, 65 Years: A Selective Catalogue* (Andover: Addison Gallery of American Art, 1996), p. 353 n. 2.

12. *Charles Sheeler in Andover: The Ballardvale Series 1946* (Andover: Addison Gallery of American Art, 1996).

13. Sotheby's, New York, *American Paintings, Drawings, and Sculpture*, 1 December 1999, lot 71.

14. Stephen Greene, artist's questionnaire, c. 1991, Addison Gallery Archives.

15. John McLaughlin, artist's questionnaire, 30 April 1969, Addison Gallery Archives.

Edward Hopper's crayon *Study for "Manhattan Bridge Loop," No. 2* (c. 1928), is one of a few black and white sketches that he drew on location as references for a picture he had planned very carefully in his mind in advance. Hopper claimed that the preliminary sketches did little to explain his painting, because the "color, design, and form" had been so simplified, but he clearly imposed on the sketch, perhaps unwittingly, the mysterious sensibility of the painting, which is in the Addison collection.[9]

Stuart Davis and Charles Sheeler also found inspiration for their geometric abstractions of the 1930s and '40s in the forms and colors of the real world. Davis claimed that he was looking around for "an accidental space definition, which corresponds obviously to geometry."[10] This approach to subject matter is clearly illustrated in the way that he emphasized the angles and triangles formed by the lines of the masts and buildings in his 1931 sketchbook drawing of the harbor in Gloucester, Massachusetts. In the resulting painting, *Red Cart* of 1932, the subject matter was reduced to yet more basic geometric forms. Davis moved the abstraction even further from reality in a contour drawing derived from the painting and squared for transfer in preparation for a 1939 print of the subject.[11]

When he was artist in residence at the Addison Gallery in 1946, Charles Sheeler was drawn to the geometric shapes of the abandoned mills of the Ballardvale neighborhood in Andover. Rather than making sketches, he recorded scenes in photographs that he used as preparatory studies for the oil painting *Ballardvale* of 1946. Three years later, Sheeler created *Ballardvale Revisited*, again from these photographs. However, this time he abstracted the scene further by sandwiching two or more negatives to produce a composite photograph that became the source for the composition of the painting.[12] Sheeler used the composite photograph to work out the forms and colors at the small scale of the Addison's opaque watercolor on board before enlarging it to the fifteen-inch-square painting in the same medium, in which he made some minor, but significant, variations in color and compositions.[13]

The later works of Stephen Greene and John McLaughlin represent the total abstraction of reality. No literal subject matter is at the core of Greene's sheet of expressive abstract watercolor studies of 1959–60. They were conceived as notes to himself in which he was playing with "hopefully meaningful forms," some of which might be used in subsequent works.[14] The Addison's three little abstract collages on paper by McLaughlin are actually models he made in 1969 after large "Constructivist" oil paintings, to help the Addison Gallery select works for an exhibition. They are, however, similar in size and medium to the studies that McLaughlin prepared for his paintings. "Sketches," he said, "in my case amount to penciled notes and construction paper blown up to one-quarter the size of the intended painting's dimensions. This is a long process often running into literally hundreds of possibilities before a composition is realized."[15]

The drawings discussed in this essay date from the late eighteenth to the late twentieth centuries. Each reflects the drawing practices and styles of a particular historical period as well as the working methods of the artist. Whatever their purpose, these studies are private expressions of an intimate nature that speak to the viewer with a simplicity and directness not generally evident in the final presentation. They reveal meaning, illuminate process, and suggest new insights into the style and significance of the work for which they were created.

The work as a **study** PORTFOLIO

BORN
10 October 1738
Springfield, Pennsylvania

DIED
11 March 1820
London, England

An American expatriate and eventually the president of the Royal Academy of London, Benjamin West was not afraid of grand themes realized on a grand scale. In 1779, he addressed King George III to challenge England's prohibition of religious art since the Protestant Reformation. Moved by West's conviction that scripture, grounded in truth, was the most natural subject for pure and "perfect" art, the king commanded he illustrate his point with some sketches.[1] West produced a series he described as "the progress of Revealed Religion from its commencement to its completion," compressing this history into thirty-five scenes in which God's authority is revealed.[2] When West presented these to the king and a committee of Anglican bishops, they agreed that his respectful treatment of the chosen subjects, "from the fall of Adam to the atonement of Christ," would "in no respect whatsoever violate the laws and usages of the Church of England."[3] With this decision, West was awarded a most ambitious commission: to design the architectural plan and painting scheme for the king's new private chapel at Horn Court, Windsor Castle. A new era of religious art in Britain, and in West's career, had begun.[4]

In *Hagar and Ishmael*, West illustrated the climax of the biblical story of the origin of Islam: we see Abraham's weary handmaiden and first-born son after he banished them to the desert and at the point of lost hope, discovered and assured by an angel that God would protect and bless Ishmael as the promised father of "a great nation."[5] Throughout the years after his royal chapel commission, West continued to explore the subject in multiple compositions in ink and oil.

JM

92 Benjamin West

HAGAR AND ISHMAEL, 1780

Iron gall ink, opaque watercolor, and chalk on beige (1), moderately thick, moderately textured (2) laid paper

18 1/8 x 21 1/8

Signed in iron gall ink l.r.: B West 1780

Museum purchase

1953.21

Hagar and Ishmael, 1776
Oil on canvas
76 x 54 1/2
The Metropolitan Museum of Art,
Maria DeWitt Jesup Fund, 1923

THE NOTES FOR THIS SECTION BEGIN ON PAGE 150

BORN
3 July 1738
Boston, Massachusetts

DIED
9 September 1815
London, England

In 1774, on the eve of the American Revolution, John Singleton Copley, America's most illustrious portraitist of the eighteenth century, left his native Boston to move permanently to England. Although a loyalist, Copley was also motivated by his ambition to paint grander subjects than portraits, by a desire to be exposed to the art of more sophisticated contemporaries, and the opportunity to study Old Master paintings. Arriving in London in June 1774, he left immediately for Rome to study and sketch Classical, Renaissance, and Baroque masterworks.

The Addison's drawing, originally known as *Battle Scene*, and now titled *The Battle over Patroclus's Body*, dates from this period.[1] It depicts the Homeric story of the revenge of Achilles against the Trojans over the death of his comrade Patroclus. At the left, the nude body of Patroclus is borne off the field.

As he provides protection for the body, Ajax turns to confront Hector, who has committed the affront of adorning himself in Patroclus's armor.[2] The opposing sides of the battle—Achilles and Patroclus on the left and Hector and the Trojans on the right—are completely contained and fully realized in deft black and white chalk delineation on two separate sheets of gray paper that have been joined. The band in the central portion caused by the overlapping of the sheets has sketchy black chalk marks, as if to simply link the two areas of action.

The role this work played ten years later in the development of Copley's famous history painting, *The Death of Major Peirson, 6 January 1781*, was first suggested by Richard Saunders in 1990 when he related the figure of dying Peirson being carried off the battlefield to the limp corpse of Patroclus in this drawing.[3]

S C F

94

John Singleton Copley

THE BATTLE OVER PATROCLUS'S
BODY, 1774–75

Chalk and charcoal on two joined sheets
of gray, medium weight (1),
slightly textured (2) laid paper

13 15/16 x 30

Unsigned

Museum purchase

1935.23

The Death of Major Peirson, 6 January 1781,
1783
Oil on canvas
97 x 144
Tate Gallery, London / Art Resource, NY

BORN
3 July 1738
Boston, Massachusetts

DIED
9 September 1815
London, England

In preparation for his major contemporary history painting *The Siege of Gibraltar* (1783–91; Guildhall Art Gallery, London), John Singleton Copley made over eighty careful studies.[1] In addition to oil portrait studies of the major participants, he sketched figure groups, detailed landscape elements, and worked out the intricate poses of figures in action.

On this sheet, one of two Copley drawings owned by the Addison that relate to *The Siege of Gibraltar*,[2] the artist sketched a helmsman balanced on a boat deck as he is about to pull the oar. The active, forward-leaning figure is given shape by swift parallel lines in black chalk. Economically applied white chalk highlights the edge of his leg, brow, cheek, and hand. On the reverse side of the sheet are four studies of a wounded, partially reclining sailor. According to the Copley scholar Jules Prown, the Addison's drawing was once the right side of a larger sheet. The left side of the sheet, which also has a helmsman on the recto and studies of a wounded sailor on the verso, is now in the collection of The Art Museum, Princeton University.[3]

SCF

96 John Singleton Copley

STUDY FOR "THE SIEGE OF GIBRALTAR," 1785–86

Chalk on blue, medium weight (2), moderately textured (2) laid paper

10 3/4 x 9

Unsigned

Inscribed in graphite l.l.: Siege of Gibraltar

Museum purchase

1947.24

BORN
3 July 1738
Boston, Massachusetts

DIED
9 September 1815
London, England

Renowned for the insightful and skillful portraiture of his early career in America, John Singleton Copley added history painting to his artistic repertoire after his immigration to England in 1774. While he continued to produce portraits, he threw himself into the construction of large-scaled, ambitious paintings devoted to classical, historical, and biblical subjects. *Saul Reproved by Samuel* is the last of approximately nine paintings of biblical scenes that Copley painted, none of them commissioned.[1]

For this work, Copley chose to depict the dramatic moment when the prophet Samuel admonishes Saul for disobeying God's order to destroy the Amalekites. The intensity of the action is reinforced by the bold scale of the figures and their tight grouping close to the forward plane of the picture. The diagonal thrust of Samuel's outstretched arm and pointing finger is echoed in the pulling backward of Saul, his soldiers, and horse, who is partially obscured by the crush of figures flanking him. In this study, Copley devoted his attention to the portion of the horse to be realized in the finished composition. The shaping of the animal's neck, head, and raised left leg are elegantly modeled in white and black chalk, while the back and rear legs are only barely suggested in a few quick black lines. Along the left and right edges of the drawing, the artist has marked a rule, probably to guide the figure's translation to the larger format of the painting. In that translation, Copley exaggerated the horse's alert stance, pulling back its head as it twists and rises up in midstride, eyes wide and nostrils flared, to emphasize the charged action of the painting.

SCF

98 ## John Singleton Copley

STUDY FOR "SAUL REPROVED BY SAMUEL FOR NOT OBEYING THE COMMANDMENTS OF THE LORD," 1798

Chalk on blue, moderately thick, moderately textured (2) laid paper

13 3/8 x 11 5/16

Unsigned

Inscribed in graphite u.l.: 1–101/2

Museum purchase

1935.21

Saul Reproved by Samuel, 1798
Oil on canvas
67 3/4 x 85 5/8
Museum of Fine Arts, Boston, Bequest of Susan Greene Dexter in memory of Charles and Martha Babcock Amory, 1925

99

BORN
7 October 1761
Boston, Massachusetts

DIED
25 May 1831
London, England

In April 1781, the Boston-born Mather Brown arrived at Benjamin West's London studio by way of Paris with a letter of recommendation from Benjamin Franklin in hand. An eager and talented young artist, he was soon admitted by West into the Royal Academy based on the quality of his drawing, becoming only the second American to receive such an opportunity.[1] He excelled in his life drawing, anatomy, and perspective courses, and was permitted to begin painting with oils within his first year. By the early 1790s, Brown's accumulated training and numerous commissions to paint both famous portraits and biblical subjects had readied him for the highly ambitious and widely popular history paintings of his mature career.[2]

Tipu Sahib Taking Leave of His Children is a study for one of Brown's early explorations in the historical genre. A perfect demonstration of the masterly skill that gained him entrée to the Academy, it depicts the first of three scenes that commemorate the military defeat of Tipu, the sultan of Mysore, by Lord Cornwallis, the British military commander-in-chief, which ended the Third Anglo-Mysore War. Within a year of the treaty of 1792, Brown composed preparatory works, including this drawing, and completed a series of paintings to record the terms of the sultan's surrender: Tipu's sons departing in sorrow from the zenana (women's quarters) of his estate; the royal children delivering his signed peace treaty to Lord Cornwallis; and Lord Cornwallis receiving the two sons as hostages.[3] Although Brown did not leave England to witness these dramatic episodes, he based his compositions on descriptive military reports and his own speculation, and presented them to a receptive London society impatient to see the popular story illustrated by the up-and-coming young American.[4]

JM

100 ## Mather Brown

TIPU SAHIB TAKING LEAVE OF HIS CHILDREN, c. 1792

Chalk on beige (1), medium weight (1), slightly textured (1) wove paper

16 5/8 x 21 15/16

Unsigned

Museum purchase

1942.22

Lord Cornwallis Receiving the Sons of Tipu as Hostages, 1792
Oil sketch, in two parts, on metal plate; remounted on board
17 9/16 x 20 1/2
The Bowes Museum, Barnard Castle, County Durham

BORN
26 April 1785
Les Cayes, Haiti

DIED
27 January 1851
New York, New York

Born in Saint-Domingue (now Haiti) and reared in France, John James Audubon came to the United States in 1803, and settled permanently in 1806. Sharing the romantic view of the American wilderness current among French artists and writers,[1] Audubon wrote that upon his arrival he was "prompted by an innate desire to acquire a thorough knowledge of the birds of this happy country" and immediately resolved to spend all of his leisure time drawing "each individual of its natural size and colouring."[2]

The stiff profile pose and relative flatness of Audubon's 1810 drawing of a crested titmouse is typical of scientific illustrations of the period and is, in fact, very similar to a depiction of the same subject in Alexander Wilson's *American Ornithology*, several volumes of which had been published by 1808. Yet, Audubon's innovative inclusion of natural habitat and graceful composition sets this drawing apart from conventional illustrations such as Wilson's.

Audubon's delicate rendering of a golden crested wren (p. 105) created ten years later shows marked improvement in his skills as a draftsman. Employing a more sophisticated mix of media, Audubon effectively captured both the iridescence of the now fully modeled bird's plumage as well as the texture of tree bark and foliage. This aesthetic and technical advance anticipates his mature style, which features complex compositions of multiple birds in densely detailed surroundings.

Soon after he made the portrait of the golden crested wren, Audubon decided to abandon his business aspirations to devote himself full-time to his artistry and dream of identifying and drawing—and eventually publishing—all the birds of America.[3] Both accurate and artistic, these early examples of what was to become Audubon's lifelong passion express the Enlightenment belief in the compatibility of art and science.

ANK

102 John James Audubon

CRESTED TITMOUSE, *PARUS BICOLOR*,
1810

Transparent and opaque watercolor
and graphite on beige (1), moderately thick,
moderately textured (2) wove paper

17 3/16 x 8 5/8

Signed in ink l.l.: J.A.

Inscribed in ink l.c.: Crested Titmouse A.W. /
Parus Bicolor / La Mélange Huppee d'Amerique. /
Red Banks 1st July 1810; in ink l.l.: No 175;
in graphite l.l.: Nyssa integrifolia / Black [Gum]

Gift of Mrs. F. Abbot Goodhue and Phoebe Milliken
in memory of F. Abbot Goodhue (PA 1902)

1964.21.1

Nyssa integrifolia
Black Gum

N.º 175.

Crested Titmouse A.W.
Parus Bicolor

La Mesange Huppée d'Amerique

J.J. Red Banks 1.st July 1810

John James Audubon

GOLDEN CRESTED WREN, *SYLVIA REGULUS*, 1820

Transparent and opaque watercolor, chalk, and graphite on beige (1), moderately thick, slightly textured (1) wove paper

17 7/8 x 11 5/8

Signed in ink l.l.: drawn by J.J. Audubon

Inscribed in ink l.c.: Golden Crested Wren A.W. / Silvia Regulus-; l.l.: Shippingport Kentucky Jany. 28th 1820 / drawn by J.J. Audubon; l.r.: Mizletoe on Black Walnut-; in graphite l.l.: #154; l.r.: Black Walnut

Gift of Mrs. F. Abbot Goodhue in memory of Elizabeth Johnson Cushing

1968.29

Golden Crested Wren A. W.
Sylvia Regulus

Shippingport Kentucky Jany 28th 1810
Drawn by J. J. Audubon

Black Walnut

Mistletoe in Black Walnut

This drawing was undoubtedly made in preparation for William Trost Richards's first major commission, a painting of Mount Vernon completed in 1855.[1] The meticulous graphite study exhibits Richards's remarkable attention to natural detail, a trait that had a number of sources: his early training as a technical draftsman; his academic study in the ateliers of Düsseldorf; and his reading of the theories of John Ruskin and the English Pre-Raphaelites, who advocated precise and reverent copying from nature.[2]

The painting was commissioned late in 1854 by the Philadelphia Art Union as a way to raise funds to purchase George Washington's estate for the nation. Like its companion organization in New York, the Art Union planned to have engravings made after the painting and sold to subscribers. Although the Union fell apart in 1855 before the subscriptions could be sold, Richard finished the painting.[3] In comparing the finished work with the drawing, one can recognize the changes Richards made in composition and technique. In the painting, the artist has chosen to center the structure in the middle ground of an expansive view overlooking the Potomac River. Carefully framed by the lush leafy canopies of the foreground trees, the venerable monument is anointed with pinky-golden sunlight.

The tiny monochromatic drawing, however, is dark with the glossy buildup of silvery graphite. The sketch's drama is enhanced by the low vantage point. Trees that the artist translated into prim upright sentinels in the painting are active here. By setting the mansion to the far left, and focusing on the dense foliage and energetic intertwining of the three gnarled trees in the foreground, in true Pre-Raphaelite fashion, Richards has made the idiosyncrasies of untamed nature the predominant subject.

SCF

106 ## William Trost Richards

MOUNT VERNON, 1854

Graphite on beige (1), moderately thick, smooth wove paper

5 3/8 x 8 5/8

Unsigned

Gift of the National Academy of Design, New York, from the Mrs. William T. Brewster Bequest

1954.20

Mount Vernon, 1855
Oil on canvas
29 1/2 x 48
The Collection of The Newark Museum,
Gift of Mr. And Mrs. Snowden Henry 1966

BORN
29 July 1824
Lovell, Maine

DIED
5 April 1906
New York, New York

In 1856, Eastman Johnson received the commission for a portrait of James Cochran Dobbin, then Secretary of the Navy, probably through the influence of his father, who worked for the Department of the Navy. The artist had recently returned to his home in Washington, D.C., after six years of study in Europe. Before going abroad, Johnson had made his living making crayon portraits, relying on his incredible natural facility for drawing. His sitters had included the Washington politicians John Quincy Adams and Daniel Webster, and the Boston literary figures Henry Wadsworth Longfellow, Nathaniel Hawthorne, and Ralph Waldo Emerson.[1] In Europe, his talent was honed in anatomy classes at the Düsseldorf Academy and by careful study of Rembrandt's self-portraits and figure studies at The Hague. Johnson began to paint in oils and, as his technical skill improved, he learned to depict his subject's face with very fine detail and expression, using broader strokes for the clothing. The Addison's study of Dobbin reflects his new confidence and sensitivity.

Johnson's training in Europe also brought him into contact with genre painting. In Düsseldorf, he apprenticed for a year in the studio of Emanuel Leutze, who was then working on his major history painting *Washington Crossing the Delaware*. Johnson also spent four years in The Hague, where he had first encountered "the splendid works of Rembrandt & a few others of the old Dutch masters."[2] The Dutch taste for scenes of domestic life and figure studies of local inhabitants struck a chord. When Johnson's European trip was cut short by his mother's death in 1855, he returned home to America armed with a new interest in genre pictures, for which he is now best known. (See the entry for Johnson's study *Berry Picking*, pp. 114–15.)

SJM

108 Eastman Johnson

STUDY FOR "JAMES COCHRAN DOBBIN, SECRETARY OF THE NAVY," 1856

Charcoal and chalk on brown, moderately thick, moderately textured (2) wove paper

29 3/8 x 21 1/2

Signed in graphite l.l.: E.J.

Inscribed in graphite l.l.: Secretary Dobbin Navy; l.c.: 1856

Museum purchase

1937.14

James Cochran Dobbin, Secretary of the Navy, 1856
Oil on canvas
44 1/2 x 38 5/8
North Carolina Collection, UNC-CH Library; Courtesy of The Dialectic and Philanthropic Societies Portrait Collection

BORN
26 November 1807
Setauket, Long Island, New York

DIED
19 November 1868
Setauket, Long Island, New York

In this delicate pencil drawing, one of four of the artist's drawings purchased by the Addison in 1942, William Sidney Mount has filled the sheet with a single composition.[1] The carefully delineated tavern interior and the deliberate hierarchical ordering of character types in this room are typical of work by Mount. At the bar, the farmer, still in his overalls, and the more elegantly dressed townsman, lift their glasses. Behind them, perched just within the edge of the door, the black man sits, literally and figuratively removed from the easy camaraderie around the bar. Outside, leaning against the door jamb with hat pulled down, a shady character eavesdrops on the action within.[2]

In 1847 Mount had written about a painter's proper subject matter:

> A painter's studio should be every where, wherever he finds a scene for a picture in doors or out—In the black smith's shop, the shoe maker's the tailor's, the church, the tavern, or Hotel, the market and into the dens of poverty and dissipation, high life and low life.... No true artist will be scared from the rich harvest before him—that is every day open to him."[3]

Mount has followed his own advice in his choice of a simple village tavern setting with local characters carrying on their daily lives. Even though the drawing is dated 10 June 1858, Mount's diary is silent about his intentions for the work. Three days before, on 7 June, after not painting for nearly two months, Mount noted, "Commenced a drawing this morning." He went on, "It is singular with me I have long intervals of rest from painting.... Rest and reflection seems [sic] like food to me."[4] Perhaps this drawing served simply as quiet reflection and nourishment for the artist.

S C F

William Sidney Mount

TAP ROOM, 1858

Graphite on cream (3), medium weight (2), smooth wove paper

7 7/16 x 11 5/16

Unsigned

Inscribed in graphite l.r.: June 10th–1858

Museum purchase

1942.11

June 10th 1858

BORN
24 February 1836
Boston, Massachusetts

DIED
29 September 1910
Prout's Neck, Scarboro, Maine

Recognized for the heroic marine paintings he made in his mature career, Winslow Homer revealed a sensitive and personal touch in earlier drawings he made in upstate New York in the 1870s. The Addison's *Milkmaid* of 1874–75 is the first of four works showing the same pensive young woman. In addition to this drawing, the earliest, she appears in the foreground of an open field on a sketchbook page in watercolor and graphite; as the central figure in a fully realized oil on canvas (1875; Delaware Art Museum); and, three years later, framed by a tree and some farm animals on a hilltop pasture in a delicately tinted watercolor.[1]

Milkmaid, a monochromatic study in white and black executed on a medium-toned paper, is remarkably modern in its blocking of shapes and forms. Homer centered the figure in the narrow vertical space of the sheet and anchored her with horizontal bands of gray tones running in counterpoint. This unusual composition was repeated in the oil painting for which this study is so clearly intended. A critic for *The Nation* who saw Homer's painting on exhibition made note of the artist's use of "several novelties of effect that strike the eye like revelations. Another artist…would hardly think of making a motive out of the horizontal stripes of a fence, relieved against a ground of very slightly differing value, so as to make the group at the fence appear like a decoration wrought upon a barred ribbon."[2]

SCF

112 Winslow Homer

A MILKMAID, 1874–75

Crayon and opaque watercolor on blue-gray, medium weight (1), slightly textured (2) wove paper

13 3/4 x 7 1/8

Signed in crayon l.l.: HOMER

Gift of Mary D. and Arthur L. Williston

1949.25

Milking Time, 1875
Oil on canvas
24 x 38 1/4
Delaware Art Museum,
Gift of the Friends of Art and other donors

In the 1870s and '80s, Eastman Johnson and his family summered on Nantucket, where wild cranberries grew on the bogs below their cliffside home. Every fall the local residents gathered in a kind of communal cottage industry to harvest the berries and bring much-needed income to the island. Johnson was fascinated at the sight of men, women, and children working side by side to bring in this uniquely American crop. Seized with his "cranberry fit," as he called his obsession, he began sketching cranberry pickers in 1875, making dozens of pencil and oil studies of individuals and groups of figures, with barrels, sacks, and wooden buckets as he worked out the composition for *The Cranberry Harvest* of 1880, now at the Timken Museum of Art.[1]

In the Addison's *Berry Picking*, probably a very early study in this series, Johnson isolated the figures from the landscape, concentrating on posture, gesture, clothing, and above all the shimmering seaside light. The brown paper stands in for the overall golden brown color of autumn, establishing a midtone that Johnson could quickly darken with watercolor or highlight with touches of opaque white. In the foreground figures, who seem to hover in barely suggested ankle-deep vegetation, Johnson recorded specific observations: the solid stance of a man with his hands in his pockets and the awkward effort of a small boy carrying large wooden buckets. Behind them, Johnson captured pickers sitting, kneeling, stooping, and bending at their backbreaking labor. In the finished painting, the artist expanded this group into a more industrious yet still tranquil scene of Yankee life.

SJM

114 Eastman Johnson

BERRY PICKING, c. 1875–80

Transparent and opaque watercolor, opaque white, and graphite on brown, medium weight (1), smooth kraft paper

7 3/4 x 19 1/2

Unsigned

Inscribed in graphite l.l. (upside down): pails + clothes / Bottle in the tree / fence up to [rail]; on verso u.r.: Berry Picking–40

Museum purchase

1935.28

The Cranberry Harvest, 1880
Oil on canvas
27 3/8 x 54 1/2
The Putnam Foundation,
Timken Museum of Art, San Diego

BORN
27 October 1856
Warren, Ohio

DIED
17 March 1919
New York, New York

Kenyon Cox, painter, muralist, writer, and critic, was one of the American Renaissance painters who sought to forge a new American art based on and incorporating the great traditions of the European Renaissance. As is the case in this drawing by Cox, American Renaissance artists—among them Augustus Saint-Gaudens, Abbott Thayer, and George de Forest Brush—turned to classically inspired depictions of the human figure to portray the ideals of beauty, truth, and virtue.[1]

The academic training of Kenyon Cox, with its emphasis on draftsmanship and craft, is revealed in this study of a heroic female figure, classically garbed and posed with one arm raised, the other holding a slender horn. The grid that overlays the drawing, strangely suggestive of the geometry and control of the

Minimalism of fifty years later, was a device to help the artist to alter the scale of the drawing in subsequent renditions. While the inscription on the lower right suggests that the image was designed for a testimonial to the musician Ignacy Paderewski, it was also used as the cover image on the program for "Sanctuary: A Bird Masque," one of the many masques, *tableaux vivants*, and charades staged in the Cornish New Hampshire art colony where Cox summered.[2] Following its Cornish presentation, the masque was given in New York and then traveled for twenty weeks to support the establishment of clubs for the care and protection of wild birds. In Cornish, Cox played the Crow in the play, while President Woodrow Wilson's daughter Eleanor was Ornis, the bird spirit, and his daughter Margaret sang the prologue, "The Hermit Thrush."[3]

S C F

116   Kenyon Cox

STUDY FOR "BIRD-SONG," 1895

Graphite on beige (1), medium weight (1), moderately textured (1), Geo. B. Hurd & Co. laid paper

20 x 15 11/16

Signed in graphite u.r.: To Louise, with thanks and love-/Kenyon Cox/July-1895.

Inscribed in graphite u.r.:
Study for / "Bird-Song."; l.r.: Programme for / Testimonial to / Paderewiski

Museum purchase

1937.40

Illustration for *Programme for the Bird Masque, Sanctuary MCMXIII*, 1913
Ink on paper
10 9/16 x 7
Dartmouth College Library

To Louise, with Steuart's own love ~
Kenyon Cox
July · 1895 ·

Study for
"Bird-Song"

117

Programme Cover
Testimonial to
Paderewski.

BORN
12 January 1856
Florence, Italy

DIED
15 April 1925
London, England

Study for Chiron captures the grace and strength of an archer's torso posed at the point of greatest tension. With a steady gaze set on sights unseen, the marksman strains before releasing his arrow. This dramatic gesture was honed by Sargent into his final depiction of *Chiron and Achilles*, one of twelve paintings and six bas-reliefs completed in 1925 for the grand staircase entrance of the Museum of Fine Arts, Boston.

Commissioned to design a bold decorative program for the Italian Beaux-Arts gateway to the museum's prestigious collection, Sargent chose to complement the grand architecture with themes of antiquity in murals, a time-honored medium for expressing lofty ideals and ideas. After finishing the building's rotunda with inventive allegorical depictions of the museum as guardian of art, Sargent ornamented the staircase with tableaux of heroic legends to further illustrate the institution's allegiance to the classical tradition.[1]

The Addison's drawing is a study for a scene of the young Achilles (eventual hero of the Trojan War) on the back of his guardian, the soaring centaur Chiron, as the elder teaches him to master his bow under the paternal watch of the god Zeus (who hovers in the form of an eagle).[2]

This study was one of hundreds Sargent produced to perfect his figural depictions so that their line and sweep in the murals would make lasting impressions from ceiling height. As an artist who preached one must "draw the figure carefully, seriously, and incessantly,"[3] Sargent valued these drawings both on principle and in practice, and shipped them across the Atlantic to refer to while completing the mural paintings on canvas in his London studio. Although Sargent died before seeing his finished works installed, his drawings and murals attest to his commitment and passion for his last, most ambitious commission.

JM

118

John Singer Sargent

STUDY FOR CHIRON, c. 1921–25

Charcoal on beige (2), moderately thick, moderately textured (1), Michallet laid paper

18 5/8 x 24 3/4

Unsigned

Inscribed in graphite l.r.: 10.8.3 (30)

Gift of Miss Emily Sargent and her sister, Mrs. Francis Ormond

1932.13

Chiron and Achilles, 1922–25
Oil on canvas
137 x 125
Museum of Fine Arts, Boston,
Francis Bartlett Donation of 1912 and
Picture Fund

119

BORN
26 September 1862
Utica, New York

DIED
24 October 1928
Florence, Italy

In 1908, Arthur B. Davies—perhaps best known for his leading role in the organization of the pivotal 1913 Armory Show—and seven fellow progressive artists organized their own exhibition as a reaction to their rejection by New York's conservative National Academy of Design in New York City.[1] The exhibition of "The Eight" included paintings by Davies, Maurice Prendergast, William Glackens, Ernest Lawson, Robert Henri, John Sloan, George Luks, and Everett Shinn.

Ironically, despite his devotion to the advancement of modern art in America, Davies could be described as "a seer of visions, this poet who would penetrate the earthly envelope and surprise the secret fervers [sic] of the soul."[2] The spiritual art of Davies has roots in European Symbolism, especially the art of Odilon Redon and Pierre Puvis de Chavannes,

in the mystical realm of the American Albert Pinkham Ryder, and in the dreams and visions of Davies himself.[3] At Sunset features a group of nude men, or perhaps the repeated figure of one man, in various poses. There is a lyrical, rhythmic quality to the soft lines of the bodies, silhouetted against a hazy landscape and sky. Interested in the multiple images of Eadweard J. Muybridge's The Human Figure in Motion (1901), Davies adopted this device, calling it "continuous composition."[4]

Davies's ethereal, visionary images had captured the eye of Lizzie P. Bliss, who would become a close friend and his most devoted patron. At Sunset, originally in the Bliss collection, came to the Addison in 1931, as one of the numerous, significant bequests by Bliss, who died just before the museum opened in 1931.[5]

GGS

120 Arthur B. Davies

AT SUNSET, c. 1910–20

Watercolor, graphite, and charcoal on beige (2), medium weight (2), moderately textured (1) laid paper

23 9/16 x 18 3/4

Signed in watercolor l.l.: A.B. DAVIES

Bequest of Miss Lizzie P. Bliss

1931.82

BORN
12 August 1882
Columbus, Ohio

DIED
8 January 1925
New York, New York

Like many of the so-called Ashcan painters, George Bellows supplemented his painting income by creating illustrations for magazines. *The Drunk* is a study for a lithograph used to illustrate an article titled "Why We Prohibit" in the May 1924 issue of *Good Housekeeping*.[1] Bellows made two prints of this subject. The Addison's drawing is virtually identical to the first stone (*The Drunk No. 1*). Bellows redrew the image for the second stone (*The Drunk No. 2*), altering the nightgown of the woman on the left as well as making slight changes to the two children and the quilt. It was this revised and more dramatic version that served as the illustration for *Good Housekeeping*.

Attracted to lithography for its immediacy and its ability to reproduce the effects of drawing, Bellows usually worked directly on the lithographic stone.[2] It therefore seems peculiar that the artist would create such a highly finished preliminary study. However,

careful planning was a hallmark of his art, and Bellows employed various compositional and color theories at different times throughout his career.

The Drunk is often cited as a prime example of the artist's use of Dynamic Symmetry. Developed by art theoretician Jay Hambidge, the system employed compositional formulas based on geometry.[3] The triangle formed by the three central struggling figures as well as the intersecting diagonals created by their straining limbs are clearly based on a geometrically structured design. The compositional underpinning lends a sense of controlled order to a scene of chaotic activity. Although some have suggested that this image lacks the spontaneity that characterizes Bellows's earlier work, it is certainly dramatic.[4] The composition, as well as Bellows's skillful use of light and shadow, and black and white, creates a stagelike theatricality befitting the climactic moment the drawing illustrates.

ANK

George Bellows

THE DRUNK, 1923–24

Lithographic crayon on beige (1), medium weight (1), smooth, Basingwerk parchment wove paper

16 x 13

Signed in lithographic crayon l.r.: Geo Bellows

Inscribed in lithographic crayon l.c.: THE DRUNK.

Museum purchase

1935.39

THE DRUNK.

123

BORN
9 September 1889
New York, New York

DIED
30 October 1930
Bilbao, Spain

The study for a painting now in the collection of the Whitney Museum of American Art, the Addison's sketch *Industry* bears all the hallmarks of Precisionism—precise technique, simplification of form, architectonic structure, a mixture of realistic and abstract design, and a focus on distinctly American subjects. Alternately described as the "Immaculate School,"[1] Precisionism was a "stylistic and thematic tendency shared by a number of artists"[2] as diverse as Dickinson, Charles Sheeler, Charles Demuth, and Georgia O'Keeffe. Reacting against the "formlessness of Impressionism and the Eight"[3] and paralleling the worldwide search for stability in the wake of World War I, Precisionists adopted a classicizing art that reordered reality.

Although very similar to the finished painting, the Addison's oil sketch is looser in execution. Employing a selective realism, Dickinson manipulated the essentially cubic forms of the industrial buildings, the planes of which he enlivened with a peppering of cables, pulleys, smokestacks, and vents. Overlaying the simplified geometry are lively surface patterns created by the play of light and shadow. Dickinson built this densely packed and essentially flat picture with a subdued palette of blacks, grays, browns, and yellows, which realistically conveys the grime of the city.[4] Yet the dynamic activity that generally accompanies an industrial setting is strangely stilled. Finding inspiration in what Louis Lozowick described as the "rigid geometry of the American city,"[5] Dickinson's rigorously constructed composition reveals an underlying order beneath chaos and confusion.

ANK

124

Preston Dickinson

STUDY FOR "INDUSTRY," early 1920s

Oil on cream (1), medium weight (1), rough (1) wove paper

9 7/8 x 7 7/8

Signed in oil l.r.: Dickinson

Museum purchase

1937.32

Industry, c. 1923
Oil on canvas
30 x 24 1/4
Whitney Museum of American Art, New York,
Gift of Gertrude Vanderbilt Whitney, 31.173

This drawing and its companion, both preparatory studies for the Addison's masterwork *Manhattan Bridge Loop*, were donated to the Addison Gallery by the artist in 1939. The gift was prompted by an unusual and highly successful collaborative project between Edward Hopper and the museum, an exhibition called *The Architecture of a Painting: Edward Hopper's "Manhattan Bridge Loop."* The normally reticent artist worked closely with the museum to create an exhibition that would "enlist students into an understanding of [the] work and the way the picture was organized and painted."[1]

For the project Hopper made one of his most incisive and illuminating statements about his art, its genesis, meaning, and making. He wrote to the Addison's first director, Charles Sawyer, "My aim in painting is always, using nature as the medium, to try to project upon canvas my most intimate reaction to the subject as it appears when I like it most; when the facts are given unity by my interest and prejudices."[2]

Relying on memory of the scene and armed with "a few small black and white sketches made from the fact" (the two drawings presently in the Addison collection), Hopper composed the painting. As he described, "The very long horizontal shape of this picture, 'Manhattan Bridge Loop' is an effort to give a sensation of great lateral extent. Carrying the main horizontal lines of the design with little interruption to the edges of the picture is to enforce this idea and to make one conscious of the spaces and elements beyond the limits of the scene itself."[3] Comparisons between a 1930s photograph of the bridge, the two preparatory drawings, and the final painting give vivid evidence of the careful way in which Hopper reordered the elements of the scene to realize his artistic goal.

SCF

126

Edward Hopper

STUDY FOR "MANHATTAN BRIDGE LOOP," NO. 2, c. 1928

Charcoal on beige (1), moderately thick, slightly textured (2) wove paper

6 3/8 x 11 1/4

Signed in charcoal l.r.: Edward Hopper

Inscribed in ink on verso u.l.: Please return to— / Edward Hopper / 3 Washington Square / New York

Gift of the artist

1940.72

CLOCKWISE FROM BOTTOM LEFT
Edward Hopper
Study for "Manhattan Bridge Loop," c. 1928
Crayon on beige (1), moderately thick, slightly textured (2) wove paper
8 1/2 x 11 1/16
Gift of the artist
Addison Gallery of American Art, 1940.71

Anonymous
"Manhattan Bridge Loop" site photograph,
c. 1930s
Vintage gelatin silver print
9 1/2 x 5 9/16
Gift of the artist
Addison Gallery of American Art, 1992.55

Edward Hopper
Manhattan Bridge Loop, 1928
Oil on canvas
35 x 60
Gift of Stephen C. Clark, Esq.
Addison Gallery of American Art, 1932.17

BORN
7 December 1892
Philadelphia, Pennsylvania

DIED
24 June 1964
New York, New York

Two important Stuart Davis drawings, added to the collection in 1998, relate to the museum's major Davis painting, *Red Cart*, of 1932. These drawings add immeasurably to our understanding of Davis's painterly intentions and working methods. *Sketchbook #3-6, Drawing for "Red Cart"*[1] is a page taken from one of the numerous sketchbooks in which Davis recorded his ideas, thoughts, and compositional testings. By the time that this ink study—derived from an actual scene of the Gloucester, Massachusetts, docks—was penned in 1931, Davis had worked out the careful balance of diagonals, shapes, and patterns that he would translate into the large oil painting of the following year. Close enough to the finished work to be a record diagram of the composition, the study and painting differ in only a few significant details. Chief among them is the addition to the painting of a checkered "ceiling" and the grommet and rope at the top right, both of which play against the painting's allusion of three-dimensionality by suggesting that the whole painting is simply a stage curtain, hung in front of our view.

Seven years after *Red Cart* was completed, Davis returned to the composition, creating a large drawing that defines in linear terms the major blocks of color in the painting. This skeletal study was then overlaid with a grid to facilitate the design's transfer to canvas. Davis's calendar entry of 18 July 1939 mentions this drawing and refers to a canvas of the same dimensions, which the artist titled *Red Cart No. 2* and painted in the summer of 1939.[2] That same summer Davis used the drawing (p. 131) as the basis for a lithograph which, in spite of the fact that it was so clearly based on the Gloucester, Massachusetts, composition, was titled *New Jersey Landscape (Seine Cart)*.

SCF

128 Stuart Davis

SKETCHBOOK #3-6,
DRAWING FOR "RED CART," 1931

Ink and crayon on beige (1), medium weight (1), smooth, Hammermill wove paper
10 3/8 x 14 3/8
Unsigned
Inscribed in graphite on verso l.l.: 3-4
Museum purchase
1998.24

Red Cart , 1932
Oil on canvas
32 1/4 x 50 1/4
Museum purchase
Addison Gallery of American Art, 1946.15

130   Stuart Davis

SCALE DRAWING FOR "NEW JERSEY
LANDSCAPE (SEINE CART)," 1939

Graphite on cream (3), thin (2),
smooth wove paper

23 x 37 1/2

Unsigned

Gift of Earl Davis

1998.23

BORN
17 December 1904
New York, New York

DIED
12 December 1999
Weston, Connecticut

In *Study for "Horseplay"* Paul Cadmus placed a beautiful young man in a formal Renaissance *contrapposto* pose in the dressing room at Jones Beach on Long Island. He made the classic, even heroic stance plausible by the implied narrative of toweling dry after a swim, but the model's passivity, the contemporary details of the setting, and the comic/aggressive locker-room play are unsettling and deliberately provocative.[1] Cadmus's extraordinary draftsmanship heightens the tension. In the final painting, the mood becomes somewhat more menacing. While the nude is only slightly modified, the expression of the seated figure snapping the towel is darker, his grin more mocking. The third man, whose back functioned in the drawing as a formal element linking the other two, now turns to leer over his shoulder, adding an undercurrent of voyeurism to the incident.

The Addison's *Study for "Horseplay"* is one of Cadmus's very few surviving early drawings of male nudes. It was made shortly after the artist returned from an extended trip to Europe, where he first studied the Italian Renaissance masters.[2] He remained devoted to their figurative tradition throughout his long career, personalizing it with his own meticulous technique, deeply felt social criticism, and provocative, homoerotic tone, challenging the prevailing notion of acceptable subject matter.

SJM

132

Paul Cadmus

STUDY FOR "HORSEPLAY," c. 1935

Ink, ink wash, and graphite on blued white, medium weight (1), slightly textured (1) wove paper

10 7/16 x 6 7/8

Signed in ink l.l.: Paul Cadmus

Museum purchase

1941.50

Horseplay, c. 1935
Oil and egg tempera on pressed wood panel
18 x 9
Private collection, courtesy DC Moore Gallery, New York

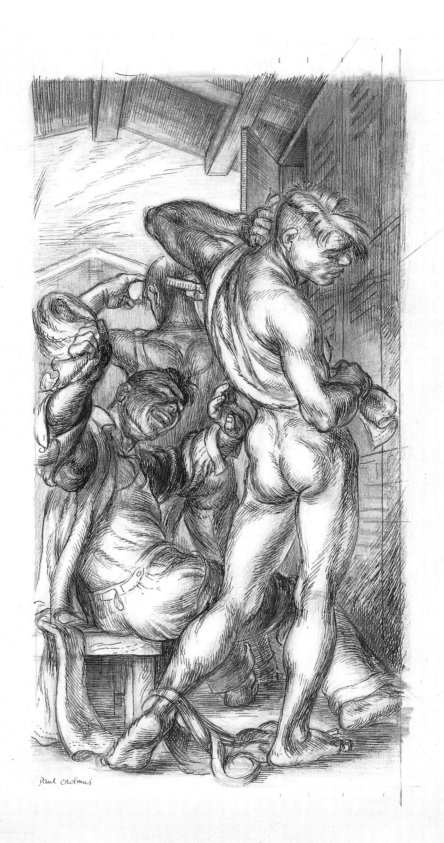

BORN
9 March 1906
Decatur, Indiana

DIED
23 May 1965
Bennington, Vermont

Although David Smith is best known for his relentless pursuit of abstract form in steel sculptures from the mid-1930s to the 1960s, he produced a series of figurative works just once in his career.[1] In the same political climate that compelled Pablo Picasso to immortalize the horrors of war in his *Guernica* of 1937, Smith felt bound to express his humanistic concerns about the destructiveness and moral degradation of war through his art. From 1937 to 1940 he worked nightly on the Medals for Dishonor, fifteen bronze medallions that poignantly memorialize his views. In a deliberately ungainly style, Smith allegorized such monstrosities as *Death by Gas*, *Bombing Civilian Populations*, and *Munition Makers* in numerous drawings, which he then hand-tooled in plaster for casting in bronze.[2]

By 1940, when the Medals were completed, Smith recalled, "War spirit had gained momentum to such an extent that it was a poor time to show them. Almost not quite ethical."[3] To clearly affirm them as "humanitarian" (not antinational) statements, he exhibited the medallions with a catalogue explaining the iconography in each.[4] The sketch chosen for the cover of this compilation, the Addison's drawing *Munitions*, portrays what Smith described as "patched skeletons."[5] Interestingly, in the final versions of both the cover and the medallion *Munition Makers*, Smith chose to include the figures who bear a bombshell and an ancient coin, two symbolically relevant metal forms for encapsulating war.

After World War II, when it could be seen through the lens of recent memory and collective healing, Medals for Dishonor was toured nationally by the American Association of University Women (1946–52). Smith gave this drawing in thanks to the organizer of the tour in April 1947.[6]

J M

134   David Smith

MUNITIONS, 1937

Ink and graphite on yellow, medium weight (1), smooth tracing paper

10 5/8 x 9 1/2

Signed in ink l.r.: David Smith

Inscribed in ink l.r.: Munitions

Inscribed in graphite on mount (since removed): Munitions, pen and ink, 1937– preliminary sketch for the exhibition / program, Medals of Dishonor

Partial gift of Ida Hoover in memory of Louise Stevens Bryant and partial museum purchase

1968.10

Munition Makers, 1939,
from Medals for Dishonor, 1937–40
Cast bronze
9 x 10 1/2
The Estate of David Smith, K97

munitions

David Smith

BORN
5 August 1920
Brooklyn, New York

George Tooker has created haunting social commentaries in egg tempera since 1946. The demanding nature of this finicky medium requires that Tooker, like the Renaissance artists he admires, resolve all of the essential visual problems before he starts to paint. Tooker considers drawing "a tool, a guide for me to use to work out my ideas and feelings. I liken the function of my final preliminary drawing to that served by the architect's blueprint for his building. All of them are truly 'messy working drawings' in every sense of the word."[1]

In *Study for "Market,"* Tooker established the central composition of five figures in a shallow frontal plane, relieved by a glimpse of deeper space just to the right of center. This figural group corresponds directly to that in the finished work. The poses, expressions, hairstyles, and clothing, as well as the awnings that enclose the space, were virtually unchanged. Details of the market scene, however, including baskets and pails, were moved or modified as the final painting emerged. The greatest difference is color. In his mind's eye, Tooker saw the range of tones of his pencil and wash drawing as tempera colors and jotted down his selected palette in the margin. Adjusted for intensity in the finished painting, Tooker's broad, dense areas of color transform delicate pencil line into solid, architectonic figures.

Unlike many artists, George Tooker does not consider his working drawings finished works of art, and for most of his career he retained all of them in his studio. In 1996 he donated his entire archive, almost two hundred drawings, as a study collection to the Addison.

SJM

136 ## George Tooker

STUDY FOR "MARKET," 1949

Graphite and watercolor on beige (2), thin (2), smooth tracing paper

28 1/8 x 28 7/16

Unsigned

Inscribed in graphite l.r.: White / Orange / Blue / Brown / Black / ~~Yellow~~

Gift of the artist (PA 1938) in memory of his parents, George Clair Tooker and Angela Montejo Roura Tooker

1996.80.92

Market, 1949
Egg tempera on gesso panel
22 x 22
Collection of John P. Axelrod (PA 1964)

BORN
16 July 1883
Philadelphia, Pennsylvania

DIED
7 May 1965
Dobbs Ferry, New York

In 1946 gallery director Bartlett Hayes invited Charles Sheeler to be the first participant in an innovative artist-in-residence program at the Addison. The program's goals were to expose the Phillips Academy community and students to art and artists, to provide much needed financial support for artists, and to enrich the Addison's collection with additions of contemporary art. In exchange for residency on campus and interaction with students, the artist was given free rein to create works of art of his or her choosing, out of which the Addison agreed to purchase one work.[1]

During his six-week stay in Andover, the painter discovered a cluster of abandoned mill buildings in the Ballardvale section of town. Sheeler, who had reached a period of creative stagnation before his visit, left Andover rejuvenated and inspired, and embarked on a prolonged period of artistic vigor. Between 1946 and 1953, Sheeler returned over and over to the imagery of the Andover mills, ultimately producing nearly twenty new works, each a complex abstract synthesis of color, form, and pattern.[2] The tiny opaque watercolor study *Ballardvale Revisited* of 1949 reveals a working method that developed from his Andover experience. To create this complex image, Sheeler laid several photographic negatives over one another, and then printed them to create a composite design of fractured overlapping planes and forms. This was then transferred onto paper, over which he laid a sheet of glass; on this glass he worked out the color composition in watercolor. Once the composition was translated onto canvas, Sheeler would return to the paper layer to meticulously replicate the color as a record of the larger painting.[3]

SCF

138 Charles Sheeler

BALLARDVALE REVISITED, 1949

Opaque watercolor and graphite on beige (1), medium weight (1), smooth wove paper
3 7/8 x 3 1/2
Signed in graphite l.l.: Sheeler– 49.
Museum purchase
1995.45

TOP TO BOTTOM
Ballardvale Mill, vertical, c. 1946
Gelatin silver print
10 x 8
Gift of Saundra B. Lane in honor of
Jock Reynolds
Addison Gallery of American Art, 1998.168

The Mill, Andover, Massachusetts, 1946
Opaque watercolor on board
4 5/16 x 5 1/4
Purchased as the gift of Sidney Knafel
(PA 1948)
Addison Gallery of American Art, 1995.27

ABOVE
Ballardvale, 1946
Oil on canvas
24 x 19
Museum purchase
Addison Gallery of American Art, 1947.21

BORN
10 December 1900
Naples, Italy

DIED
10 May 1964
Malibu, California

In the wake of the horrors of World War II, Rico Lebrun became engrossed in the subject of the Crucifixion of Christ, explaining that his "choice of the theme, Crucifixion, was prompted by the constantly repeated history of man's blindness and inhumanity."[1] From 1948 through 1951, he boldly explored this weighty subject in a cycle of several hundred drawings and paintings, culminating in *The Crucifixion*, an immense painting which was completed in 1950 for his exhibition at the Los Angeles County Museum of Art and then installed in 1958 as part of his striking triptych at Syracuse University.[2]

In the thematically related drawing *Helmet Heads with Flares*, bared teeth and fierce eyes peer out from under steel helmets as two figures march in file with fists and torches raised. Since the target of this brutish advance is left undefined, these could just as easily be modern-day troops as ancient Roman soldiers who threaten such menacing violence.[3] Lebrun exploits the visceral impact of both interpretations, reinforcing the evocative power of his fragmented figures with the emotional power of his heavily drawn strokes. Rehashed contours, vines of tangled lines, and obscured erasures merge with sharp details—hinged armor, flared nostrils, thick skulls, fire's glare—into a ferocious close-up view of human aggression. In this mid-century work, Lebrun bridges past and present, using a style both rooted in modernist figuration and pointing toward Abstract Expressionism.[4]

JM

140 ## Rico Lebrun

HELMET HEADS WITH FLARES
(STUDY FOR "THE CRUCIFIXION"), 1951

Chalk on beige (1), moderately thick, smooth wove paper

17 7/8 x 24 1/8

Signed in ink and graphite l.r.: Lebrun / 1951

Inscribed in graphite on verso u.l.:
$150 (7) Carnegie Tech. / Helmet Heads with Flares / 1951- Chalk on white paper.

Gift of Cleve Gray (PA 1936)

1965.9

The Crucifixion, 1950
Oil on compressed paper board
192 x 312
Courtesy of the Syracuse University Art Collection

BORN
19 September 1917
New York, New York

DIED
18 November 1999
Valley Cottage, New York

On a single sheet of thick paper, Stephen Greene compiled a set of compositional notes that allow the viewer insight into his iconography, his way of constructing work, and his engagement with color. According to the artist, this drawing contains "forms that have stayed with me for a long time and they change, shift but some of the basic assumptions remain.... It is basically a sketch, playing with hopefully meaningful forms—saying 'Here I am, this is what I'm about.'"[1]

What Greene was about as an artist was complex—adventurous and energetic, enigmatic and probing, overt and private, bold yet delicate. In the two studies at the left of the sheet, one senses his delight in the contrast of crisp, straight edges and curving organic forms. Dropped into the sure graphite framework are clear true colors that hold their own against the white, untouched paper. In the composition to the right, layers of transparent washes pool between black arcing forms, the fragile fluid colors

suggesting dimension and depth that play against the flat picture plane. Below the scribed studies hang bright red-orange propeller-like shapes, a green-edged gearbox, bonelike forms defined in fine black line or suggested in a touch of white wash—serving both as citations of the artist's characteristic imagery and as skillfully distributed components to balance the overall composition of the sheet.

Often referred to as a student of Philip Guston and the mentor of Frank Stella, Greene's gutsy idiosyncrasy as a painter earns him his own accolades. As art historian and critic Karen Wilkin has written, "Greene's strongest paintings are cranky, lush, seductive, scary, and hard to forget";[2] his "painfully beautiful" drawings, she writes, are "disquieting and lyrical series of evocative images."[3]

SCF

142 Stephen Greene

UNTITLED, c. 1959–60

Transparent and opaque watercolor, graphite, and collage on cream (1), moderately thick, very smooth Arches wove paper

14 15/16 x 22 1/4

Signed in graphite l.r.: Stephen Greene

Inscribed in graphite l.l.: for Cleve + Francine Gray

Gift of Cleve (PA 1936) and Francine duPlessix Gray, Addison Art Drive

1991.62

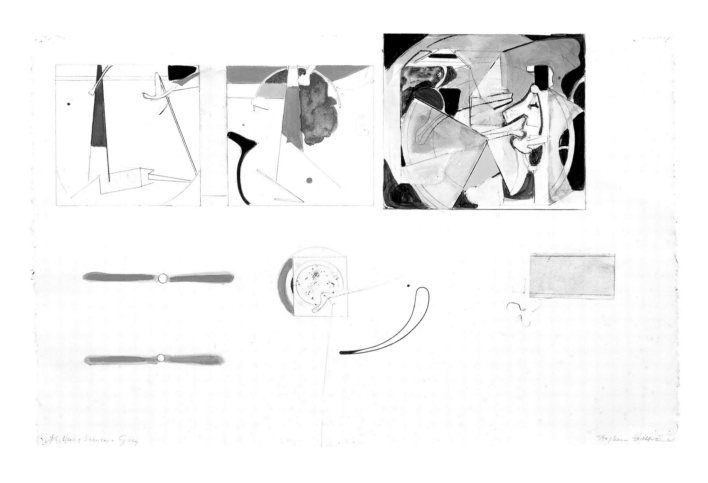

BORN
23 February 1931
Cincinnati, Ohio

In the 1960s Tom Wesselmann's paintings turned to imagery adopted from popular American culture—the commercial logo, the billboard, the printed page. While Pop artists like Andy Warhol and Claes Oldenburg used this imagery for its associative character or its ability to make social commentary, Wesselmann was attracted to the visual, formal qualities it provided.[1] In the Great American Nude series begun in 1961,[2] Wesselmann combined appropriated images and found objects with painted nudes that the critic Lucy Lippard called a fusion of "the arabesque and brilliant colour of Matisse with the sinuous line of Modigliani and a more rigorous framework traceable to Mondrian."[3]

The Addison's drawing is a study for the large work *Great American Nude #51* of 1963. In the painting, Wesselmann incorporated stars, stripes, a bowl, fruit, a glimpse of picture-postcard landscape, and a languishing pinup into a tight, flat composition, the intense energy of which relies as much on color, pattern, and form as it does on allusions to popular media. Wesselmann's nudes, with their splayed poses and lack of humanizing features—eyes and nose—have been described as "blank schemata animated only at the erogenous zones of mouth, nipple, and groin."[4] Yet, the artist subdues their eroticism, enlarging, streamlining, and transforming them into negative spaces cutting across the composition.

Where the painting is fierce and charged, Wesselmann's preparatory drawing is elegant and whisper-soft, sensual versus overt, personal rather than emblematic. Its delicate silvery line traverses the edges of the woman's rib cage and pelvic bone, catching the drape of her stomach at rest, defining the hollow of her belly button and armpit. As this enticing, singular figure was translated onto canvas, she metamorphosed into a band of flat, undulating flesh-color, becoming landscape and still life as well as nude.

S C F

144 ## Tom Wesselmann

STUDY FOR "GREAT AMERICAN NUDE #51," 1963

Graphite on beige (2), moderately thick, slightly textured (1) wove paper

18 x 23 7/8

Signed in graphite l.r.: Wesselmann 63

Inscribed in graphite on verso l.r.: D6372; l.l.: 6060B

Museum purchase

1966.41

Great American Nude #51, 1963
Oil and collage on canvas
120 x 144
Collection of Guenther Sachs, St. Moritz

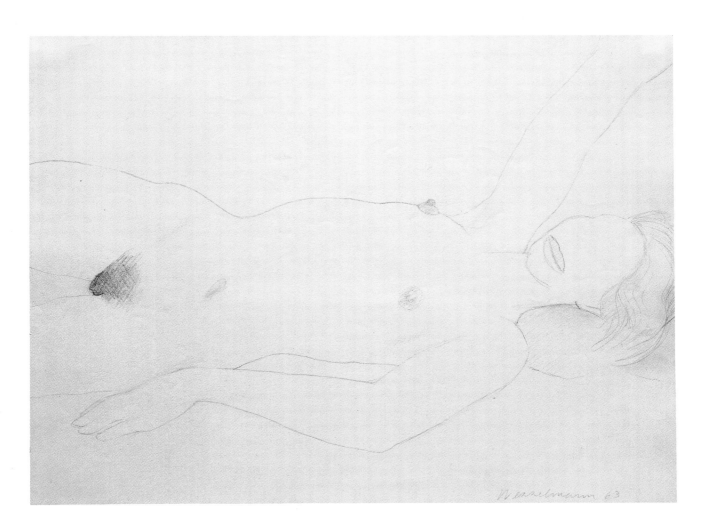

Wesselmann 63

BORN
21 May 1898
Sharon, Massachusetts

DIED
22 March 1976
Dana Point, California

John McLaughlin sought to make purely abstract art that evoked nothing else but itself—"I am not in the least concerned with mood as such, but rather strive to transcend the particular."[1] He strove to produce a static, refined, contemplative, and timeless art. McLaughlin was influenced by Asian art, and also admired the Russian Constructivist Kasimir Malevich, citing his radical *White on White* of 1918 as a point of departure.

The Addison's collages were sent to the gallery in 1969 in preparation for the exhibition *Seven Decades, Seven Alumni of Phillips Academy*. As the artist explained, "they are mini-copies of paintings as substitutes for photos not readily at hand."[2] Despite what one might assume, they were not studies for paintings. However, they do bear a relationship to the artist's working method. His use of cut construction paper was central to McLaughlin's process. Sometimes he worked in full scale, placing forms directly on the canvas. Other times, he would work in one-quarter scale. In either event, the artist noted, these studies were disposed of.

Paper Model for "No. 16" reveals the artist's increasingly reductive move away from geometric forms (p. 149). The *Paper Model for "Untitled"* is a horizontal work of five zones and three colors (p. 148). The palette is restricted further, and the collage is perceived as a whole, not as a pictorial surface "read" from one side to another. The most radical, *Paper Model for "No. 2,"* is dominated by a large, flat black zone with smaller white zones above and below. The black evokes both solid and void, its simplification being reminiscent of Malevich. It is based on the Addison's painting, *No. 2*. Despite its diminutive size, it captures the gestalt and essential character of the oil itself.

ADW

146   John McLaughlin

PAPER MODEL FOR "NO. 2," 1969

Collage of moderately thick, slightly textured (1) wood pulp paper

6 x 7 1/2

Signed and inscribed in graphite on verso u.c.: TOP / John McLaughlin / Title #2, 1969 / 48 x 60 / oil & acrylic

Gift of the artist

1991.201

No. 2, 1969
Oil on canvas
48 x 59 1/2
Museum purchase
Addison Gallery of American Art, 1969.32

148 John McLaughlin
PAPER MODEL FOR "UNTITLED,"
1969

Collage of moderately thick, slightly
textured (1) wood pulp paper

4 x 4 3/16

Signed and inscribed in graphite on verso
u.c.: TOP / McLaughlin / Oil & casein /
32 x 38 / Addison #3

Gift of the artist

1991.202

PAPER MODEL FOR "NO. 16," 1969

Collage of moderately thick, slightly
textured (1) wood pulp paper

6 1/16 x 4 5/16

Signed and inscribed in graphite on verso
u.c.: TOP / McLaughlin / o/c Title: #16, 1960
/ 48 x 34 / #7 Addison list

Gift of the artist

1991.203

BENJAMIN WEST, HAGAR AND ISHMAEL

1. See Robert C. Alberts, *Benjamin West: A Biography* (Boston: Houghton Mifflin, 1978), pp. 157–58.
2. Allen Staley, *Benjamin West: American Painter at the English Court* (Baltimore: The Baltimore Museum of Art, 1989), p. 72.
3. Alberts, pp. 158, 159.
4. Ibid., pp. 159–60.
5. See Genesis 21:8–21.

JOHN SINGLETON COPLEY, THE BATTLE OVER PATROCLUS'S BODY

1. Jules David Prown, *John Singleton Copley in England 1774–1815* (Cambridge: Harvard University Press, 1966), p. 250, ill. 336, listed as *Roman Conquest*.
2. William L. Pressly, "The Challenge of New Horizons," in Emily Ballew Neff, *John Singleton Copley in England* (Houston, Tex.: Museum of Fine Arts; London: Merrell Holberton, 1995), pp. 28, 142, cat. 20, ill. p. 142.
3. Richard H. Saunders, "Genius and Glory: John Singleton Copley's The Death of Major Peirson," *The American Art Journal* 22, no. 3 (1990): 5–39.

JOHN SINGLETON COPLEY, STUDY FOR "THE SIEGE OF GIBRALTAR"

1. Jules David Prown, *John Singleton Copley in England 1774–1815* (Cambridge: Harvard University Press, 1966), pp. 322–37, ill. 489–585.
2. The other sheet owned by the Addison contains studies for the foreleg of General Elliot's horse. See ibid., ill. 551.
3. Ibid., pp. 455–56.

JOHN SINGLETON COPLEY, STUDY FOR "SAUL REPROVED..."

1. Jules David Prown, *John Singleton Copley in England 1774–1815* (Cambridge: Harvard University Press, 1966), p. 351, ills. 610–12.

MATHER BROWN, TIPU SAHIB TAKING LEAVE OF HIS CHILDREN

1. Dorinda Evans, *Benjamin West and His American Students* (Washington, D.C.: National Portrait Gallery, 1980), pp. 74–75. Following in the footsteps of American Joseph Wright, Brown was allowed to take classes at the Academy for no charge.
2. Ibid., pp. 80–95.
3. See the National Galleries of Scotland's Website produced in conjunction with the exhibition *The Tiger and The Thistle: Tipu Sultan and the Scots in India*, 2000, <www.nationalgalleries.org.uk/tipu/tipu325.htm> (31 January 2003).
4. Dorinda Evans, *Mather Brown: Early American Artist in England* (Middletown, Conn.: Wesleyan University Press, 1982), pp. 112–13.

JOHN JAMES AUDUBON, CRESTED TITMOUSE and GOLDEN CRESTED WREN

1. Theodore E. Stebbins, Jr., "Audubon's Drawings of American Birds, 1805–38," in *John James Audubon: The Watercolors for "The Birds of America"* (New York: The New York Historical Society, 1993), pp. 6–7.
2. John James Audubon, "Account of the Method of Drawing Birds Employed by J.J. Audubon, Esq. F.R.S.E.," in *John James Audubon: Writings and Drawings* (New York: Literary Classics of the United States, 1999), p. 753.

3. The resulting publication, *The Birds of America*, included 435 plates and was published in 1838. The Addison's collection includes the four-volume set.

WILLIAM TROST RICHARDS, MOUNT VERNON

1. Linda S. Ferber, *William Trost Richards: American Landscape & Marine Painter 1833–1905* (Brooklyn: The Brooklyn Museum, 1973), pp. 17–18.
2. Ibid., p. 24.; see also Linda S. Ferber and William H. Gerdts, *The New Path: Ruskin and the American Pre-Raphaelites* (Brooklyn: The Brooklyn Museum, 1985).
3. Ferber, pp. 48–51.

EASTMAN JOHNSON, STUDY FOR "JAMES COCHRAN DOBBIN"

1. Teresa A. Carbone and Patricia Hills, *Eastman Johnson: Painting America* (New York: The Brooklyn Museum of Art in association with Rizzoli International Publications, 1999), pp. 12–13.
2. Eastman Johnson to Andrew Warner, 25 November 1851, quoted in ibid., p.19 n. 52.

WILLIAM SIDNEY MOUNT, TAP ROOM

1. When first purchased this drawing was identified as "One Sheet of Studies with tap room"; at some later date, for an undisclosed reason, the title was changed to "Study for Tap Room." Since the sheet does not contain multiple studies, nor has a published final painting for which this is a study been found, the name has been changed.
2. For a discussion of the use of these types in mid-nineteenth-century American genre painting, see Elizabeth Johns, *American Genre Painting: The Politics of Everyday Life* (New Haven: Yale University Press, 1991).
3. Ibid., p. 311.
4. Ibid.

WINSLOW HOMER, A MILKMAID

1. See Nicolai Cikovsky, Jr., and Franklin Kelly, *Winslow Homer* (Washington, D.C.: National Gallery of Art; New Haven: Yale University Press, 1995), pp. 118–21.
2. Quoted in ibid., p. 118.

EASTMAN JOHNSON, BERRY PICKING

1. Eastman Johnson to Jervis McEntee, 12 October 1879, quoted in Teresa A. Carbone and Patricia Hills, *Eastman Johnson: Painting America* (New York: New York: The Brooklyn Museum of Art in association with Rizzoli International Publications, 1999), p. 98.

KENYON COX, STUDY FOR "BIRD-SONG"

1. See Richard Guy Wilson et al., *The American Renaissance: 1876–1917* (Brooklyn: The Brooklyn Museum; New York: Pantheon Books, 1979) for an in-depth discussion of this movement.
2. See Susan Faxon Olney et al., *A Circle of Friends: Art Colonies of Cornish and Dublin* (Durham, N.H.: University Art Galleries, 1985) for discussion of the colony in Cornish and its participants.
3. Ibid., p. 55.

JOHN SINGER SARGENT, STUDY FOR CHIRON

1. See Carol Troyen, *Sargent's Murals in the Museum of Fine Arts, Boston* (Boston: Museum of Fine Arts, 1999), p. 22. Sargent's commission for the redesign of the museum's

rotunda lasted 1917–21, and produced eight murals and twelve bas-reliefs. The ensuing commission for the staircase ran 1921–25.

2. Ibid., see p. 44.

3. Thomas Fox, quoted in Troyen, p. 14: "Sargent's favorite model, an African American hotel worker named Thomas McKeller, posed for many figures, both male and female." That sketches of him were translated into figures in the museum's rotunda murals is documented. Although the Addison study relates to the later commission, McKeller may have been the model for this drawing as well.

ARTHUR B. DAVIES, AT SUNSET

1. Bennard B. Perlman, *The Lives, Loves, and Art of Arthur B. Davies* (Albany: State University of New York Press, 1998), pp. 154–55.

2. Ibid., p. 165.

3. Elizabeth Milroy, *Painters of a New Century: The Eight & American Art* (Milwaukee: Milwaukee Art Museum, 1991), p. 105.

4. Perlman, p. 226.

5. Susan C. Faxon et al., *Addison Gallery of American Art, 65 Years: A Selective Catalogue* (Andover: Addison Gallery of American Art, 1996), pp. 328, 351. The connection between Davies, Bliss, and the Addison is memorialized in Davies's painting *Mountain Beloved of Spring*, donated to the Addison Gallery as its first accessioned object.

GEORGE BELLOWS, THE DRUNK

1. The date of this issue has been erroneously cited as February 1924 in several Bellows publications.

2. Although some of his early prints were created by the transfer process (a lithograph drawn on paper, transferred onto stone, and then printed), Bellows's printer, Bolton Brown, was quoted in the *New York Evening Post* of 7 May 1921 as saying, "George Bellows is drawing directly on the stone, rather than reaching results by means of transfer paper." See Lauris Mason, *The Lithographs of George Bellows: A Catalogue Raisonné* (San Francisco: Alan Wofsy Fine Arts, 1992), p. 23.

3. Bellows first became acquainted with Dynamic Symmetry in the fall of 1917 when he attended a lecture by Hambidge. A staunch supporter of the theory from that point on, he came to regard it as "more valuable than the study of anatomy."

4. See, for example, Suzanne Boorsch, "The Lithographs of George Bellows," *Art News* 75 (March 1976): 60–62.

PRESTON DICKINSON, STUDY FOR "INDUSTRY"

1. The term "immaculate" was first used to describe the condition of the factory roofs in the Whitney's version of *Industry*. See Henry McBride, "Art News and Reviews," *The New York Herald*, 4 November 1923.

2. Ruth Cloudman, *Preston Dickinson 1889–1930* (Lincoln, Neb.: Sheldon Memorial Art Gallery, 1979), p. 20.

3. Gail Stavitsky, "Reordering Reality: Precisionist Directions in American Art, 1915–1941," in *Precisionism in America 1915–1941: Reordering Reality* (New York: Harry N. Abrams in association with Montclair Art Museum, 1994), p. 34.

4. Richard Lee Rubenfeld, "Preston Dickinson: An American Modernist, with a Catalogue of Selected Works; Volumes I and II," Ph.D. diss., University of Ohio, Columbus, 1985, 2:377.

5. Stavitsky, p. 153.

EDWARD HOPPER, STUDY FOR "MANHATTAN BRIDGE LOOP," NO. 2

1. Charles Sawyer to Edward Hopper, 17 October 1939, Addison Gallery Archives.

2. Edward Hopper to Charles Sawyer, 19 October 1939, Addison Gallery Archives.

3. Ibid.

STUART DAVIS, Drawings for "RED CART" and "NEW JERSEY LANDSCAPE (SEINE CART)"

1. According to the Stuart Davis catalogue raisonné project, this drawing was the sixth page of sketchbook 3, and is referenced in Davis's calendar entry of 7/12/39: "Made new analysis & drawing of 1931 sketch "Red cart," (letter from the project to the museum, 27 April 2001, Addison Gallery Archives).

2. Information about the unlocated painting, *Red Cart No. 2*, is from the Stuart Davis catalogue raisonné project, ibid.

PAUL CADMUS, STUDY FOR "HORSEPLAY"

1. Richard Meyer, "Paul Cadmus," *Art Journal* 57, no. 3 (Fall 1998): 81.

2. Justin Spring, *Paul Cadmus: The Male Nudes* (New York: Universe, 2002), pp. 17–25.

DAVID SMITH, MUNITIONS

1. See *David Smith by David Smith*, ed. Cleve Gray (New York: Holt, Rinehart and Winston, 1968), p. 27–29: "From 1936 after I came back from Europe I was impressed by Sumerian Seals—Intaglio concept in general—a collection of war medals I had seen in British Museum. I decided to do a series of Anti-war medallions called 'Medals for Dishonor.'"

2. Stanley E. Marcus, *David Smith: The Sculptor and His Work* (Ithaca: Cornell University Press, 1983), p. 59.

3. Smith, p. 29.

4. Ibid. The *Medals for Dishonor* were exhibited in November 1940 at the Willard Gallery, New York. William Blake and Christina Stead (his wife) wrote for the catalogue.

5. Smith quoted from the 1940 catalogue in Jeremy Lewison and David Smith, *David Smith: Medals for Dishonor 1937–1940* (London: The Henry Moore Centre for the Study of Sculpture, Leeds City Art Galleries, 1991), p. 32: "Patched skeletons take up their old duties—the / shell-bearer, the spearman, the shepherd, the cripple. / The banner of death-dollars flies from the stub of / a mediaeval soldier's arm. An ancient coin is held / aloft—the 'pen is mightier than the sword' but the / soldier still clings to the tommy-gun. / The antediluvian land tortoise comes forward with / low-hanging buttocks. From the imprint of past ages / emerge shellholes and ancient coins marked by the / gain of the merchants of death."

6. Lura Beam to Bartlett Hayes, 4 January 1968. In the letter Beam explains that she acquired the work when "David came to the house bringing two drawings, one for me [later given by Beam to Ida Hoover] and one for Louise Stevens Bryant who was to route his one-man AAUW exhibition I was assembling for 1946–47. We had it on the road until 1952." In the postscript of a letter from Beam to Hayes, 23 February 1968, Beam notes "I have ascertained that he brought me the drawing in the early spring of 1947, when I was assembling his one-man show for Dallas in April, 1947." The original backing of drawing was letterhead of the National Headquarters of the American Association of University Women Washington D.C.

GEORGE TOOKER, STUDY FOR "MARKET"

1. Quoted in Ildiko Heffernan, *George Tooker: Working Drawings* (Burlington, Vt.: Robert Hull Fleming Museum, University of Vermont, 1987), p. 8.

CHARLES SHEELER, BALLARDVALE REVISITED

1. Bartlett H. Hayes, Jr., to the Addison Gallery Associates, 1 October 1946, Addison Gallery Archives.

2. Karen E. Haas, "Charles Sheeler in Andover: The Ballardvale Series," exhibition brochure, Addison Gallery of American Art, 1996.

3. Carol Troyen and Erica Hirschler, *Charles Sheeler: Paintings and Drawings* (Boston: Little, Brown, 1987), p. 214.

RICO LEBRUN, HELMET HEADS WITH FLARES

1. James Thrall Soby, foreword in *Rico Lebrun: Drawings* (Berkeley and Los Angeles: University of California Press, 1961), p. vi.

2. Ibid.; and Domenic J. Iacono, "Interior Murals and Sculptures," entry no. 7 in *Guide to the Murals and Sculpture on the Campus of Syracuse University*, <sumweb.syr.edu/suart/campus1.htm> (31 January 2003).

3. For the story of Jesus's torch-lit arrest preceding his crucifixion, see John 18:1–12.

4. See Iacano.

STEPHEN GREENE, UNTITLED

1. Stephen Greene, artist's questionnaire, c. 1991, Addison Gallery Archives.

2. Quoted in *Stephen Greene Recent Paintings* (Lowell: University Gallery at University of Massachusetts, Lowell, 1999), p. 7.

3. Quoted in *Stephen Greene: A Retrospective Exhibition of Work Produced from 1963 to 1973* (Philadelphia: Tyler School of Art, Temple University, 1974), n.p.

TOM WESSELMANN, STUDY FOR "GREAT AMERICAN NUDE #51"

1. As Thomas H. Garver noted, Wesselmann himself rejected the term Pop art, "because of the emphasis it places upon the social rather than the visible quality of the images he uses in his art." See Garver, *Tom Wesselmann: Early Still Lifes, 1962–1964* (Newport Harbor, Calif.: Newport Harbor Art Museum, 1971), n.p.

2. According to Garver, "the idea for the 'Great American Nudes' came to Wesselmann when he dreamed of the red, white and blue colors of the flag." The title also carries a sly association with such generic titles as the Great American Novel, as pointed out in Tatsumi Shinoda, "Sensuality in Blank Space," in *Tom Wesselmann: Recent Still Lifes and Landscapes* (Tokyo: Galerie Tokoro, 1991), n.p.

3. Lucy R. Lippard, *Pop Art* (New York: Frederick A. Praeger, 1966), p. 111.

4. Lawrence Alloway, *American Pop Art* (New York: Collier Books in association with the Whitney Museum of American Art, 1974), p. 24.

JOHN MCLAUGHLIN, Paper Models

1. Quoted in *John McLaughlin Paintings 1949–1975* (New York: André Emmerich Gallery, 1979), n.p.

2. John McLaughlin to Bartlett H. Hayes, 30 April 1969, Addison Gallery Archives.

151

The work as a **product** "ARE WATERCOLORS SERIOUS?" CAROL CLARK

The query "Are Watercolors Serious?," posed in 1878 by a critic for the *New York Times*, boldly stated the plight of the exhibited watercolor, and by extension any work of art on paper. According to the *Times*, "critics... deliberated over sketches as if they were elaborate works in oil, and the public, instead of frankly enjoying the light bit of work, done in a comparatively short space of time, wanted to know what was meant by such carelessness on the part of the painter." The *Times* critic persisted: watercolors should "be sketchy, and hence unpretentious" for they are "serious in the sense that the lightest thing can embody a great thought of a master," but "they were not meant to convey the greatest and most complex forms of art."[1] It was a backhanded compliment. Why was a watercolor that embodied an artist's "great thought" not a "complex form of art"? This seeming contradiction goes to the heart of the matter.

To consider this question from another perspective: How can we possibly know when an artist thought a work fully realized rather than a record of, or a step in, an artistic process? We can't. Judging "finish" is a complex and ultimately fruitless effort, for what looks incomplete to one is considered fully realized by another, and inclusion in an exhibition does not necessarily mean a work bears the artist's stamp as "final product." At least some nineteenth-century exhibitions that featured works of art on paper included a category called "sketches" to distinguish preliminary drawings or studies from works considered "finished." My discussion also bears upon the difference between drawing's distinct roles. I am here concerned with the social and cultural grid of artistic practice where works on paper are offered for public contemplation, consideration, and purchase. More commonly perhaps, we think of drawing as a personal, solitary vehicle of self-expression, a quality that has distinguished it from painting since the Renaissance. In this construction of drawing as a private act, its contemplation is a window into the private process of creativity. Although exhibition practices have changed over the decades, critical response remains a telling factor as we attempt the unattainable—uncovering the vexed notion of artistic intention.

When the *New York Times* critic asked his question "Are Watercolors Serious?" in 1878, despite artists' success in making watercolors acceptable as exhibitable works of art, the established hierarchy prevailed: oil painting was still at the top. In some rare cases, artists put oil painting to the service of watercolor and effectively reversed the hierarchy. Notable among them was Thomas Eakins, who made oil studies in preparation for his small, tightly finished watercolors. Some of these studies were twice the size of the exhibited watercolors themselves. Eighteen seventy-eight, the year of the *Times* article, was a moment of ascendancy for watercolor, which had become an established "movement" in the 1860s, spawning regional and national organizations to promote the medium's practice and exhibition. American followers of John Ruskin championed watercolor in the late 1850s and 1860s, and beginning in 1867 the American Watercolor Society mounted an annual exhibition at the National Academy of Design in New York City.[2] Public exhibition of watercolors enhanced their market value. They were regarded as perfectly suited to decorate the middle-class home: smaller and less formal, they were also more affordable than oil paintings. Like prints, they brought new buyers into the art market.

Despite this comfortable niche, in the 1870s watercolors competed with oils for acceptance by critics and the buying public. One signal of this rivalry was the practice of enclosing exhibition watercolors in gilt mats and elaborate frames, and enlarging the size of the paper supports, to make them appear in scale and presentation more like paintings in oil on canvas. Critics, too, became protective of the medium:

> Many persons imagine that a water-color is nothing more or less than a sort of cheap oil-painting; that it can be done in about a quarter of the time that it takes to execute a work in oil; that it will soon fade; that it makes "no show whatever" when hung beside oils and that, consequently it ought to be sold at about half the price of a work in that medium. We need hardly say that all these conclusions are entirely wrong, utterly false in fact, and based on an entire ignorance of the process of painting in water-colors, and of the first principles of art.[3]

This critic's defensiveness embraced the medium's perceived fragility—that its colors were fugitive and its paper support less stable and therefore not as permanent as canvas. Debates about watercolor's durability, and consequently its marketability, dogged the medium's acceptance from the start. The American Society of Painters in Water-Color responded in 1868 with the publication of a pamphlet definitively titled *Water-Color Painting: Some Facts and Authorities in Relation to Its Durability*. Interestingly enough, today's conservators and curators are sensitive to watercolors' evanescence, limiting their exposure to light and shortening their time on view in museums and even in private homes. Some watercolors may be finished products and intended for exhibition, but wise stewardship often keeps them out of sight.

Usually relegated to life in a Solander box, a watercolor's appearance in exhibitions like *On Paper* at the Addison Gallery marks a rare and special occasion.

Within four years of the *Times*'s question "Are Watercolors Serious?" the American Watercolor Society enjoyed its most successful exhibition, an event that turned out to be the organization's watershed. Records for attendance and sales at the society's 1882 show soared to heights not reached for the rest of the century, but the jury's rejection of the work of many determined artists generated America's first watercolor "Salon des Refusés."[4] This controversy marked the end of the Society's proselytizing in the art world. Watercolors were no longer the realm of tourists, amateurs, and women, or suitable only for plein-air sketching; they were now accepted as finished, exhibitable works of art. The society had won its battle and retired from active engagement in this war.

The efforts of organizations like the American Watercolor Society bore fruit for the turn of the century, which was another notable moment for watercolor. Group and solo exhibitions promoted sales around 1910 of works in significant numbers by Winslow Homer and John Singer Sargent to major museums like the Metropolitan Museum of Art, the Brooklyn Museum, the Museum of Fine Arts, Boston, and the Worcester Art Museum. Each of these artists promoted his own watercolors. Sargent actively and successfully created a market for them to divert attention from his career as a society portraitist. Homer declared to his own New York dealer, "You will see, in the future I will live by my watercolors." Whether he meant in sales or reputation, or both, is not known.[5] Although other artists, notably John La Farge, produced important bodies of independent work in watercolor at this time, the names of Homer and Sargent are forever linked and juxtaposed as a domestic and a cosmopolitan exemplar of the medium that they defined for early-twentieth-century artists.

Marsden Hartley, one of the modernists who was often compared with Homer, observed in 1921: "There is then a fine American achievement in the art of water-color painting [which] may safely be called at this time a localized tradition. It has become an American realization."[6] His conclusions are strands in the fabric of American exceptionalism and cultural nationalism, and his statement reflects the fact that watercolor was the medium chosen (if for very different reasons) by many early-twentieth-century artists, from Post-Impressionist Maurice Prendergast to modernists John Marin, Georgia O'Keeffe, Arthur Dove, and Charles Demuth. Dealers, too, fostered the medium's avant-garde status, none more assiduously than Alfred Stieglitz at his "291" gallery. The medium also had a special appeal in New England, where shows were organized and museums pursued purchase of modernist works on paper. The Addison itself, soon after it was founded in 1931 with a collection of highly important American oil paintings, emphasized the exhibition and purchase of watercolors and drawings, many of which were patently independent works of art rather than studies or sketches. The reasons for these acquisitions were far ranging: financial, a quest to give greater breadth to a teaching collection, and a desire to acquire challenging works of contemporary art. The result was a focus that has continued to this day.[7]

The fluid, informal, experimental techniques of drawing and watercolor that appealed to this group of early-twentieth-century artists engaged the Abstract Expressionists as well. By the mid-twentieth century the hierarchical separation of mediums that favored oil for the most serious work had begun its final collapse as artists freely chose new mediums and supports. Today drawing occupies what one critic calls "a privileged position" because "its boundaries, compared to the blurred edges of other categories, remain precisely defined...continu[ing] a tradition that began with the earliest manifestations of Western art."[8] Perhaps as a consequence of this "privileged position" drawings enjoy a special prominence in both contemporary and historical exhibitions today.

Notes

1. *New York Times*, 3 February 1878. I am indebted to the research and ideas of many scholars of American watercolors, notably Kathleen Adair Foster, whose 1982 Yale dissertation, "Makers of the American Watercolor Movement: 1860–1890," broke new ground and built upon Theodore E. Stebbins, Jr.'s comprehensive exhibition and book, *American Master Drawings and Watercolors: A History of Works on Paper from Colonial Times to the Present* (New York: Harper & Row, 1976). More recently, several museum curators have written enlightening essays to accompany catalogues of their watercolor collections: Susan E. Strickler, ed., *American Traditions in Watercolor: The Worcester Art Museum Collection* (New York: Abbeville Press, 1987); Sue Welsh Reed and Carol Troyen, *Awash in Color: Homer, Sargent, and the Great American Watercolor* (Boston: Museum of Fine Arts in association with Little, Brown and Company, 1993); and Linda S. Ferber and Barbara Dayer Gallati, *Masters of Color and Light: Homer, Sargent, and the American Watercolor Movement* (Washington, D.C.: Smithsonian Institution Press in association with The Brooklyn Museum, 1998). More popular treatments ofthe subject include Donelson F. Hoopes, *American Watercolor Painting* (New York: Watson-Guptill, 1977) and Christopher Finch, *American Watercolors* (New York: Abbeville Press, 1986).

2. The American Society of Painters in Watercolor, founded in 1866, shortened its name in the following decade.

3. "The Water-Color Collection," *New York Times*, 9 February 1873, quoted by Gallati, "The Exhibition

Watercolor in America," in *Masters of Color and Light*, p. 45.

4. See Kathleen A. Foster, "The Watercolor Scandal of 1882: An American Salon des Refusés," *Archives of American Art Journal* 19, no. 2 (1979): 19–25.

5. For Homer and Sargent, see in particular Ferber, "Watercolors by Winslow Homer at The Brooklyn Museum of Art," and Gallati, "Controlling the Medium: The Marketing of John Singer Sargent's Watercolors," chapters four and five in *Masters of Color and Light*. Homer's statement to Charles R. Henschel of Knoedler's is quoted by Ferber, p. 93. It is often cited, first by Lloyd Goodrich, *Winslow Homer* (New York: Macmillan for the Whitney Museum of American Art, 1944), p. 159.

6. *Adventures in the Arts* (1921; repr. New York: Hacker Art Books, 1972), p. 101, as cited by Gallati, "Language, Watercolor, and the American Way," in *Masters of Color and Light*, p. 160. For discussions of watercolors and modernism, see this chapter by Gallati, and Troyen, "A War Waged on Paper: Watercolor and Modern Art in America," in *Awash in Color*.

7. I am indebted here to Charles Sawyer, first director of the Addison (and later my own teacher at the University of Michigan), and appreciate our recent e-mail exchange.

8. Dieter Schwarz, "'Not a Drawing': Some Thoughts about Recent Drawing," in Pamela Lee and Christine Mehring, *"Drawing is another kind of language": Recent American Drawings from a New York Private Collection* (Cambridge, Mass.: Harvard University Art Museums; Stuttgart: Daco-Verlag Günter Bläse, 1997).

The work as a **product** PORTFOLIO

BORN
Circa 1751
Lancashire, England

DIED
26 February 1811
New York, New York

The well-established English portraitist James Sharples, Sr., his third wife, Ellen, and two sons and daughter, all of whom were artists, arrived in New York in 1793. Armed with letters of introduction, Sharples traveled up and down the East Coast making likenesses. As William Dunlap wrote in his history of the American arts:

> His successful practice in this country was in crayons, or past[e]ls, which he manufactured for himself; and suited, in size, the diminutive dimensions of his portraits, where were generally en profile, and, when so, strikingly like.... The portrait was finished in about two hours, the likeness generally induced an order for a copy, and brought as sitters all who saw it. His price for the profile was $15; and for the full-face... $20.[1]

This portrait of an unidentified yet distinguished gentleman, finely drawn in pastel on the artist's favored thick, moderately textured, grayish tan paper (in this case now turned brownish), was of the twenty-dollar variety. The sitter has a forthright, quiet demeanor typical of Sharples's work. As a later historian claimed, "In all these portraits the purpose of the artist seems to have been sturdily honest.... There are no experiments in idealizing, no ambitious attempts to portray exceptional character."[2] This portrait's skillfulness is a testament to the meticulous application for which Sharples was known. After his travels, the artist settled in Philadelphia, where he took on portrait commissions of such famous American leaders as George Washington, John Adams, and James Monroe.[3] Sharples and his family moved back to England in 1801. After returning to New York in 1809, Sharples died there two years later.[4]

S C F

158 James Sharples

PORTRAIT OF A MAN, c. 1793–1801

Pastel on gray-brown, moderately thick, slightly textured (1) wove paper

9 1/2 x 7 7/16

Unsigned

Museum purchase

1936.37

BORN
14 November 1833
Philadelphia, Pennsylvania

DIED
8 November 1905
Newport, Rhode Island

The Philadelphia-born landscape and marine painter William Trost Richards was an enthusiastic advocate of the theories and practices of the American Pre-Raphaelite movement. Encouraged by the lessons of the English writer and artist John Ruskin, the Americans formed an association, published journals, and supported each other in the search for truth in nature. "The landscape of an American Pre-Raphaelite was to serve both science and art, conceived and rendered 'in such a way that the poet, the naturalist and the geologist might have taken large pleasure from it.'"[1]

Richards's works of the 1860s reveal his dedication to Pre-Raphaelite ideals in their minutely detailed, close-up study of natural vegetation. Although he often worked in oil, his extraordinary technical ability in watercolor gives proof of the American adherents'

"special affection for this medium."[2] In the Addison's watercolor, Richards's virtuoso technique has been put to the service of an uncharacteristically broad vista, as if he were attempting to meld the meticulous Pre-Raphaelite touch with the sweep of the earlier Hudson River School panorama. The breathless polish and elegant luminosity of this work relates it to other landscapes painted during the artist's travels in Italy during his extended European trip of 1866–67.[3] In these works Richards maintained his exacting mastery of the watercolor medium, yet eschewed his usual emphasis on the minute details of foreground.

Despite its panoptic viewpoint, this watercolor landscape still adheres to the model of Ruskin, who stated, "The only rule which I have, as yet, found to be without exception respecting art is that all great art is delicate."[4]

SCF

William Trost Richards

160

DAWN, c. 1867

Transparent and opaque watercolor on blue, moderately thick, slightly textured (1) wove paper

4 1/2 x 9 11/16

Unsigned

Stamped in ink on verso u.l.: 184

Museum purchase

1992.113

BORN
11 July 1834
Lowell, Massachusetts

DIED
17 July 1903
London, England

In September of 1879, Whistler embarked on a journey to Venice, prompted by bankruptcy in the wake of his infamous trial with John Ruskin, and with a commission by London's Fine Arts Society for a series of a dozen etchings of the Italian city. What began as a three-month stay became fourteen months and resulted in more than forty etchings, several oil paintings, and one hundred pastels.[1] When the artist finally returned to London, the Fine Arts Society hosted exhibitions of his work that helped to restore both the artist's tarnished reputation and lost finances.[2] Whistler was characteristically proud of his Venetian efforts. In a letter to a friend about the pastels, he wrote, "seriously I think you can form no idea of their bright beauty—their merry lightness and daintiness."[3]

Campanile Santa Margherita is located in a Venetian *campo* of the same name, in one of the western quarters of the city where Whistler lived and worked. In Whistler's day, the square was bounded by Venetian confraternities and cheap cafés, and bustled with the activity of its market.[4] Whistler captured the scene with delicate, descriptive black lines and pastel highlights reflecting the bright, varied colors of Venice. The artist exploited the warm, brown tone and visible flecks of the paper to enliven the space of the square and to serve as the background color of the building facades and tower walls, lending a textured reality to the scene. Visible pinholes along the edge of the drawing provide evidence that Whistler devoted at least nine sittings to this work, and scholars believe that he added his signature butterfly at the lower right base of the tower at the request of the pastel's first owner.[5]

GGS

162

James McNeill Whistler

CAMPANILE SANTA MARGHERITA,
1879–80

Chalk and pastel on brown, medium weight (2), slightly textured (1) wove paper

11 7/8 x 7 3/8

Signed in pastel l.r.: [butterfly monogram]

Inscribed in chalk on verso l.l: N:39 -
11 1/2 x 6 1/2

Gift of anonymous donor

1928.37

163

BORN
24 February 1836
Boston, Massachusetts

DIED
29 September 1910
Prout's Neck, Scarboro, Maine

On the Cliff, Cullercoats, depicting three young women walking on a bluff high above the shore, is one of the powerful images Winslow Homer produced in the English coastal town of Cullercoats during his twenty-month stay in 1881–82. In his English watercolors Homer focused on the hardy fishermen who made their living from the sea and the majestic women who waited for them on shore. One of the first art critics to comment on the shift between Homer's earlier genre painting and those of the English experience was Marianne Van Rensselaer, who, in a November 1883 article, compared "the awkwardly truthful gestures of his New England figures, with the sculptural grace of these fisher-girls."[1] The painter and critic Kenyon Cox wrote in 1913 that from Homer's experience with "these robust English fishwives… he learned the meaning of classic breadth and serenity, and his idea of figure drawing was transformed and enlarged."[2]

For *On the Cliff, Cullercoats*, Homer chose a low vantage point to isolate and frame three women against the ominous cloud-filled sky. He further intensified their immediacy by eliminating the foreground and allowing the edge of the picture plane to cut the forward figure below the knees. Poised on the very edge of the cliff, one in front of another as if inextricably bound by the cumbersome fishing nets they carry, they form a tight horizontal shape that references the noble stance and timeless gravity of a classical Greek monument.[3] In this work and in similar compositions made from his English experience, Homer venerated the power, humanity, and nobility of the working women he portrayed.

S C F

164 # Winslow Homer

ON THE CLIFF, CULLERCOATS, c. 1881–82

Watercolor and charcoal on cream (2), moderately thick, moderately textured (2) wove paper

15 x 21 1/4

Signed in watercolor l.l.: Winslow Homer

Gift of anonymous donor

1930.15

BORN
24 February 1836
Boston, Massachusetts

DIED
29 September 1910
Prout's Neck, Scarboro, Maine

Dog on a Log and *Casting*, two of eleven Winslow Homer watercolors in the Addison collection, are brilliant testaments to the artist's mastery of the medium.

Dog on a Log was one of more than eighty-seven watercolors Winslow Homer produced in the Adirondacks between the fall of 1889 and 1900.[1] The early watercolors of this period have been described as "among the most formally and technically beautiful and powerful and explicitly expressive watercolors he ever made."[2] *Dog on a Log* is part of a large series dealing with deer hunting and the dubious practice of hounding, in which dogs drove the deer into the water, where hunters waited for the kill. In this sheet, the hunting dog, momentarily poised on a half-submerged log, is bathed by sunlight that has broken through the deep forest. The expectant animal, his jaw almost aquiver, is framed by exuberantly layered green and blue vegetation sparkling with flecks of red in a composition of breathtaking anticipation, rich color, and radiant light.

In *Casting*, painted eight years later on one of the artist's trips to Quebec (p. 169), Homer focused not on the process of hunting but on the solitary pursuit of the fly fisherman. Homer eschewed the jewel-like tones of his Adirondacks pictures for mastery of subdued tonalities and controlled composition.[3] Watery films of blue-gray tones used to define the vegetation and the rocky river edge alternate with the bands of unpainted paper and golden touches that suggest the mounting sprays of water. Deftly scribing into the still-wet passages with his brush end, Homer created a vertical sequence of tree trunks across the background, and, with one final sweep, he picked out the sinuous fishing line in back cast as it prepares to roll into the crystalline stillness of the river pool.[4]

S C F

166 Winslow Homer

DOG ON A LOG, 1889

Watercolor and graphite on cream (3), thick, moderately textured (3) wove paper

14 x 20 1/16

Signed in watercolor l.r.: HOMER 1889

Bequest of Miss Candace C. Stimson

1946.120

Winslow Homer
CASTING, 1897

Transparent and opaque watercolor
and graphite on cream (1), thick, moderately
textured (2) wove paper

13 15/16 x 20 7/8

Signed in watercolor l.l.: WH 1897

Gift of anonymous donor

1928.22

BORN
31 March 1835
New York, New York

DIED
14 November 1910
Providence, Rhode Island

John La Farge's watercolor *Spearing Fish, Samoa* relates to a sixteen-month-long trip the artist made with his close friend, the writer Henry Adams. Starting in August of 1890, the two wound their way westward around the globe, stopping in Hawai'i, Samoa, and Tahiti, going on to Fiji, past Australia to Singapore, Java, and Ceylon, and returning finally to New York in November 1891. La Farge returned with a substantial number of sketches and watercolors made on the trip, as well as photographs he and Adams had taken, and purchased postcards.

La Farge made productive and continuous use of photography in his work, beginning early in his career.[1] The South Seas images were no exception, as the La Farge scholar James Yarnall notes: "Many highly finished watercolors were painted both in the South Seas and after La Farge's return to New York, using various pictorial sources including annotated drawings, watercolor sketches, photographs, and books."[2]

Using a photograph taken by Charles Spitz about 1885–90, La Farge created this watercolor. While he closely adopted the composition of his model, he expanded the viewpoint, and with delicate washes of blues, greens, and warm tans imbued the scene with the shimmering heat and light of the tropics. The figure of the fisherman, elegantly balancing his long spear, anchors the focus and provides a human counterpoint to the compact, lushly green atoll floating just off the shore.

La Farge showed the watercolor both in his 1893 exhibition of South Seas scenes at Doll and Richards, Boston, and in the major exhibition *Paintings, Studies, Sketches, and Drawings: Mostly Records of Travel 1886 and 1890–91*, which he organized for exhibition in New York and then at the Paris Salon.[3]

SCF

170

John La Farge

SPEARING FISH, SAMOA, c. 1892–93

Transparent and opaque watercolor on beige (1),
medium weight (2), smooth wove paper

16 3/8 x 23 3/4

Unsigned

Museum purchase

1937.11

BORN
10 October 1858
St. John's, Newfoundland, Canada

DIED
1 February 1924
New York, New York

Maurice Brazil Prendergast has been called America's first modern painter, combining in his work a social commentary on American life at the turn of the century with a style characterized by flat surfaces carefully composed through the use of harmonious color.[1] Prendergast painted *Float at Low Tide, Revere Beach* shortly after his return from Paris, where he received his only formal art instruction.[2] In his early watercolors, he translated what he had learned from the French Impressionists and American expatriate James McNeill Whistler into a unique style, reflective of life in the American cities of Boston and New York.

In the Boston of the 1890s, increasing industrialization led to a rise in prosperity, which in turn afforded money and leisure time to the working class. The beaches to the north and south of Boston, such as Revere Beach, were popular holiday destinations.[3]

Prendergast, a lover of crowds and spectacles, often joined the masses of people on these summer weekend outings. He depicted the figures in this work as a group of fashionable yet unspecific people, blurring class distinctions. They embody the meeting of urban life and nature, one of the recurring themes in Prendergast's art.[4] The strong vertical and horizontal lines of the float dominate the composition and separate the expanses of color, while the space is made ambiguous by the patterning of the water and the high line of the horizon. The flat space organized by color and the focus on design reflect the influence of Japanese prints and Art Nouveau posters, while the jewel-like colors of his Impressionist palette emphasize the brilliance of light along the coast.

GGS

172 Maurice Prendergast

FLOAT AT LOW TIDE, REVERE BEACH,
c. 1896–97

Watercolor and graphite on cream (3), moderately thick, moderately textured (1) wove paper

13 13/16 x 9 3/4

Signed in ink l.r.: Maurice B. Prendergast

Gift of Mrs. William C. Endicott

1942.2

BORN
10 October 1858
St. John's, Newfoundland, Canada

DIED
1 February 1924
New York, New York

Maurice Prendergast's *Venice* includes iconic elements of this picturesque city's charm.[1] Gondolas drift under a whimsically bowed bridge teeming with finely dressed tourists who spill out onto surrounding walkways and stone steps. Above the quiet bustle float, like magic, stone buildings, between which are strung red banners that glow with local color. All is captured through Prendergast's sketchy pencil lines and blunt watercolor strokes that either melt into loose pools of transparent color or snap together with crystalline clarity.

Prendergast made this painting during an extended visit to Italy between July 1898 and late 1899, much of which was spent in Venice.[2] The Addison's watercolor, like most of Prendergast's Venetian work, uses the architecture of the city as a structural frame: the building facades and flags define the space, as if they were a theatrical backdrop in front of which plays the lively activity of street, bridge, and canal.

Unusual among Prendergast's work, this watercolor sports a visible seam running across the darkness of the buildings' open second-story windows, suggesting that Prendergast joined two sheets to make a conscious readjustment of his original composition. The seam neatly divides the image into a lower portion that contains the throngs of foreigners flocked in a tourist location and an upper portion that includes the tops of buildings and large red banner bearing the image of a golden winged lion, the symbol of Saint Mark, patron saint of Venice. In the combination of the two, Prendergast seems to unite two worlds: the charm of a specific neighborhood during festival season (above) with the reality of Venice's tourist industry (below) to make a modern painting that captured both realities of European life at the dawn of the twentieth century.

JM

174 Maurice Prendergast

VENICE, c. 1898–99

Watercolor and graphite on two joined sheets of cream (1), moderately thick, slightly textured (2) wove paper

17 1/4 x 15 1/2

Signed in ink l.l.: Maurice Prendergast

Graphite sketch on verso

Bequest of Miss Lizzie P. Bliss

1931.96

BORN
10 October 1858
St. John's, Newfoundland, Canada

DIED
1 February 1924
New York, New York

At the turn of the twentieth century, America experienced a dramatic expansion of industry that resulted in the growth of cities and an increase in immigrant population. In turn, the distinctions between classes became more marked, while the space they shared became more congested.[1]

In this image of Central Park, Prendergast chose to depict the mingling of social classes as they escape to a communal refuge from the pressures of city life.[2] Although there is a mixing of social levels, all are unified through their fashion, leisurely pursuit, and unidentifiable features. Small children play in front of a fountain while their parents relax on the park benches. The figures are organized around the fountain, whose upward spray constitutes the main, vertical axis of the composition. The eye circles the fountain, led by the explosions of red in the dress of the children in the foreground, to the pinks and blues along the bench surrounding the fountain, to the small, red parasol of a woman disappearing down the path between trees. These bright bursts of color stand out against the muted greens, browns, and dark blues that dominate the work.

A resident of Boston for most of his mature life, Prendergast had his first one-person exhibition at the prestigious Macbeth Gallery in New York City in 1900 and thereafter spent part of each year in that city.[3] Central Park was one of the sites most frequently depicted by the artist, and, though different in setting and tonality, this image is similar in spirit to such coastal New England paintings as *On the Pier, Nantasket* (see next entry).

GGS

176 Maurice Prendergast

IN CENTRAL PARK, NEW YORK,
c. 1900–1903

Watercolor and graphite on cream (1), moderately thick, slightly textured (1) wove paper

12 1/4 x 20

Signed in ink l.r.: Prendergast

Inscribed in graphite on verso u.l.: Central Park New York

Gift of anonymous donor

1928.48

BORN
10 October 1858
St. John's, Newfoundland, Canada

DIED
1 February 1924
New York, New York

In *On the Pier, Nantasket*, fashionable people promenade under a protective canopy, socializing in the clean, fresh air along the Atlantic coast. Playful children and dogs dot the low band of sidewalk, while the adults process at the center of the composition. The compression of the flat pictorial space makes the meeting of the sea and sky appear as if it is both behind the figures and above them, indicating perspective while counteracting it. The columns of the pier punctuate the lateral motion of the figures, lending cadence to the composition. The sheltering roof and the dark band along the bottom of the picture serve to frame the image's upper and lower boundaries. Though the composition is thus enclosed from above and below, the columns' regularity and the open sides establish a temporal rhythm to the procession that leads one to wonder who will appear as this group of figures continues down the pier.

In 1898, Prendergast had traveled to Italy, where he spent time studying the light and color of Venice and was exposed to the artistic tradition of Venetian painters. The influence of Vittore Carpaccio, a sixteenth-century Venetian artist who created narrative paintings with an emphasis on horizontal, lateral motion, can be seen in the processional quality of this painting.[1] The brilliant colors of Prendergast's early watercolors are intensified here, catching the light off the ocean and dazzling the eye. While incorporating European artistic traditions, Prendergast's images of coastal New England helped to promote tourist trade to the area as well as the idea of an American holiday.[2]

GGS

178 ## Maurice Prendergast

ON THE PIER, NANTASKET,
c. 1900–1905

Watercolor and graphite on white, moderately thick, moderately textured (3) wove paper

12 1/2 x 19 3/8

Signed in ink l.r.: Prendergast

Gift of anonymous donor

1928.49

BORN
22 May 1844
Allegheny City, Pennsylvania

DIED
14 June 1926
Chateau de Beaufresne, France

By the time Mary Cassatt drew this pastel portrait of a young boy, she had achieved critical success in her adopted city of Paris under the encouragement of Edgar Degas and the Parisian artists known as the Independents. Absorbing the influences of Degas's form and color, Manet's structure, Courbet's painterliness, and Japanese prints' emphasis on asymmetry, compositional flattening, and simplification, Cassatt painted the people and urban settings of her own experience, earning a reputation as the most distinguished painter of mother and child subjects.[1]

The Addison's portrait *Little Boy in Blue (No. 2)* of about 1906 was executed during a decade when she worked frequently in pastel.[2] It is one of three pastels of the same subject.[3] In each the elegantly dressed and coiffed

boy sits on a settee, his head turned slightly to his right. In the Addison's portrait, the artist devoted careful attention to the depiction of the boy's long curls and bangs and his pink and white complexion, leaving the background, the settee, and the details of his vibrant blue coat more loosely defined. The child's long hair and sweet, even sentimental expression may be the reason that Macbeth Gallery titled the work *Yvonne* at the time of its transfer to the Addison Gallery.[4] Cassatt's Paris dealer, Durand-Ruel, whose inventory number still exists in chalk on the back of the stretcher, more aptly called the work "Jeune garcon au col blanc [Young boy in the white collar]."[5]

SCF

180 ## Mary Cassatt

LITTLE BOY IN BLUE (NO. 2), c. 1906

Pastel on brown, medium weight,
moderately textured (3) wove paper

25 1/2 x 19 3/4

Signed in pastel l.r.: Mary Cassatt

Gift of anonymous donor

1930.300

181

BORN
9 September 1889
New York, New York

DIED
30 October 1930
Bilbao, Spain

One of the earliest images of suburbia produced by Preston Dickinson, this drawing was probably created sometime during the winter of 1915–16, around the time the artist moved to Valley Stream, Long Island, to live with his widowed sister.[1] Made soon after his return to New York after a four-year stay in Paris, Dickinson's drawing is both a reflection of his European sojourn and an early manifestation of the Precisionist style for which he is best known.

Although he went to Paris to study at the École des Beaux-Arts and the Academie Julian, it was Dickinson's exposure to the Parisian art world and his independent visits to museums and galleries that had the greatest effect on his work. In this drawing, the choice of a thin paper as well as the calligraphic quality of line and the emphasis on flat design reveal the artist's interest in the Japanese ukiyo-e prints he would have seen in Paris. Dickinson roots his "picture of the floating world" within a gridlike composition of horizontals and verticals, to make a wintry world that is simultaneously ethereal and earthbound.[2]

The tension created between the delicacy of the paper and medium and the underlying architectonic structure is echoed in the dynamism Dickinson created between realism and abstraction. Carefully detailed and realistic renderings of rooftops, melting snow, and the picket fence exist harmoniously alongside simplified forms of trees and an electrical pole animated by just a few deft strokes of charcoal. Pushing these crisply drawn elements to the edges of his composition, Dickinson allowed floating expanses of soft rice paper to hold the central focus. In its balance of objective reality and abstract design, this carefully constructed drawing anticipates the Precisionist movement that was to emerge in the 1920s.

ANK

182   Preston Dickinson

LANDSCAPE (HOUSE AND TREES),
c. 1915–16

Crayon on beige (1), thin (2),
slightly textured (1) tracing paper

11 11/16 x 9 5/8

Signed in graphite l.l.: Dickinson

Museum purchase

1935.56

BORN
2 August 1880
Canandaigua, New York

DIED
23 November 1946
Huntington, New York

In 1910 and 1911 Arthur Dove produced a series of small oil paintings that were unlike anything he had made before. Although inspired by nature, these daring abstractions were completely nonrepresentational. What makes this transformation so remarkable is that up until this point, Dove's work was fairly conservative.[1] In 1908, the artist traveled to France, where he was initially inspired by Impressionism and then Fauvism. After returning to New York in 1909, a competent yet still somewhat derivative painter, Dove continued his search for artistic identity. His breakthrough abstractions of 1910–11 reveal the beginnings of a personal style and a lifelong interest in expressing the essence of the natural world through pure abstract form.

Although the 1910–11 sketches were not shown in Dove's lifetime, a subsequent group of ten pastels was included in his first one-person show at Alfred Stieglitz's "291" gallery in 1912. Made up of forms distilled from but not imitating nature, these pastels (later known as "The Ten Commandments") placed Dove in the forefront of the American avant-garde. Unfortunately, the arduous demands of growing crops and raising chickens on his farm in Westport, Connecticut, prevented Dove from fully capitalizing on his newfound notoriety.

One of the few works he created in the ensuing decade,[2] the Addison's drawing extends Dove's efforts to communicate the underlying essence rather than outward appearance of nature. *Drawing*, 1913, depicts the very forces that make up and animate nature. Densely packed and overlapping, the fractured forms seethe and roil just below the picture plane. Threatening to burst, this heaving land-scape suggests the gathering energy before a storm, or the "pulsating surge of nature's growth."[3] Composed of only a few reduced and repeated shapes, the drawing supports Dove's conviction that to "simplify is to work toward truth."[4]

ANK

184 Arthur Dove

DRAWING, 1913

Charcoal on brown, medium weight (1), slightly textured (1) wove paper

21 7/16 x 18

Unsigned

Museum purchase

1959.18

BORN
15 November 1887
Sun Prairie, Wisconsin

DIED
6 March 1986
Santa Fe, New Mexico

Produced in 1919, this striking charcoal composition marks a pivotal moment in O'Keeffe's early career. After exploring the expressive possibility of the flatness of the picture plane with lush pools of water-color and swirling charcoal abstractions in nearly one hundred fifty works on paper from 1915 to 1918, O'Keeffe arrived in New York in June 1918 to a creative rebirth in which she destroyed a number of these earlier works and delved into a wholly new investigation of form through oil painting to achieve a personal imagery.[1]

A rare work on paper from this early oil painting phase, *Black Lines* synthesizes both O'Keeffe's mastery of flat tone from her previous work and her initial experimentation with tight-cropped, cleanly contoured volumes that would emerge as her stylistic signature.[2] With two sharp black bolts piercing through a defined edge into a smoothly shaded volume, the work resonates with a powerful tension between the abstract weight of light and dark, sharp flatness and smooth volume, and motion and stillness. Considering the resulting image in light of her later enlargements of flower details, we can let ourselves imagine what this pure abstraction might be: a puncture? a bee sting? a piercing note of music?

JM

186 Georgia O'Keeffe

BLACK LINES, 1919

Charcoal on beige (1), moderately thick, slightly textured (2), Michallet laid paper
24 5/8 x 18 3/4
Unsigned
Museum purchase
1959.22

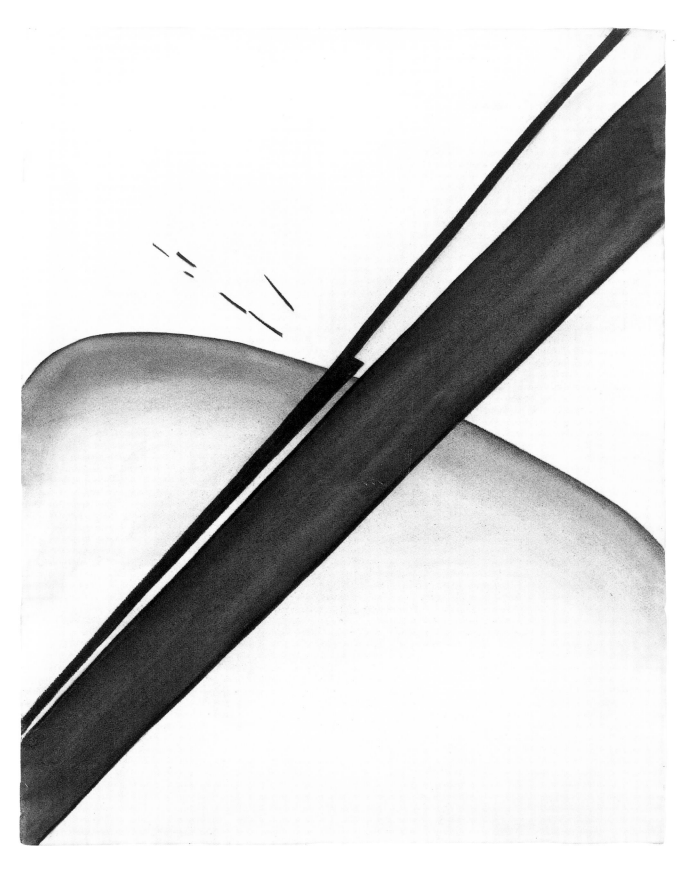

BORN
23 December 1872
Rutherford, New Jersey

DIED
1 October 1953
Cape Split, Maine

In August of the summer he painted *Blue Sea, Crotch Island*, John Marin wrote to his dealer, Alfred Stieglitz, to describe his approach to painting.

> I don't paint rocks, trees, houses, and all things seen, I paint an inner vision. Rubbish. If you have an intense love and feeling towards these things, you'll try your damdest to put on paper or canvas, that thing. You can transpose, you can play with and on your material, but when you are finished that's got to have the roots of that thing in it and no other thing.[1]

This watercolor, energetically executed in the artist's characteristic wet swathes of color and dashing line, is testament to Marin's abiding passion for the rhythms, colors, and balance of nature. As Marin described in his staccato, stream-of-consciousness way,

> This—a work of Art—A Consummate sense of Construction based on those vital lines about which the parts move. A consummate draughtsmanship. A consummate awareness of color weights— of balance—of rhythm. Not that you have painted a violin but that you have the rhythmic flow shows that you have music aboard.[2]

Addison Gallery director Charles Sawyer first saw this watercolor at Edith Halpert's Downtown Gallery in 1934. She had received it on consignment from Stieglitz earlier in the year. Sawyer was particularly taken with the work, and after borrowing it for the Addison's summer exhibition, *Watercolors by Contemporary Americans*, in 1935, he immediately negotiated its purchase.[3]

SCF

188   John Marin

BLUE SEA, CROTCH ISLAND, 1923

Watercolor and charcoal on cream (3), very thick, rough (2) wove paper

17 3/16 x 20 1/2

Signed in watercolor and charcoal l.r.: Marin '23

Inscribed in graphite on verso c.: Blue Sea off Crotch Island

Museum purchase

1935.46

BORN
8 November 1883
Lancaster, Pennsylvania

DIED
23 October 1935
Lancaster, Pennsylvania

Plums is a masterwork by one of America's modern virtuosos of watercolor.[1] Charles Demuth's extraordinary technical control transcended the seductive qualities of transparent immediacy that is sometimes the *raison d'etre* of the medium. In *Plums* Demuth flaunted his skill, but he also explored difficult intellectual problems of composition and color. A branch of plums is the subject of this still life, unusual in that it was not assembled from individual objects but was apparently *selected* from an unseen tree. The composition, a triangle of overlapping elements cascading down the page, was influenced by Cubism. The illusion of physical space is constrained by tension between the three-dimensional objects and the air around them. At the center of the image the background seems as solid as the fruit. Demuth used saturated brown and black washes to silhouette leaves of lighter shades of green or no color at all. Elsewhere, Demuth blotted away wet paint, creating a dappled effect. The overall impression is of rustling leaves, each one changing as the light touches it.

Charles Demuth was a central figure in American modernism in the 1920s and early 1930s. He maintained close personal and professional relationships with Marsden Hartley, Georgia O'Keeffe, Alfred Stieglitz, and the poet William Carlos Williams. He lived abroad for extended periods and exhibited regularly in New York. In the early 1920s, at the height of his artistic career, Demuth was diagnosed with diabetes, a little understood disease at the time. He suffered debilitating attacks that forced him to retreat to the comfort of his family home in Lancaster, Pennsylvania. There he could work from the fruit and flowers in his mother's garden without overtaxing his strength. *Plums* is one of a series of remarkable watercolors Demuth executed there in 1925.[2]

SJM

190 Charles Demuth

PLUMS, 1925

Watercolor and graphite on cream (2), medium weight (2), slightly textured (1), Whatman wove paper

18 1/8 x 12

Signed in graphite l.r.: C. Demuth 1925

Museum purchase

1934.5

BORN
17 November 1904
Los Angeles, California

DIED
30 December 1988
New York, New York

Isamu Noguchi was a world-renowned sculptor of abstract forms in stone and in bronze, steel, and other metals. He was also an extremely talented draftsman, and at various times in his career turned to drawing both figurative images and abstractions. As part of his earliest training in New York as an academic sculptor, he must have studied figure drawing.[1] In 1927, Noguchi worked as an assistant in the Paris studio of sculptor Constantin Brancusi, where he produced hard-edged opaque watercolor drawings that would inform his own early abstract sculpture. After an exhibition of these first abstract sculptures was not a commercial success, Noguchi turned to portrait heads to raise money to continue his studies in Paris and the Far East. In China, he apprenticed himself to the master painter Qi Baishi and learned the very difficult technique of traditional ink painting.[2] By 1930–31, the young

Japanese American artist was thoroughly engaged in both Eastern and Western traditions and well on his way to bridging the gap between the two cultures through his own personal brand of modernism.[3]

The Addison's *Standing Nude* is an exquisitely finished charcoal drawing. This woman appears as if from a mist, her voluptuous curves created almost entirely from delicate shading rather than line drawing. Even at this early stage in his career, Noguchi reached for essential volumetric form, expressed in smooth surface treatment suggestive of polished white marble.[4]

SJM

192 Isamu Noguchi

STANDING NUDE, c. 1931

Charcoal on cream (2), very thick, smooth wove paper mounted on board

19 1/4 x 12 3/8

Unsigned

Gift of Winslow Ames (PA 1925)

1964.22

BORN
11 March 1876
Marion, Massachusetts

DIED
24 October 1971
Bennington, Vermont

In the winter of 1941, the Detroit Institute of Arts presented an exhibition and concert devoted to the work of Carl Ruggles. It was a fitting confluence of the two art forms that had engaged Ruggles throughout his life. Included in that exhibition was the Addison's charcoal drawing, *Polyphonic Stanza*, which had been purchased from the artist in 1937.

By all accounts, Carl Ruggles was an eccentric Yankee, "a rather colorful and 'homespun' character."[1] His close friend Rockwell Kent described him as "a strange, intense little man, a bald egg-headed little man, with eyes that were alight with fervor."[2]

A contemporary of the musicians Charles Ives, Henry Cowell, and Charles Seeger, Ruggles's musical contributions are well known and highly respected; his name is far less well-known in painterly circles. It is possible that Ruggles's interest in art was first piqued by Kent, who used him as the model for a painting of Captain Ahab. He also cultivated friendships with the artists Boardman Robinson,

Henry Schnakenberg, Thomas Hart Benton, and Herbert Meyers. After his retirement Ruggles devoted most of his time to painting and exhibited at various Northeast locations.

In contrast to his music, over which he agonized and labored, he painted easily and quickly, creating hundreds of works.[3] In *Polyphonic Stanza* that ease of execution is evident in the swirling plumes that rise and intertwine with the banking cloud forms above. The energetic patterns of the drawing bear a close relationship to a description of Ruggles's music—"atonal but not serial, and filled with shifting lines and rhythms."[4] The art historian and music critic Alfred Frankenstein echoes that assessment of Ruggles's art: "At the best his pictures have an inspired, mystical, radiant, jewel-like quality which is by no means unlike the spirit of his tonal reactions."[5]

SCF

194

Carl Ruggles

POLYPHONIC STANZA, 1930s

Charcoal on cream (2), thick, rough (2) wove paper

12 x 12 3/16

Signed in ink l.l.: Carl Ruggles

Gift of Friends of Southern Vermont Artists

1937.70

BORN
26 July 1893
Berlin, Germany

DIED
6 July 1959
Berlin, Germany

When the German artist George Grosz arrived in New York in 1932 to teach summer school at the Art Students League, he had already made a name for himself both in Germany and the United States as "the merciless critic of German bourgeoisie and German institutions."[1] His positive summer experience and deteriorating conditions in Germany convinced him to move permanently to the United States. In January of 1933, just eighteen days before Hitler became chancellor of Germany, Grosz landed in New York.

Quickly moving beyond his German roots, Grosz embraced a country he believed was filled with hope and endless opportunity. In a letter to a friend he wrote,

> New York—I love this town. I have seen tramps sleeping on newspapers in Union Square…Broadway aglow at night; workers in overalls suspended between steel girders…Wall Street and shouting brokers at the stock exchange…sweet girls stripped to the applause of the men…. This town is full of pictures and contrasts.[2]

Between 1932 and 1935 Grosz traversed New York City, filling pads with quick sketches that captured the diversity of metropolitan street life. These he brought back to his studio to transform into finished watercolors. The Addison's portrait, made the year after his immigration, is such a work. In it, Grosz's keen acumen for gesture and perception of character is realized with his customarily lively line and fluid, fuzzy-edged watercolor[3] in a work that has left behind the satirical and biting to celebrate the gracious humanity of an anonymous subway rider. That he chose as a subject an elegantly dressed black woman and portrayed her with dignity and appreciation is indicative of his enthusiastic embrace of the American promise.

SCF

196

George Grosz

PORTRAIT OF A LADY (ON THE SUBWAY), 1933

Transparent and opaque watercolor on cream (2), moderately thick, moderately textured (2), Fabriano wove paper

26 3/8 x 19

Signed in ink l.r.: GROSZ / 33 / N YORK

Inscribed in graphite l.l.: Colored girl; in graphite on verso l.l.: 78 / LG Nr.4 / Schwarze Lady 1933; stamped l.l.: George Grosz Nachlass; in ink l.l.: 1 81 2 ; in graphite l.c.: K. Nr. 707 / PMG 81

Gift of Lilian and Peter M. Grosz (PA 1945) in memory of Michael Grosz (PA 1974)

1992.24

BORN
3 December 1897
New York, New York

DIED
4 January 1977
Great Neck Estates, New York

In 1932, in preparation for the exhibition *Murals by American Painters and Photographers*, the Museum of Modern Art invited sixty-five artists to submit sketches for a mural that addressed some aspect of "the Post-War World." While the interpretation and technique were left up to the artist, each was asked to design a three-part composition and make an enlarged finished version of one of the study's three sections. *Unemployed (Prosperity Around the Corner)* is the left frame of the mural study submitted by William Gropper. A biting commentary on American industrialism and capitalism, the triptych drawing and accompanying panel were so critical of the establishment that MoMA trustees considered eliminating them from the exhibition.[1]

By the time this drawing was created Gropper had established himself as one of America's foremost graphic artists.[2] A native of New York's Lower East Side and a student of Robert Henri and George Bellows, Gropper combined in his work the Ashcan School's

interest in contemporary everyday life with a keen sense of social responsibility. The product of a deft hand, sharp wit, and deep sympathy for the oppressed, Gropper's satirical drawings, many of which served as illustrations in newspapers and magazines, are a masterful blend of art and social expression.

The Addison's drawing depicts the "prosperity" predicted by President Hoover several years before his defeat in the 1932 presidential campaign. In the midst of a fervent speech, Hoover is surrounded by signs and symbols of the times: racism, postwar disillusionment, gangsterism, police brutality, moral debauchery, and government corruption. Opposite this dense jumble of activity, Gropper has placed a faint, almost visionlike scene suggesting the outcome of Hoover's false prediction: closed factories and widespread unemployment. Absolutely alive with action and movement, Gropper's striking design delivers a powerful ideological and aesthetic punch.

ANK

William Gropper

UNEMPLOYED (PROSPERITY AROUND THE CORNER), 1932

Ink and graphite on beige (2), moderately thick, rough (1) wove paper

21 1/16 x 14

Signed in ink l.r.: GROPPER

Museum purchase

1936.45

BORN
9 April 1893
Ashtabula Harbor, Ohio

DIED
10 January 1967
West Seneca, New York

The weatherbeaten buildings, the heavy sky, the overarching tree, the melancholy and foreboding mood of the scene that Charles Burchfield has captured in *The Sky Beyond* resonate with a sense of the familiar, even if one cannot pinpoint the exact building, or exact tree, pictured. As fellow painter Edward Hopper said of Burchfield's art, "By sympathy with the particular he has made it epic and universal. No mood has been so mean as to seem unworthy of interpretation."[1]

The art of Charles Burchfield defies categorization, as it comprises realist, expressionist, abstract, visionary, and Regionalist elements.[2] He was a painter of the world around him who celebrated the wonders of a forest in spring, a backyard in the summer sun, and an old farmhouse in the approach of a winter storm. Throughout his life, Burchfield sought to capture the light, movement, and mood of a scene, recording an impression reflective of the found, natural world and of his own emotions. Burchfield was influenced by nineteenth-century Christian pantheism, which promoted the idea of a oneness between God and nature, as well as by Transcendentalism and Romanticism.[3] *The Sky Beyond* merges realistic yet obliquely viewed buildings, expressionistic brushwork, and a Romantic mood conveyed through gathering clouds in a composition so focused on these elements as to render the scene monumental, sublime, and spiritual; a vision seen and then given form by the artist.

GGS

200

Charles Burchfield

THE SKY BEYOND, 1940

Watercolor on cream (2), moderately thick, slightly textured (1) wove paper mounted on board

28 1/16 x 22 15/16

Signed in watercolor l.r.: CEB [monogram] / 1940

Gift of Mrs. Elizabeth P. Metcalf

1954.24

BORN
1 January 1889
St. Louis, Missouri

DIED
29 January 1962
New York, New York

After architectural training in St. Louis, in 1912 Hugh Ferriss moved to New York City, where he earned a significant reputation as an architectural delineator. Taking lucrative commissions from architectural firms, advertisers, and magazines, he transformed buildings and products into lush, dark, evocative renderings that were powerful tributes to the Machine Age aesthetic. His 1929 publication, *The Metropolis of Tomorrow*, an artistic manifesto on the city of the future, established him as an urban visionary and theorist as well.[1]

By the 1940s, Ferriss's enchantment with the city of skyscrapers was over. Honored with a travel award from the Architectural League of New York, Ferriss set out across the country to record contemporary architecture. Eighteen thousand miles later, Ferriss returned with drawings that celebrated the drama and romance of monuments of American engineering. In his characteristic chiaroscuro style, Ferriss captured the "massive power plants, trim airports, handsome broadcasting stations and telephone buildings, gleaming factories and farflung highways"[2] that were the 1940s equivalents of city skyscrapers that had so engaged him in the twenties. When these charcoal drawings were exhibited at the Whitney Museum of American Art under the title *The Power of America in Buildings*,[3] *Newsweek* raved, dubbing Ferris "this country's No. 1 artist of architecture." *Time*'s review called him "U.S. Architecture's most grandiose seer."[4]

The Addison's drawing, depicting a train trestle viewed from below at a moment of explosion or fire, is not listed in Ferriss's meticulous job books, suggesting that it was made for his own pleasure and not for a commission.[5] The dramatic viewpoint, the theatrical light, the tiny awestruck figure, and the insistently angular diagonals and abstracted structure are evidence of the very best of Ferriss's mature compositional style and mastery of the charcoal medium.

SCF

202 Hugh Ferriss

TRESTLE, c. 1940

Charcoal on beige (1), moderately thick, moderately textured (1) Whatman illustration board

25 9/16 x 18 1/8

Signed in charcoal on verso c.: Hugh Ferris[s]

Gift of Mr. John Davis Hatch, Jr.

1961.19

BORN
28 January 1912
Cody, Wyoming

DIED
11 August 1956
East Hampton, New York

This untitled, two-sided drawing is one of a number of drawings made by Jackson Pollock about 1943 that explored the emotional and dramatic impact of dark black passages in combination with his characteristically sinuous lines.[1] On the recto, the small sheet is dominated by a powerful interplay of shapes—faces with open mouths and the limbs of bodies—appearing and disappearing into a background alternately solidly black and densely screened by crosshatching. The figural intensity is reinforced by the vigor with which the artist pressed with his pen nib to raise ink-saturated paper fibers on the surface.

When the work was first acquired by the Addison, it was erroneously called *Study for "Mad Moon-Woman."*[2] However, the drawing has no visual or compositional relationship to that painting. Pollock, an inveterate draftsman, was dedicated to making drawings as works distinct and significant in their own right.[3] In a 1950 interview, he claimed, "I approach painting in the same sense as one approaches drawing; that is, it's direct. I don't work from drawings, I don't make sketches and drawings and color sketches into a final painting."[4]

On the verso of the sheet is a sgraffito drawing of black on green (p. 207).[5] On this side, the artist coated the entire expanse of paper with a light green, opaque, water-based paint, into which, with needle-thin lines, he scribed an unsettlingly obscure imagery—a sharply profiled man, his hand holding a cigarette, glaring at a fetus-like form over which floats an unintelligible inscription. While its composition seems incomplete and unresolved, the work is allied with other drawings of about 1943 in which coiling and looping lines suggesting strange beasts and humanlike forms dance across the pages.

SCF

204 Jackson Pollock

Untitled (recto), c. 1943

Ink and opaque watercolor on beige (2),
medium weight (1), smooth wove paper

7 5/16 x 5 5/16

Signed in ink l.c.: J. Pollock

Gift of Mr. and Mrs. Allan Stone (PA 1950),
Addison Art Drive

1991.87a

206   Jackson Pollock
Untitled (verso), c. 1943

Ink on opaque watercolor ground on paper
1991.87b

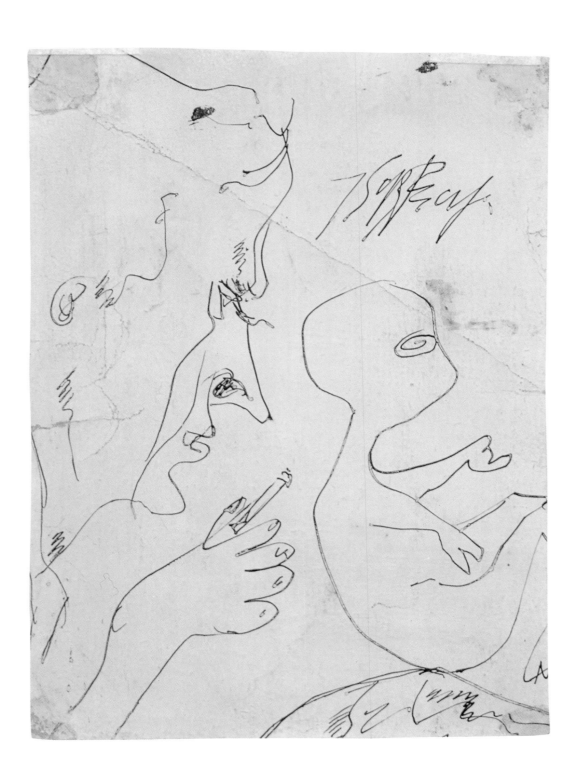

BORN
25 September 1903
Dvinsk, Lithuania

DIED
25 February 1970
New York, New York

Personages is one of over seventy watercolors that the Abstract Expressionist painter Mark Rothko made during the mid-1940s. The Addison's watercolor marks a rare moment of exploration using works on paper, which Rothko, an artist generally known for his large paintings in oil, would not repeat until the late 1960s.[1]

In the forties the artist employed watercolor to test and explore issues of transparency and luminosity in ways not possible with oil paint.[2] In these light and magical watercolors, the artist laid on fluid washes of close-hued grays and tans, what one critic called "pale and uninsistent colours,"[3] between and over which play calligraphic forms suggestive of the underlying universality of myth, an imagery that engaged many of the Abstract Expressionists during this period of time.

In the Addison's watercolor, typical of works of this period, and indeed of the large oils that were to follow, the artist has controlled the composition within horizontal bands. Framed by the upper and lower striations of gray, the central band of tan is inhabited by a pattern of lines, swirls, and dabs of color that jab and push up and down at the borders of the confining horizontals. Lying "just at the periphery of recognition,"[4] two almost-figures seem to dance at the left of the sheet, perhaps to an ethereal musical score, as suggested by the free-form grid of lines and curves on the right. Delighting in the materiality of watercolor and paper and playing with the contradictions of flat picture plane and raised surface, Rothko has overlaid translucent veils of tone with marks that alternate between thin dragged lines of intense opaque color, swirls of vaporous color, and ragged white lines created by aggressive incising of the paper surface.

s c f

208   Mark Rothko

PERSONAGES, c. 1946

Watercolor and pastel on cream (3), thick,
rough (1) wove paper
22 x 29 7/8
Signed in watercolor l.r.: MARK ROTHKO
Promised gift of Jacob and Ruth Kainen
PL96.4

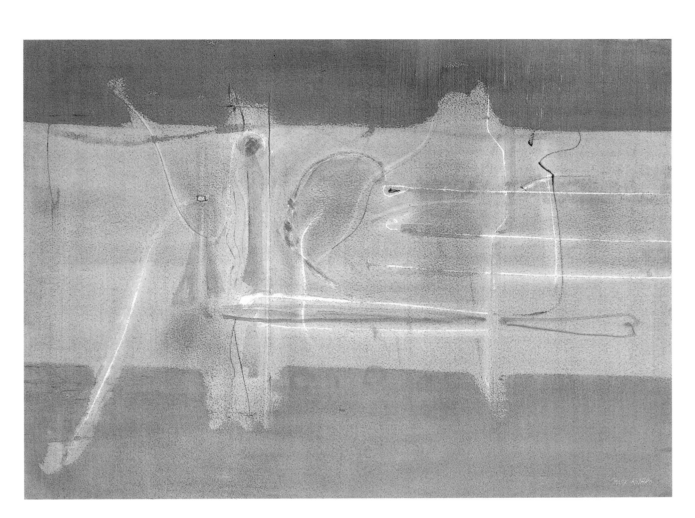

BORN
8 June 1916
St. Paul, Minnesota

DIED
25 October 1992
New York, New York

In the mid-1940s Richard Pousette-Dart began to exhibit his art with Abstract Expressionist painters such as Jackson Pollock and Willem de Kooning. Despite often diverging aesthetic concerns, these are the artists he would be linked with throughout his career.

Although there are often distinctive characteristics of Pousette-Dart's work in a given period, it is hard to generalize as he frequently shifted among various painting idioms. His work of the early 1940s tended to have bold outlines and compartmentalized structures, often with an insistent, gridlike framework that was counterbalanced with spheres, ovoids, and curlicue forms. The paintings and works on paper of this time commonly maintain a figurative aspect, the structures of which are laid down against atmospheric fields of color. These works maintain vestigial ideogrammatic forms revealing a continued interest in Native American, particularly Northwest Coast, art.

After 1944, perhaps influenced by critic Clement Greenberg's polemical concerns with the edges of paintings, Pousette-Dart's works achieved a more all-over quality.[1] In this untitled watercolor of 1946, the glyphs metaphorically and literally bleed together and to the edges of the paper. The figurative elements are submerged, layered, and fused with the surface. The forms are not centralized within the confines of the paper, they are subjects in and of themselves spanning edge to edge. "What he paints and his means of painting are not inseparable."[2] The compartmentalization dissolves in the fluid brushiness of the water-based pigments. The evanescent, glowing colors are evidence of Pousette-Dart's growing fascination with stained glass. This watercolor, with its vibrant yellows, aqua blues, and hints of green and reddish brown, seems to glow from within. Pousette-Dart's passion for Bach's music is also suggested in the counterpoint of forms and the harmonization of colors.

ADW

210

Richard Pousette-Dart

Untitled, 1946

Transparent and opaque watercolor and ink on cream (3), thick, moderately textured (3) wove paper

5 15/16 x 9 1/16

Unsigned

Museum purchase

1947.10

BORN
14 March 1903
New York, New York

DIED
4 March 1974
New York, New York

Adolph Gottlieb was one of the pioneers of Abstract Expressionism. He trained with the realist painter John Sloan, and in his early career he belonged to a prominent group of avant-garde artists called The Ten.[1] In his later work he moved to an exploration of the power of abstraction, and developed a style increasingly concerned with the formal and expressive possibilities of art. The Pictographs of the 1940s represent his first mature style, combining the influence of numerous painting traditions with the structure and vision of contemporary poetry.[2]

Vigil of Cyclops is a Pictograph, composed of enigmatic symbols isolated in rectilinear compartments along the surface of the picture plane. The image reveals a rich interplay of influences: grids and symbols derived from the art of The Ten, patterning and sandy coloring derived from Navajo pottery and primitive art, flattening of space and form derived from Cubism, and division of the surface derived from Surrealism.[3] The appropriation of Greek mythology as subject matter was the inspiration of many artists who felt that the violence and tragedy of myth was appropriate in a climate recovering from the devastation of World War II. Gottlieb's Pictographs and later art also have a strong connection to Imagist poetry, which emphasized idea over narrative.[4] Gottlieb started his Pictographs by placing one symbol into a compartment and using free association to arrive at the others, experiencing a kind of revelation through the process of art-making.[5] He stated: "Painting is the making of images. If the painter's conception is realized in the form of an image, we are confronted with a new natural object which has its own life, its own beauty and its own wisdom."[6]

GGS

212 Adolph Gottlieb

VIGIL OF CYCLOPS, 1947

Opaque watercolor and chalk on beige (1), thick, slightly textured (1) wove paper

24 x 18

Signed in opaque watercolor l.r.: Adolph Gottlieb 1947

Inscribed in graphite on verso c.: 24 x 18 / Vigil of Cyclops / 1947

Gift of Mr. and Mrs. Samuel M. Kootz

1948.4

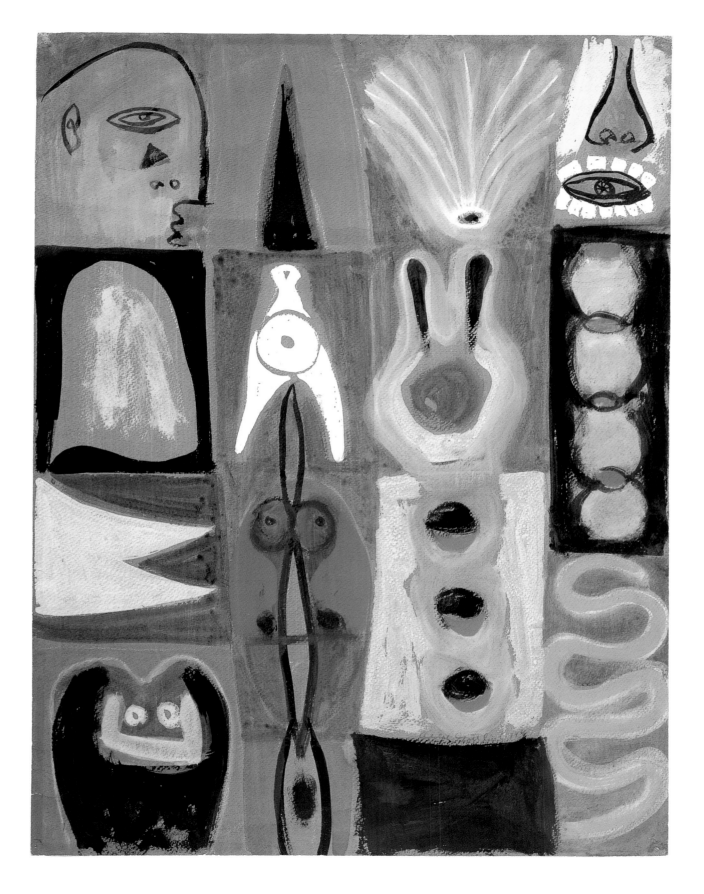

BORN
21 March 1880
Weissenburg, Bavaria

DIED
17 February 1966
New York, New York

By 1947, Hans Hofmann's shift from naturalistic painting toward full abstraction was accelerating, and recognition of his work was on the rise.[1] Two events of 1944 in particular led to the stylistic metamorphosis of his color compositions: After twelve years of teaching in New York, Hofmann showed his work at Peggy Guggenheim's gallery, Art of This Century, and immediately earned the endorsement of the influential critic Clement Greenberg. In addition, a hernia operation forced him to work almost exclusively indoors. Hofmann's increased exposure to the work of emerging artists (including Jackson Pollock and William Baziotes) at Guggenheim's gallery combined with his limited access to painting subjects inspired rapid iterations of abstractions.[2]

His continual practice of extracting and refining new images out of the same sources in his studio—still life objects and reproductions of other artists' work—resulted in a confident calligraphic shorthand for his familiar forms. The vertical "periscope" shapes anchored by a spread base seen in the upper left and center of *Untitled VII 13*[3] are derived from driftwood trunks propped on roots that Hofmann kept in his Provincetown studio.[4] Centering the image is a loosely contoured "half-moon" visage (facing upward), an icon adapted from forms in Pablo Picasso's portraits and, more immediately, Pollock's paintings of "moon women," shown at Art of This Century in 1943.[5]

With this vocabulary of form mastered, Hofmann could then test his ideas about color and its powers of abstraction ("Form only exists through color and color only exists through form") and expression ("I want the fullness of myself realized through color").[6] Through the immediacy of works on paper, what he called his "free creations," he explored both the spatial effects and emotional connotations of specific color-form relationships.[7]

JM

214 ## Hans Hofmann

UNTITLED VII 13, 1947

Oil on beige (1), moderately thick, smooth wove paper

17 1/16 x 14 1/8

Signed in oil l.r.: VII 13 / 47 / hans hofmann

Museum purchase, Culpeper Foundation Fund, in memory of Bartlett H. Hayes

1991.64

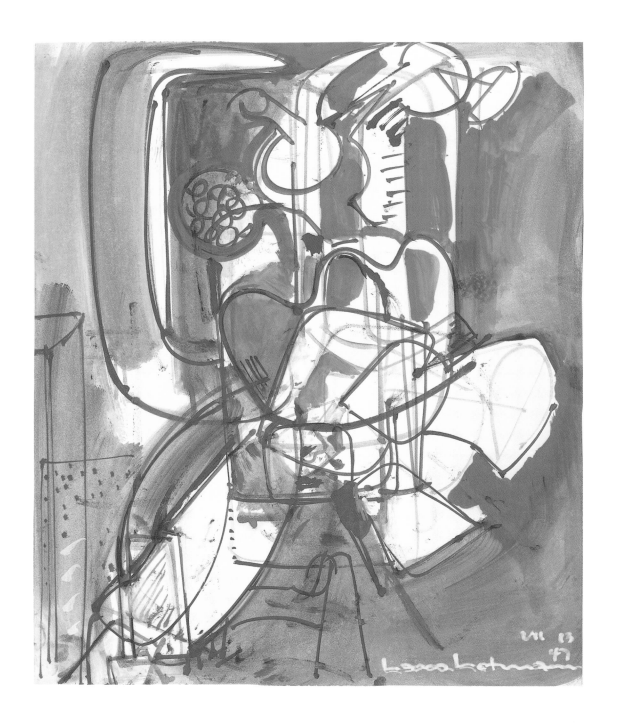

BORN
14 March 1898
Paris, France

DIED
3 July 1954
Dorset, Vermont

Reginald Marsh first went to Coney Island in the early 1920s, on assignment as an illustrator for the *New Yorker*. It became his favorite subject, luring him from the city three or four days a week every summer for thirty years: "I like to go to Coney Island because of the sea, the open air, and the crowds—crowds of people in all directions, in all positions, without clothing, moving—like the great compositions of Michelangelo and Rubens."[1] *Crowded Day at Coney* was painted in Chinese ink, a medium Marsh adopted after many years of experimentation with oils, tempera, and watercolor. According to the art historian Lloyd Goodrich, it liberated the artist. "Without the distraction of color, in these Chinese ink drawings he attained the greatest graphic freedom in all his work. In their fullness of form, linear vitality, and plastic inventiveness, they were among his most original creations."[2] The dramatic contrast between "sea serpents" in the dark sea and sun worshippers in the dazzling light celebrates this exuberant freedom.

Marsh was an inveterate sketcher. From 1925 until his sudden death in 1954, he recorded every imaginable detail of life on the Lower East Side of Manhattan in small homemade books of bound paper. These sketches formed the basis for finished work, including the Chinese ink drawings, made later in the studio. The Addison's sketchbook pages are filled with quick studies of figures and faces, perhaps at Coney Island, and the bizarre inhabitants of places, like the adjoining Luna Park, that always caught Marsh's eye (pp. 218–19). Alzonia the Turtle Girl, Jean the Human Ant, and Fifi the Sheep-headed Girl were for Marsh just more to love in the weird and wacky world of Coney Island.

SJM

216 Reginald Marsh

CROWDED DAY AT CONEY, 1948

Ink, ink wash, and crayon on cream (3),
very thick, rough (2), Arches wove paper
22 1/2 x 29 5/8
Signed in ink l.r.: REGINALD / MARSH / 1948
Gift of Louis F. Kemp (PA 1925)
1996.76

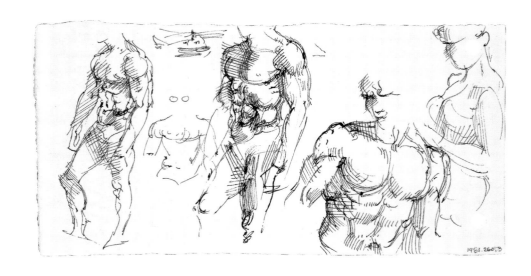

218   Reginald Marsh
       Sketchbook, c. 1954

       Ink and graphite on eight unbound sheets
       of cream (1), medium weight (2), slightly
       textured (1) wove paper

       4 x 7 5/8

       Unsigned

       Gift of Gene Pyle

       1981.260.1a–8b

       TOP TO BOTTOM
       Page 3b [Four male torsos and one female]
       Ink and graphite on paper
       1981.260.3b

       Page 6b [Various heads and headless figures]
       Ink and graphite on paper
       1981.260.6b

Page 8b Alzonia, The Turtle Girl...
Ink and graphite on paper
1981.260.8b

219

BORN
23 July 1909
New York, New York

DIED
27 August 1979
New York, New York

In 1950, twenty-five of the most important abstract artists of the day, among them Willem de Kooning, Hans Hofmann, Robert Motherwell, Barnett Newman, and David Smith, gathered at Studio 35 for a discussion about art-making. Norman Lewis was among them. When participants were asked how to know when a work was finished, Lewis responded, "I have stopped, I think, when I have arrived at a quality of mystery."[1]

Lewis's *New Moon*, purchased from the artist's 1951 exhibition at Marian Willard's prestigious New York gallery, is indeed a mysterious work. Its tender and ethereal quality is worlds apart from the aggressive, exuberant character of other Abstract Expressionists' work, and even distinctly different from the work for which Lewis first was known.

Born in New York City, Lewis first was exposed to art-making in the Harlem studio of sculptor Augusta Savage in 1933,[2] and he supported himself as an art teacher under the Federal Arts Project from 1936 to 1939. Motivated by his ardent political beliefs, his work of that period was a social realism that focused on the lives of urban black Americans. By the mid-1940s Lewis was questioning this subject matter. Beginning to feel "the development of one's aesthetic abilities suffers from such emphasis," in the late forties, Lewis found what he considered a more universal aesthetic voice in abstraction.[3]

New Moon belongs to a group of works Lewis produced in the fifties in which he explored the process of painting with drybrush. With exacting control, Lewis drew very light washes of oil across the paper to create soft tones of color gathered around the most fragile lines of ink, all balanced across the sheet in a manner that has been described as "a movement…almost like a ballet."[4]

SCF

220 Norman Lewis

NEW MOON, 1951

Ink, charcoal, and crayon on cream (2), moderately thick, smooth wove paper

19 1/8 x 24 1/8

signed in graphite l.r.: May 1951/Norman Lewis

Museum purchase

1952.10

BORN
20 July 1889
Hoboken, New Jersey

DIED
17 April 1954
Morristown, New Jersey

Inspired by a 1949 exhibition of the work of the German artist Kurt Schwitters, the artist and poet Anne Ryan spent the last six years of her life making the delicate collages of paper, fabric, and found objects that were to be the work for which she is best known.[1]

Ryan came to art-making in 1938 after her marriage had ended and with three small children in her care. Moving from New Jersey to Mallorca, then in 1933 to Greenwich Village, she became part of a circle of artists that included Tony Smith, Barnett Newman, Fritz Bultman, and Hans Hofmann. It was Hofmann who encouraged her first forays into painting. In 1941 she took up printmaking at Atelier XVII under Stanley William Hayter.[2]

Collage spoke to Ryan's poetic sensibilities in ways that neither paint nor printing ink could. Through such layered and textured works, she could revel in the way the frayed edge could confound the crispness of the cut fabric fragment, in the counterpoint of fragile tissue against rough-woven burlap, in the potential of gesture in a length of thread, or in the subtle variations of seemingly monochromatic tones. Working alternately with debris and carefully chosen fragments, with some compositions balanced and gridded and others more automatic and gestural, she mined the expressive character of the medium. She wrote of the magic of art-making and the artist as the conduit for finding and releasing cosmic meaning and revelation:

> The rights of the imagination are greater than any other rights. In the secret country where the solitary mind exists, where it is possible for only one, the self, to enter, all colors, arcs, patterns, images, have steady room for themselves to move about and resolve at last under the fingers.[3]

SCF

222

Anne Ryan

NO. 1, 1951

Collage of fabrics, wood pulp, wax paper, and photo-offset printed paper mounted on illustration board

17 7/8 x 23 11/16

Signed in color pencil l.r.: A. Ryan; signed in marker ink on verso l.r.: A. Ryan

Inscribed in marker ink on verso u.l.: For Show / 1951 / Parson's Gallery / Oct 15- Nov 3; l.l.: April 17, 1951

Gift of Miss Elizabeth McFadden

1960.8

223

BORN
29 March 1913
Brunoviski, Latvia

In the 1940s Hyman Bloom created a series of paintings depicting dead bodies.[1] Radiantly captured in richly applied, jewel-like color, these disturbing images portray the human body in the process of decay and metamorphosis. A decade later Bloom turned to paintings and drawings of dissections and autopsies observed in local hospitals. The paintings of the 1950s were more analytical than those of a decade earlier. "My concern was the complexity and color beauty of the internal works, the curiosity, the wonder, and the feeling of transgressing boundaries which such curiosity evokes."[2] The Addison's *Cadaver No. 1* of about 1952 is a probing study of the body as both container laid open and structure revealed, a series of complex voids and solids spiraling between mystery and revelation. Captured in virtuoso draftsmanship of Baroque-like swirling red chalk lines,

the composition, as Holland Cotter has observed, "is arranged as a complex, multi-layered visual puzzle which only gradually introduces us to the subject itself."[3]

In 1952, Addison director Bartlett Hayes was asked to recommend works by young artists deserving of greater recognition for an exhibition in Dallas. Among the works he chose was "a fairly large, red conté drawing… one of a series recently executed and exhibited by Hyman Bloom" which he recommended as of "extraordinary quality."[4] Fifteen years later, in 1969, William and Saundra Lane donated this startling and ambitious work to the Addison.

SCF

224

Hyman Bloom

CADAVER NO. 1, c. 1952

Crayon on beige (2), moderately thick, smooth wove paper

54 3/4 x 37 3/4

Unsigned

Gift of Mr. and Mrs. William H. Lane

1969.11

BORN
7 March 1885
Altmar, New York

DIED
3 January 1965
New York, New York

The Pamet River in Truro, Massachusetts, is a "meandering creek" running across the narrow part of northern Cape Cod.[1] Milton Avery captured the sandy sweep of the Pamet River Valley in September 1956, on his way to Provincetown, where he and his wife decided to spend the following four summers.[2]

As in all of Avery's mature works, the subject matter of this one, a tranquil stretch of landscape, has been reduced to essential shapes and unusual color harmonies, balanced across the flatness of the picture plane. As Avery explained,

> I like to seize the one sharp instant in nature, to imprison it by means of ordered shapes and space relationships. To this end I eliminate and simplify, leaving apparently nothing but color and pattern. I am not seeking pure abstraction; rather the purity and essence of the idea—expressed in its simplest form.[3]

The Addison's watercolor presages in transparent medium the shift to more abstract compositions that Avery's paintings would take in 1957. Against the solid light pink sky, the artist has laid in large triangular stretches of intense yellow and pea green, each tempered with an overlay of allied color. These quiet passages are contrasted with dark, mottled shapes created of overlapping strokes of various greens and black that hold the compositional elements in tight interlocking color forms.

Lyrical watercolors like *Pamet River* drew the admiration of Avery's artistic colleagues, even those who worked in a dramatically different language of abstraction. Calling Avery a "great poet," Mark Rothko wrote of his "courage in a generation which felt that it could be heard only through clamor, force and a show of power.... Avery had that inner power in which gentleness and silence proved more audible and poignant."[4]

SCF

226

Milton Avery

PAMET RIVER, 1956

Watercolor on beige (1), thick, slightly textured (1) wove paper

20 x 26

Signed in graphite l.l.: Milton Avery 1956

Inscribed in graphite on verso u.c.: PAMET RIVER / 1956; u.r.: 8891 (c)

Gift of Elaine Graham Weitzen

2003.2

BORN
3 June 1926
New York, New York

When Peggy Guggenheim's Art of This Century gallery presented Charles Seliger's first one-person exhibition in 1945, he was just nineteen, the youngest of the Abstract Expressionists. Today he is the last of a generation that included Jackson Pollock, Adolph Gottlieb, Willem de Kooning, Mark Tobey, and Mark Rothko.[1]

Seliger's work, like that of Pollock, is founded in the automatic, gestural, and spontaneous. However, he rejects the grand gesture. For him, "the expression of subjective elements in huge scale is almost always a failure…the subjective is an intimate revelation."[2] Starting with a "subconscious, non-rational approach,"[3] Seliger lays on paint. Out of that initial impulse he meticulously revises and adjusts, in a process that is both excavation and accumulation, to reveal the embedded poetry. Francis O'Connor points out that "like his fellow Abstract Expressionists at their purest, [Seliger] operates on the level of analogy, evoking and suggesting the unseen with meticulously rendered visual tropes crafted in paint."[4]

Vineyard Haven is as poetic as any of his works, yet its inspiration was particular rather than subconscious. As Seliger explained,

> Most of the time my "landscapes" are of a cerebral nature. This is one of the few paintings I have done directly from nature. This was painted during my first visit to Martha's Vineyard—after looking at the landscape and lovely sunsets I found myself forgetting I was on vacation (and not going to work)—and painted this picture.[5]

While its motivation was unusual, the painting, neither literal or even specifically referential, embodies Seliger's signature qualities in its careful mediation of "the knowable and the unknowable" and its characteristic metamorphosis "into the realm of the ideal and the lyrical."[6]

SCF

228

Charles Seliger

VINEYARD HAVEN, 1957

Opaque watercolor and ink on cream (3), medium weight (1), smooth wove paper mounted on board

10 15/16 x 13 15/16

Signed in ink l.r.: Seliger / '57

Gift of Elaine Graham Weitzen

1962.8

BORN
16 July 1883
Philadelphia, Pennsylvania

DIED
7 May 1965
Dobbs Ferry, New York

Sun, Rock, Trees was prompted by a trip Charles Sheeler had made to Yosemite with his friend Ansel Adams in 1956. It was an exhilarating experience, as Sheeler wrote to their mutual friend, the collector William Lane:

> This is it—the place where those who prefer our way of life may come— my America! I need a new dictionary of adjectives to convey a glimpse of what I am seeing and feeling here—it is something I have not experienced before. The Yosemite is wonderful as you have known…maybe I can manage one day within a frame to put something down. I hope![1]

The Addison's work is the first of three versions of this abstracted fragment of dense woodland.[2] It reveals an important way of working for Sheeler in which he drew broad compositional outlines on a paper support and tried out various color balances in opaque watercolor on a transparent overlay of glass or Plexiglas, which allowed him to remove and reapply paint.[3] The Addison's work is unusual in that it still retains its paper underlayer as well as in the careful correlation between the design on the paper and that on the acrylic sheet. Rather than following his usual practice of creating a line drawing, Sheeler blocked in the composition on the paper with pools of monochromatic watercolor. He more completely developed the interwoven forms of rocks and foliage on the Plexiglas overlay, adding highlights of color and a variety of opaque and transparent washes, while either wiping away or leaving unpainted sections through which the paper composition can be seen. Compared with the single-surfaced painting for which this was a study, Sheeler's sandwich of plastic and paper is made dynamic through the shifting shadows that play across the paper when light is transmitted through the acrylic layer.

SCF

230 Charles Sheeler

SUN, ROCKS, TREES, 1959

Watercolor, ink, and graphite on cream (1), moderately thick, smooth wove paper and opaque watercolor on Plexiglas

6 3/4 x 9 3/4

Unsigned

Museum purchase

1966.27

BORN
28 March 1921
Chicago, Illinois

DIED
3 February 1999
East Wallingford, Vermont

"I've always thought that one of the great elements of great art is drawing."[1] Looking at Norman Bluhm's explosively painted untitled work of 1959 one might first think it has little to do with drawing. At a glance, the drips, splashes, and slashes seem aggressive. This work, made using opaque watercolor and ink on a raw brown paper, at a scale that seems less than intimate, is deceiving. Bluhm was a pilot during World War II, and his experience of flying had an effect on his work.[2] This drawing, with its rapidly ascending and descending strokes and lacking a horizon line, has a weightlessness. The earth-tone paper serves as a backdrop for his aerobatics. The raining rivulets of white, blue, and black are in fact tender and delicate. And the harmonious intermingling of pigments is exquisite.

This untitled work was made in New York three years after Bluhm returned from a decade in Paris, where he had studied the plein-air paintings of Cézanne, Corot, and particularly the late Monet. Bluhm's art was consistently, although at times obliquely, concerned with nature.[3] This work bears the radical influence of Willem de Kooning and particularly Franz Kline, both of whom he knew.

For Bluhm, like the older Abstract Expressionists, the brushstroke is a mark, a structure, a gesture. Instead of trying to "cover one's tracks" as in the work of many an old master, these painters made their marks evident. Drawing, which for Bluhm was an underpinning of all great art, is laid bare. The stroke became means and subject. Here the drawing is a painting and vice versa. This drawing is an end in itself, not a trial run for something else. His luminescent color—including white—and the lyrical quality of the drips makes his accomplishment distinctive.

ADW

232 Norman Bluhm

Untitled, 1959

Ink and opaque watercolor on brown, moderately thick, smooth wove paper

48 1/8 x 39 7/8

Signed in graphite l.r.: bluhm / 59'

Gift of Charles O. Wood III and Miriam M. Wood in honor of Carolyn Bluhm

2002.38

233

Barnett Newman produced eighty-three drawings during his lifetime. Neither sketches nor studies, they "convey the certainty of a finished work of art." However, it is significant that Newman's bursts of drawing activity in the 1940s (fifty-seven works) and in 1959–60 (twenty-five works) preceded highly productive periods of painting. His drawings served as a warm-up, a readying of the mind, and an investigation of materials and materiality.[1]

This is one of fifteen drawings in a fourteen-by-ten-inch format that have been associated with Newman's celebrated painting cycle Stations of the Cross. Although the two bodies of work overlap somewhat in date—the first and second stations were completed two years before the group of drawings—it seems that the flurry of ink drawings may have helped Newman to crystallize the conception of the Stations series.[2]

Each of Newman's drawings is a deliberate statement with specific characteristics, shared but not duplicated by another. This is attested by the fact that the artist produced—or saved, as the case may be—so few drawings. In this cycle of drawings there is great sensitivity to material, and the variety of effects he achieved with merely ink and brush is extraordinary, from hazy luminescence to silky sensualness. Despite the seeming spontaneity of this sheet, with its energetic, brushy open area, little is left to chance. Yet one has the sense of light breaking through—a metaphorical cracking of the dawn or the light of creation.

Brenda Richardson has noted that it is "unique in Newman's work" and has "no parallel in the paintings." She pointed out that "the black-on-black inking in the drawing includes a sweeping diagonal which is almost unprecedented by this artist so identified with the perpendicular.... [He] habitually employed a brush stroke which was definitely either vertical (usually) or horizontal."[3]

ADW

BORN
29 January 1905
New York, New York

DIED
4 July 1970
New York, New York

234

Barnett Newman

Untitled, 1960

Ink on cream (1), moderately thick, rough (1) wove paper

13 15/16 x 9 15/16

Unsigned

Gift of Mrs. Barnett Newman in honor of Frank Stella (PA 1954)

1999.28

235

BORN
24 December 1903
Nyack, New York

DIED
29 December 1972
Flushing, New York

Joseph Cornell is best known for box constructions that encapsulate complex universes of fantasy and infatuation made with humble objects from dime stores and desk drawers. Finding resonance in materials of seemingly slight significance—sand, magazine clippings, wooden balls, pocket change, postal stamps—Cornell set them in contexts that could create worlds of meaning. Awe-inspired by stars (both the celestial bodies and worldly celebrities), he often created works with astral themes in homage to his favorite luminaries (including ballet dancers, actresses, and artists).[1] Although reclusive, Cornell's earnest yet mysterious assemblages sparked connections with other artists, including Marcel Duchamp and Andy Warhol, who elevated mass-produced objects or imagery to the iconic in their respective generations.

By the early 1960s, Cornell turned from boxes to collage on board as his medium of choice. Straightforward in its construction, collage allowed him to experiment with the boldest and most current imagery of his career.[2] Cornell's *Homage to Brancusi* is coolly minimal in composition but characteristically layered in theme. Affixed to its stained surface is a postmarked Romanian stamp issued in 1967 to commemorate the work of renowned sculptor Constantin Brancusi ten years after his death.[3] Cornell encircled the pictured girl with compass lines and a constellation of punctures filled with the white pencil leads that made them. Collectively, the elements seem a revision of Leonardo da Vinci's *Study of Proportions*, with Cornell's signature focus on a female figurehead and stars replacing the famed image of man on his axis. Since he never met Brancusi, it is possible that this is more subtly a private homage to Cornell's close friend Duchamp, who had once been curator of a Brancusi exhibition, and whose own health was failing at the time this collage was created.[4]

JM

236 Joseph Cornell

HOMAGE TO BRANCUSI, c. 1967

Stain, postal stamp, stamp impression, and color pencil on wove paper mounted on particle board

14 7/8 x 11 7/8 x 1 1/2 (with frame)

Signed in ink on verso l.r.: Joseph Cornell

Gift of Fiona and Michael Scharf (PA 1960) in honor of Jock Reynolds, Mr. Enthusiasm

1998.110

BORN
18 November 1933
McPherson, Kansas

Bruce Conner—painter, draftsman, sculptor, printer, collagist, assemblagist, filmmaker, photographer—has been described as "an original...a terrific contradiction. He's from Kansas, and when you meet him he can seem like the most normal Midwestern man—like a classically constructed Kansan house. But then there are all these odd corners and nooks; he's got quite an attic stuck on him, and there are strange things going on in it."[1]

Since his appearance in the San Francisco Beat culture of the 1950s, Conner has created work that is indeed strange and difficult to categorize. His early assemblages, densely intertwining stockings, newspaper, wax, and varied found objects, suggested decay, fragmentation, brutality, or social struggle. A year in Mexico from 1961 to 1962 marked a transition toward a more private, even spiritual vision, and an increasing interest in drawing, paper-based collage, and film.[2]

While the spare composition of *Water* is unusual in Conner's oeuvre, the work, made the year after his return from Mexico, prefigures both the Mandala drawings of the mid-sixties and the densely layered engraving collages of the eighties. As is always the case for Conner, this work challenges the viewer with enigmatic and disquieting images. Disparate elements—meandering graphite lines, a fragment of a wood engraving, decaying plastic tape and burned plastic, stamps, string—play across the sheet. Black dots contrast with flesh-toned adhesive bandage circles and colored foil stars; assertive black shapes intersect soft graphite passages in counterpoint to delicate tracery lines. A hooded eye emerges as if to compensate for the blankness of the figure's eye sockets. In final contrariness for an artist who is known not to sign work and who once staged his own posthumous exhibition, a stamped sequence of the artist's name fades down a column from the top center of the page.

SCF

238

Bruce Conner

WATER, 1963

Ink, graphite, stamp impression, string, burnt plastic bag, gold foil stamps, pressure-sensitive tape, adhesive bandage, wood engraving, and color pencil on cream (2), medium weight (1), moderately textured (1) wove paper

26 1/8 x 21

Unsigned

Inscribed on verso l.r.: Water/7/14/63

Museum purchase

1964.17

Bruce
Bruce Conner
Bruce Conner
Bruce Conner
Bruce Conner

239

BORN
22 November 1923
Lynn, Massachusetts

For the last thirty-five years the Massachusetts-born Beverly Hallam has lived in Maine, where the rock-strewn shore, clear light and expansive skies, and blowsy summer flowers have inspired her art-making. While her subjects are drawn from her everyday surroundings, her artistic methods are experimental. She relishes the unanticipated, delighting in the exploration of new materials and the conjunction of unexpected materials and methods.[1]

In the early 1950s, Hallam moved toward abstraction in paintings that she executed in an adventurous range of materials—from oil to encaustic to acrylic, variously combined with mica, talc, sand, automotive paint, gold leaf, and found objects. By the end of the decade, dissatisfied with the growing sculptural character of her assemblages, the artist returned to two-dimensional work.[2] By 1963 Hallam began to make monotypes in earnest.

She alternately experimented with oil paint or lithographic ink, which she applied to the glass plate with brushes or rollers, often working over the unique impression with pastel. As she explained,

> In making "Arabesque" I worked rapidly with oil on plate glass, establishing the black and some broad patches of color. While wet, I covered it with rice paper, rubbed my hand over it and pulled it off. When dry, it was finished with pastel.[3]

In the exuberant work that resulted, the bold black structure of the Picasso vase grounds the swirls of intense yellow, red, brown, gray, and black floral forms that dance across the soft cream color of the fragile rice paper.

SCF

240

Beverly Hallam

ARABESQUE, 1966

Oil monotype and pastel on cream (3), medium weight (1), slightly textured (1) rice paper

24 1/2 x 20

Signed in pastel l.l.: Hallam; in graphite l.r.: Hallam 65

Inscribed in graphite on verso l.l.: Arabesque 1966

Museum purchase in honor of Christopher Cook

1998.95

BORN
5 November 1949
New Haven, Connecticut

In 1980 the loops and doodles of Carroll Dunham's meandering line that had been seeking to reinstate and reveal the procedures of drawing began also to respond to the more heated desires of the imagination.[1] Charting the erogenous zones that the organic loops and doodles had formerly been willing only to allude to, by 1982 Dunham's seemingly uninterrupted line had become the cartographer of fiery and delirious realms that he referred to as "sexual galaxies," where line's formal articulation of the flatness of the plane was interchangeable with the vagrant sensuality of the imagination. *Untitled* is one of the group of twelve related drawings that inaugurates this transition.

Dunham's line-driven erotics were slowly arrived at; his risks have always been both daring and methodical. When Dunham started making art in 1976, he propelled his drawing into simple gestures on a modulated, monochrome ground that looked back on Surrealist automatism through Cy Twombly and Jackson Pollock. He wanted his line, like that of the Minimalist and Process artists Robert Mangold, Brice Marden, and Robert Ryman, to grow out of and become one with the plane rather than be a closed representation imposed upon it.

By 1980, when this work was made, Dunham's hairpin curves and mounds began to acquire more allusiveness—inclining toward the intestinal, the vaginal, and the phallic—while retaining a clarity of process. The days of the month recorded on the Addison's *Untitled* drawing mark the duration of the making, and have a feature that has, to this day, remained part of Dunham's diaristic, psychosexual formality. Still interacting on a modulated monochrome field, his open-ended linear forming is poised to burst out of its cocoon into the Technicolor adulthood of the work to follow.

K K

242 ## Carroll Dunham

UNTITLED, 1980

Opaque watercolor, graphite, and dry pigment on cream (1), very thick, rough (1) wove paper

30 1/2 x 22 1/4

Signed in graphite u.l.: CD 1980

Inscribed in graphite u.c.: April 30 May 1; c.r.: April – 20, 21, 22; l.r.: 4/26

Museum purchase

1984.232

243

BORN
31 May 1952
Flushing, New York

John Newman's abstract sculptures and drawings hinge on dramatic tension—between the formal and the physical, contour and dimension, skin and innards. In each, bipolar forces wrestle in contentious visual play: axes twist in opposite directions, radials compete for dual perspectives, surfaces fluctuate from inner to outer, scale vacillates from macro to micro, and contrary textures and colors collide. Newman compounds these opposed extremes by loading his work with multivalent references to the organic, mathematical, sexual, and surreal. The result: animate geometries that flex and torque under pressure, each about to burst with distinctive personality.

The huge looming figure introduced in this work of 1991 reappears in a lithograph Newman dubbed *Jaw Breaker*.[1] That title alludes both to the candy-striped "fireball" clamped within the tubular blue vise, and that which is "difficult to pronounce," or in this case, difficult to "swallow" (accept, understand, or define).[2] Is this an image of digestive compression inward or a tumor swelling outward? Is the vessel a benign sweet or a malignant cancer? The contorted shape glows with a red halo and writhes like a muscle or vein blocked in strain. Which force will prevail: a pop or a crunch?

Since the late 1970s, Newman has been intrigued by the conflicting emotions that can be elicited from form. Frustrated by his peers' minimalist tendencies toward industrial process, serial repetition, and neutral geometry, he instead found inspiration in the classic past, including the connotative volumes of ancient Japanese armor, representative of both attractive power and repulsive fear, of outer protection and inner aggression.[3] By 1990, he again turned to the old masters: inspired by the modeled figures, balanced tensions, and mathematical compositions in the Renaissance drawings of Raphael, Newman began drawing such sculpturally defined tubular forms "carved" out of geometric shapes and radials as seen here.[4]

JM

244

John Newman

UNTITLED, 1991

Grease pencil, chalk, pressure-sensitive tape, graphite, and color pencil on beige (1), moderately thick, smooth wove paper

89 7/8 x 56 3/8

Unsigned on recto

Partial gift of the artist and partial museum purchase, Frederick H. Morrison Fund

1991.94

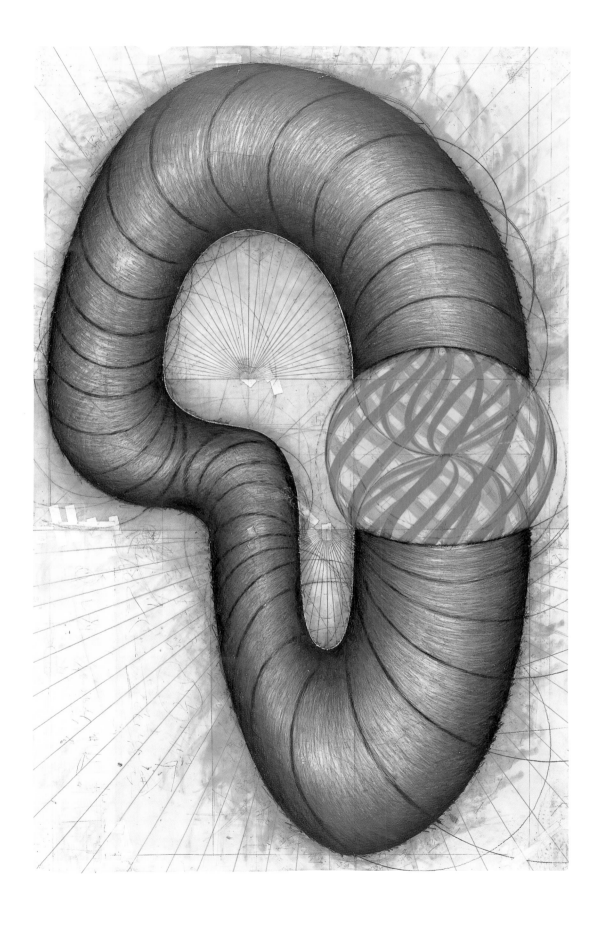

BORN
27 June 1950
Bridgeport, Connecticut

The image world in all its diversity and multiplicity of unstable meanings is the stage for the enactment of Jane Hammond's art. She creates networks of heterogeneous images encompassing fields ranging from cultural history and religion to magic and phrenology. Begun without a specific notion of where she is heading, her works on paper are process driven. Hammond typically begins by laying a foundation of small, often faintly applied pictographs as background, a fertilizer for her process. The images are often repeated, sometimes as ghosts, as here with the cartoon head that derives from a Hokusai-like Japanese image. These elements, along with the repeated red gouache, acrylic dots, and the rubber-stamped stippled pattern create a field of possibilities out of which springs the large, bold, central image in the foreground—a running figure that was lifted from a do-it-yourself book on sculpture.

The images Hammond applies and her techniques for doing so respond to one another and to the shape and texture of the rice paper itself, setting off a chain reaction that teeters on the edge of explosiveness. Her ideograms are put on top, behind, and intertwined to create new hybrids. She challenges herself and viewers with the density limits of information. The use of multiple artistic techniques—from linoleum block prints to solvent transfers—further complicates the reading.

Works such as *Players* produce a primordial network of images that actualize the qualities of thought itself. Her "drawing" is associative but not "free association" in the Surrealist sense. Hammond has said that "free association may not be free at all…. It's like five witnesses providing different accounts of an accident." After all, the connections are in the viewer's mind, "the figures don't know about each other."[1]

ADW

246   Jane Hammond

PLAYERS, 1992

Graphite, solvent transfers, color photocopy, crayon, linoleum block prints, stamp impression, transparent and opaque watercolor, and acrylic on two joined sheets of cream (2), medium weight (1), slightly textured (1) rice paper

38 1/2 x 36 1/8

Unsigned

Gift of Klaus Kertess (PA 1958)

2003.26

BORN
13 January 1959
Havana, Cuba

Through its title text, symbolic imagery, material presence, and grand scale, José Bedia's *Islote Inaccessible, Lejano, Solo* reflects the rich layers of his cultural roots, religious affiliations, personal iconography, and artistic practice. In white ink, he grounds the composition with text that references the "isolated island," a bold black form—at once a sharp-chinned head and an impenetrable cliff-faced rock—emerging from an implied horizon line. The smaller silhouettes of a perched bird and a lone boatman stand out against the eight-foot span of the mottled surface of the hand-made, crushed bark *amate* paper.

Beyond its striking appearance, the work derives much of its powerful meaning from Bedia's cultural perspective as a Cuban American and an initiate of Palo Monte, an Afro-Cuban religion that shares many universal beliefs with animistic practices of Native American and African communities across the globe. By centering this image around the concept of "island," Bedia not only alludes to the complex experience of a Cuban islander cut off from the outside world by stone-faced bureaucrats, but deliberately depicts the land as spirited and animate, a fundamental belief of his religious practice.[1] As do his installations of full-room wall-paintings combined with objects of sacred significance, this drawing envelops the viewer with the materiality and spirituality inherent in its surface: the *amate* paper not only enfolds us with its physical scale, but its history as a medium for ceremonial offerings by the Aztecs and other indigenous peoples amplifies the drawing's power to communicate with mystical portent.[2]

J M

248 José Bedia

ISLOTE INACCESIBLE, LEJANO, SOLO, 1994

Ink on brown, dark brown, and beige (2), thick, rough (2) *amate* paper

46 7/8 x 93 1/2

Signed in ink l.r.: J Bedia 94

Inscribed in ink l.c.: ISLOTE INACCESIBLE, LEJANO, SOLO

Gift of John P. Axelrod (PA 1964)

2003.4

BORN
1 June 1949
Brooklyn, New York

Works on paper are integral to Terry Winters's art. His work, in all media, is a single, larger investigation of systems. For Winters, drawing is a mark-making system, a sign composed of gesture and material residue. Each mark carries its own code that is in turn modified and augmented by every other mark. The accumulation of these marks in a work and their effect on the viewer are tempered by the viewer's associations, perceptions, and visceral responses. Thus, every mark is a link in a chain of actions and reactions that lead outward from the work of art connected to ever-larger systems.

Scattering Conditions, 5, is from a set of nine drawings. These works were commissioned for an exhibition of eight artists who were invited to create artworks in response to an archive of photographs held by the relief organization American Jewish Joint Distribution Committee. The archive consists of fifty thousand images picturing the travels, travails, and tragedies of the Jewish communities from every part of the globe.

Winters wanted these drawings to "occupy a position…between the inexactness of memory and the precision of photography." This series is intentionally ambiguous and not meant "to lock specific meanings into forms."[1] In effect, Winters used the images as points of departure to leech out their significance and effect. The trajectories, matrices, and junctions of the *Scattering Conditions* drawings relate to his fascination with mapping. The linear and circular forms and the points suggest movement, directionality, and locations. As he wrote, "I started to develop this group of drawings by using simple component parts to build complex structures that suggested migration, something moving, separating, forming lines of flight. Territories were being described and occupied."[2]

J M

250 Terry Winters

SCATTERING CONDITIONS, 5, 1998

Ink, charcoal, graphite, and acrylic on white, thick, smooth wove paper

44 1/4 x 30 1/4

Signed in graphite in image l.l.: TW / 1998

Inscribed in graphite in image u.l.: 5

Gift of the artist

2003.41

BORN
30 September 1966
Jackson, Michigan

Exploring the interface between nature and culture, Jason Middlebrook's work addresses oppositions of decay and renewal, chaos and order, and the organic and the synthetic. Drawing from childhood experiences in rural California and building on the legacy of earthworks artists such as Robert Smithson, much of Middlebrook's art deals with the notion of entropy. As the artist has explained, "decay is an inevitable process that urbanites forget about. In the natural world we are surrounded by death, it's part of the recycling process. I'm interested in the complexity of that process."[1]

In *Site Lines*, this gradual process is accelerated as fragments of organic and man-made elements rocket through space destined for what threatens to be an apocalyptic implosion. In the midst of this kaleidoscopic chaos emerges a radically simplified order. Echoing the hierarchies of and divisions between nature and culture, images of floating protozoa, blood cells, brains, DNA strands, plant forms, rocks, and contemporary works of art are organized into distinct strata. Yet, these divisions quickly dissolve as they hurtle toward a vanishing point in which all distinctions between natural and cultural objects collapse. Though advancing to what appears to be a finite end, the delicate and luminous beauty of Middlebrook's images does not diminish as the elements recede, suggesting that, as in nature, every end sparks a new beginning. The vanishing point is also a starting point. Following a reabsorption and unification of creative energy, the process will begin again as a new order, as fragile and luminous as the first, rises out of decay.

Revealing the layers above and beneath earth and skin, Middlebrook offers us a new line of sight—a comprehensive landscape in which the geological, biological, and man-made possess equal weight and are all part of a single and ever-shifting life force.

ANK

252 ## Jason Middlebrook

SITE LINES, 2002

Ink, acrylic, graphite, and photocopy transfer on bright white, moderately thick, smooth wove paper

46 7/8 x 107 1/8

Signed in graphite on verso l.l.: Jason Middlebrook

Inscribed in graphite on verso l.l.: "Site Lines," 2002

Purchased as the gift of Harriett Ames Charitable Trust

2002.59

253

JAMES SHARPLES, PORTRAIT OF A MAN

1. William Dunlap, *History of the Rise and Progress of the Arts of Design in the United States*, 2 vols. (New York: George P. Scott and Co., 1834), 2:70–71.
2. Essay by J.W. Palmer, *Lippincott's Magazine* of December 1871, quoted in Katharine McCook Knox, *The Sharples: Their Portraits of George Washington and His Contemporaries* (New Haven: Yale University Press, 1930), p. 9.
3. Attribution of Sharples portraits is often confused because Ellen made credible copies of her husband's work when a portrait proved to be especially successful. So too, the three children became proficient in portraiture (Knox, p. 19).
4. Ibid., p. 44.

WILLIAM TROST RICHARDS, DAWN

1. John Ruskin quoted by Linda S. Ferber in "'Determined Realists': The American Pre-Raphaelites and the Association for the Advancement of Truth in Art," in Linda S. Ferber and William H. Gerdts, *The New Path: Ruskin and the American Pre-Raphaelites* (Brooklyn: The Brooklyn Museum, 1985), p. 13.
2. Kathleen A. Foster, "The Pre-Raphaelite Medium: Ruskin, Turner, and American Watercolor," in Ferber and Gerdts, p. 79.
3. Spanierman Gallery to Elizabeth Block, 7 July 1995, Addison Gallery Archives; see also Barbara Novak and Annette Blaugrund, *Next to Nature: Landscape Paintings from the National Academy of Design* (New York: National Academy of Design, 1980), pp. 139–40; and *Watercolors by William Trost Richards* (New York: Berry-Hill Galleries, 1989), p. 9, for other European inspired landscapes.
4. Foster, p. 87.

JAMES MCNEILL WHISTLER, CAMPANILE SANTA MARGHERITA

1. Margaret F. MacDonald, *Palaces in the Night: Whistler in Venice* (Berkeley and Los Angeles: University of California Press, 2001), pp. 13–16, 34.
2. Ibid., pp. 99–101.
3. Ibid., p. 37.
4. Richard Dorment and Margaret F. MacDonald, *James McNeill Whistler* (London: Tate Gallery Publications, 1994), p. 181.
5. Ibid.

WINSLOW HOMER, ON THE CLIFF, CULLERCOATS

1. Quoted in Nicolai Cikovsky, Jr., and Franklin Kelly, *Winslow Homer* (Washington, D.C.: National Gallery of Art; New Haven: Yale University Press, 1995), p. 178.
2. Kenyon Cox, "Winslow Homer," in *What is Painting? "Winslow Homer" and Other Essays* (New York: W.W. Norton, 1988), p. 26.
3. See Helen A. Cooper, *Winslow Homer Watercolors* (Washington, D.C.: National Gallery of Art; New Haven: Yale University Press, 1986), pp. 113–16, for discussion of composition in Homer's Cullercoats watercolors.

WINSLOW HOMER, DOG ON A LOG and CASTING

1. Helen A. Cooper, *Winslow Homer Watercolors* (Washington, D.C.: National Gallery of Art; New Haven: Yale University Press, 1986), pp. 165–66; see also David Tatham, *Winslow Homer in the Adirondacks* (Syracuse, N.Y.: Syracuse University Press, 1996).
2. Nicolai Cikovsky, Jr., and Franklin Kelly, *Winslow Homer* (Washington, D.C.: National Gallery of Art; New Haven: Yale University Press, 1995), p. 260.
3. Cooper, pp. 196–207.

4. Paul Schullery, "The Fly-Fishing Stories in Winslow Homer's Art," in Patricia Junker with Sarah Burns, *Winslow Homer: Artist and Angler* (Fort Worth, Tex.: Amon Carter Museum; San Francisco: Fine Arts Museums of San Francisco, 2003), p. 76.

JOHN LA FARGE, SPEARING FISH, SAMOA

1. See James Yarnall, "John La Farge's *Portrait of the Painter* and the Use of Photography in His Work," *American Art Journal* 18, no. 1 (1986): 4–20; and idem, "New Insights on John La Farge and Photography," *American Art Journal* 19, no. 2 (1987): 52–79.
2. James Yarnall, "Nature and Art in the Painting of John La Farge," in *John La Farge* (Pittsburgh: Carnegie Museum of Art; Washington, D.C.: National Museum of American Art, Smithsonian Institution; New York: Abbeville Press, 1987), p. 113; and idem, *Recreation and Idleness: The Pacific Travels of John La Farge* (New York: Vance Jordan Fine Art, 1998), pp. 139–41.
3. Two other works owned by the Addison were included in La Farge's exhibition as well: the watercolor *Water-Fall of Urami-No-Taki*, c. 1886, made during his first trip to Japan, and the oil painting *Maua, a Samoan*, that La Farge painted on his visit to that island with Henry Adams in 1891.

MAURICE PRENDERGAST, FLOAT AT LOW TIDE

1. Hedley Howell Rhys, *Maurice Prendergast 1859–1924* (Cambridge: Harvard University Press, 1960), p. 15.
2. Nancy Mowll Mathews, *Maurice Prendergast* (Williamstown, Mass.: Williams College Museum of Art; Munich: Prestel, 1990), p. 12.
3. Ibid., p. 14.
4. Ibid.

MAURICE PRENDERGAST, VENICE

1. This text is excerpted from the author's entry "Venice" in Susan C. Faxon and Nancy Mowll Mathews et al., *Maurice Prendergast: Learning to Look* (Andover: Addison Gallery of American Art, 2001), p. 13.
2. Nancy Mowll Mathews, *Maurice Prendergast* (Williamstown, Mass.: Williams College Museum of Art; Munich: Prestel, 1990), p. 17.

MAURICE PRENDERGAST, IN CENTRAL PARK

1. Victor W. Henningsen III, "In Central Park, New York," in Susan C. Faxon and Nancy Mowll Mathews et al., *Maurice Prendergast: Learning to Look* (Andover: Addison Gallery of American Art, 2001), p. 15.
2. Nancy Mowll Mathews, *Maurice Prendergast* (Williamstown, Mass.: Williams College Museum of Art; Munich: Prestel, 1990), p. 14.
3. Ibid., p. 19.

MAURICE PRENDERGAST, ON THE PIER

1. Hedley Howell Rhys, *Maurice Prendergast 1859–1924* (Cambridge: Harvard University Press, 1960), p. 32.
2. Nancy Mowll Mathews, *The Art of Leisure: Maurice Prendergast in the Williams College Museum of Art* (Williamstown, Mass.: Williams College Museum of Art, 1999), p. 22.

MARY CASSATT, LITTLE BOY IN BLUE (NO. 2)

1. Adelyn Bohme Breeskin, *Mary Cassatt 1844–1926* (Washington, D.C.: National Gallery of Art, 1970), p. 17.
2. E. John Bullard, *Mary Cassatt Oils and Pastels* (Washington, D.C.: National Gallery of Art, 1972), p. 18.

254 Notes

3. See Adelyn Bohme Breeskin, *Mary Cassatt: A Catalogue Raisonné of the Oils, Pastels, Watercolors, and Drawings* (Washington, D.C.: Smithsonian Institution Press, 1970), p. 182.

4. Macbeth Gallery receipt, Addison Gallery Archives.

5. Breeskin 1970, p. 182.

PRESTON DICKINSON, LANDSCAPE

1. Although the Addison drawing is undated, a similar winter scene (location unknown) is signed and dated 1916. See Richard Lee Rubenfeld, "Preston Dickinson: An American Modernist, with a Catalogue of Selected Works; Volumes I and II," Ph.D. diss., University of Ohio, Columbus, 1985, 2:341.

2. Ibid., 1:106.

ARTHUR DOVE, DRAWING

1. The sudden shift in Dove's work is surely due in part to his meeting, in late 1909 or early 1910, Alfred Stieglitz, who became a lifelong friend and supporter of his work. See Debra Bricker Balken, "Continuities and Digressions in the Work of Arthur Dove from 1907 to 1933," in *Arthur Dove: A Retrospective* (Andover: Addison Gallery of American Art; Cambridge: The MIT Press; Washington, D.C.: The Phillips Collection, 1998), pp. 17–35.

2. Dove's output during this time was limited to mostly charcoal drawings, a few pastels, and an occasional painting.

3. Balken, p. 24.

4. Ann Lee Morgan, *Arthur Dove: Life and Work, with a Catalogue Raisonné* (Newark: University of Delaware Press, 1984), p. 65.

GEORGIA O'KEEFFE, BLACK LINES

1. Barbara Buhler Lynes, "Inventions of Different Orders," in *O'Keeffe: On Paper* (Washington, D.C.: National Gallery of Art, 2000), p. 41.

2. See Lynes, pp. 49–51.

JOHN MARIN, BLUE SEA, CROTCH ISLAND

1. John Marin to Alfred Stieglitz, 14 August 1923, in *Letters of John Marin*, ed. Herbert J. Seligmann (New York: An American Place, 1931).

2. *John Marin by John Marin*, ed. Cleve Gray (New York: Holt, Rinehart, and Winston, 1977), p. 118.

3. See correspondence between Charles Sawyer and Edith Halpert, May–June 1935, Addison Gallery Archives.

CHARLES DEMUTH, PLUMS

1. The best and most recent evaluation of Demuth's work is Barbara Haskell, *Charles Demuth* (New York: Whitney Museum of American Art and Harry N. Abrams, 1987).

2. Thomas E. Norton, ed., *Homage to Charles Demuth: Still Life Painter of Lancaster* (Ephrata, Penn.: Science Press, 1978), p. 96.

ISAMU NOGUCHI, STANDING NUDE

1. *Isamu Noguchi: Beginnings and Ends* (New York: Pace Gallery, 1994) n.p., quoting unpublished statements by Isamu Noguchi for the 1986 Venice Biennale.

2. Robert J. Maeda, "Isamu Noguchi and the Peking Drawing of 1930," *American Art* 13, no. 1 (Spring 1999): 84–93.

3. For more on Noguchi's abstract drawings and Chinese ink paintings, see Bruce Altshuler, "Isamu Noguchi: Early Drawings from Paris and Bejing," *Drawing: The International Review* 16, no. 4 (November–December 1994): 73–77.

4. According to Noguchi himself, this drawing was probably made in Paris in early 1931 on the way back to Beijing, artist's questionnaire, early 1969, Addison Gallery Archives.

CARL RUGGLES, POLYPHONIC STANZA

1. Charles Sawyer to Christopher C. Cook, 20 July 1978, Addison Gallery Archives.

2. Marilyn Ziffrin, *Carl Ruggles: Composer, Painter, and Story-teller* (Urbana: University of Illinois Press, 1994), pp. 41–42.

3. Ibid., p. 142.

4. Allen Sweet, "Ruggles, Carl Sprague (Charles)," *AskART*, <www.askart.com/biography> (4 April 2003).

5. Ibid.

GEORGE GROSZ, PORTRAIT OF A LADY

1. George Grosz, *George Grosz: An Autobiography*, trans. Nora Hodges (New York: Macmillan, 1983), p. 235.

2. Hans Hess, *George Grosz* (London: Studio Vista, 1974), pp. 175–76.

3. As Abram Lerner wrote in his introduction to Frank Gettings, *George Grosz: The Hirshhorn Museum and Sculpture Garden Collection* (Washington, D.C.: Smithsonian Institution Press, 1978), p. 3: "The line is unmistakably Grosz, as is the fluid watercolor technique with its fuzzy, invading edge."

WILLIAM GROPPER, UNEMPLOYED

1. See Nelson A. Rockefeller, "The Governor Lectures on Art," *New York Times Magazine*, 9 April 1967, pp. 28–31, 117–24.

2. Gropper was not recognized as a painter until his first one-person show of paintings in 1936 at the ACA Galleries in New York.

CHARLES BURCHFIELD, THE SKY BEYOND

1. Henry Adams, "Charles Burchfield's Imagination," in *The Paintings of Charles Burchfield: North by Midwest* (New York: Harry N. Abrams in association with the Columbus Museum of Art, 1997), p. 124.

2. Michael D. Hall, "Burchfield's Regionalism: The Middle Border and the Great Divide," in ibid., p. 75.

3. Joseph S. Trovato, introduction to *Charles Burchfield: Catalogue of Paintings in Public and Private Collections* (Utica, N.Y.: Munson-Williams-Proctor Institute, 1970), p. 12.

HUGH FERRISS, TRESTLE

1. For an assessment of Ferriss's visionary work, see Carol Willis, "Drawing Towards Metropolis," in Hugh Ferriss, *The Metropolis of Tomorrow* (1929; reprint, New York: Princeton Architectural Press, 1986), p. 149.

2. "Ferriss' Future-Perfect," *Time*, 18 May 1942, pp. 42–43.

3. These drawings were published in Ferriss's second book, *Power in Buildings: An Artist's View of Contemporary Architecture*, originally published in 1953 by Columbia University Press.

4. "Power of America," *Newsweek*, 11 May 1942, p. 69; "Ferriss' Future-Perfect."

5. Record of Work 1922–1961, Hugh Ferriss Papers, Drawings and Archives Department, Avery Architectural and Fine Arts Library, Columbia University, New York.

JACKSON POLLOCK, Untitled

1. This image is cat. no. 701 in Francis V. O'Connor and Eugene Victor Thaw, eds., *Jackson Pollock: A Catalogue Raisonné of Paintings, Drawings, and Other Works*, 4 vols. (New Haven: Yale University Press, 1978), 3:209.

2. The drawing was called *Sitting Nude* when it was sold as lot 168 in the sale of Sotheby's, London, *Impressionist and Modern Paintings, Drawings and Sculpture*, 30 November 1967, Addison Gallery Archives.

3. As the catalogue raisonné noted, the volume of individual sheets and sketchbooks in a wide variety of media and techniques remaining in Pollock's studio at his death gave testament to the importance he assigned to his drawings (O'Connor and Thaw, 3:vii).

4. Ibid., 3:xxi.

5. While the verso is incorrectly listed in the catalogue raisonné as a separate work, there is no doubt that this is the reverse of one single sheet of paper. The catalogue identifies this drawing as no. 754, c. 1945, ink on dark blue paper, 11 1/2 x 8 3/4 (ibid., 3:247).

MARK ROTHKO, PERSONAGES

1. Lisa Mintz Messinger, *Abstract Expressionism: Works on Paper* (New York: The Metropolitan Museum of Art; Atlanta: High Museum of Art, 1992), pp. 111–12.

2. Diane Waldman, *Mark Rothko, 1903–1970: A Retrospective* (New York: Harry N. Abrams in collaboration with The Solomon R. Guggenheim Foundation, 1978), p. 48.

3. Introduction to one-person exhibition held in January 1945 at Peggy Guggenheim's Art of This Century gallery, quoted in ibid., p. 44.

4. William C. Seitz, *Abstract Expressionist Painting in America* (Cambridge: Harvard University Press; Washington, D.C.: National Gallery of Art, 1983), p. 30.

RICHARD POUSETTE-DART, Untitled

1. See Konrad Oberhuber, "Material Awareness of Spirit: Richard Pousette-Dart and His Works on Paper," in Ingrid Ehrhardt and Katja Hilbig, eds., *The Living Edge: Richard Pousette-Dart, Works on Paper* (Frankfurt: Schirn Kunsthalle Frankfurt, 2001), p. 34.

2. Ibid., p. 61.

ADOLPH GOTTLIEB, VIGIL OF CYCLOPS

1. April Kingsley, *Adolph Gottlieb: Works on Paper* (San Francisco: Art Museum Association of America, 1985), pp. 9–11.

2. Ibid., p. 20.

3. Ibid., pp. 15, 19.

4. Ibid., pp. 20–21.

5. Robert Doty and Diane Waldman, *Adolph Gottlieb* (New York: Whitney Museum of American Art and F.A. Praeger, 1968), p. 19.

6. Kingsley, p. 23.

HANS HOFMANN, UNTITLED VII 13

1. See Irving Sandler, "Hans Hofmann: The Dialectical Master," in Cynthia Goodman, *Hans Hofmann* (New York: Whitney Museum of American Art; Munich: Prestel, 1990), p. 86.

2. Cynthia Goodman, *Hans Hofmann*, Abbeville Modern Masters 10 (New York: Abbeville Press, 1986), pp. 53–55.

3. This form can also be seen in related 1947 paintings, including: *Ecstasy* (Berkeley Art Museum, University of California), *Gestation* (collection of Frank Stella), and *Exaltment* (Addison Gallery of American Art).

4. See Cynthia Goodman, "Hans Hofmann: A Master in Search of the 'Real,'" in Goodman 1990, p. 61 and illustration p. 190.

5. Goodman 1986, p. 51: "Hofmann also kept a copy of the catalog from that [Pollock] show among his papers."
6. Quoted in Goodman 1990, p. 31.
7. Goodman 1986, p. 55.

REGINALD MARSH, CROWDED DAY AT CONEY and Sketchbook

1. Lloyd Goodrich, *Reginald Marsh* (New York: Harry N. Abrams, 1972), p. 38.
2. Ibid., p. 163.

NORMAN LEWIS, NEW MOON

1. Robert Goodnough, ed., "Artists' Sessions at Studio 35," *Modern Artists in America*, 1st series (New York: Wittenborn Schultz, 1952), p. 12.
2. Norman Lewis, interview with Henri Ghent, Smithsonian Archives of American Art, <artarchives.si.edu/oralhist/lewisn68.htm> (12 April 2003).
3. Norman Lewis, "Application for Guggenheim Fellowship, 1949," quoted in *Norman Lewis: From the Harlem Renaissance to Abstraction* (New York: Kenkeleba Gallery, 1989), p. 65. Despite his turn to abstraction, Lewis continued to champion African American artists who were struggling for the recognition that came more easily to their white counterparts. He was a founding member of both the SPIRAL group and the Cinque Gallery, which provided opportunities for support and exhibition of African American artists.
4. Quoted in Ann Eden Gibson, "Black Is a Color: Norman Lewis and Modernism in New York," in *Norman Lewis Black Paintings 1946–1977* (New York: The Studio Museum in Harlem, 1998), p. 21.

ANNE RYAN, NO. 1

1. Sarah Faunce, *Anne Ryan Collages* (Brooklyn: The Brooklyn Museum, 1974), pp. 6–7.
2. John Bernard Myers, "Anne Ryan's Interior Castle," *Journal of the Archives of American Art* 15, no. 3 (1975): 8–11.
3. Anne Ryan, c. 1947, quoted in *Anne Ryan: Collages* (New York: Marlborough Gallery, 1974), p. 7.

HYMAN BLOOM, CADAVER NO. 1

1. See Isabelle Dervaux, *Color & Ecstasy: The Art of Hyman Bloom* (New York: National Academy of Design, 2002), pp. 18–22.
2. Ibid., p. 24.
3. Holland Cotter, "Introduction," in *Hyman Bloom* (New York: Chameleon Books, 1996), p. 9.
4. Bartlett H. Hayes to John W. O'Boyle, 21 September 1954, Addison Gallery Archives.

MILTON AVERY, PAMET RIVER

1. National Park Service, Cape Cod National Seashore, Places, Pamet Valley, <www.nps.gov/caco/places/pametvalley.html> (11 April 2003).
2. Marla Price, *Milton Avery: Works from the 1950s* (Fort Worth, Tex.: Modern Art Museum of Fort Worth, 1990), p. 7.
3. Quoted in Robert Hobbs, *Milton Avery* (New York: Hudson Hills Press, 1990), p. 166.
4. Mark Rothko, "Commemorative Essay," in Barbara Haskell, *Milton Avery* (New York: Whitney Museum of Art, 1982), p. 181.

CHARLES SELIGER, VINEYARD HAVEN

1. John Yau, "Charles Seliger and His Syncretic Abstraction," in *Charles Seliger: Chaos to Complexity* (New York: Michael Rosenfeld Gallery, 2003), p. 3.
2. Francis V. O'Connor, *Charles Seliger: Redefining Abstract Expressionism* (Manchester, Vt.: Hudson Hills Press, 2003), p. 87.
3. Seliger, quoted by Melvin P. Lader, "Introduction," in O'Connor, p. 8.
4. O'Connor, p. 87.
5. Charles Seliger, artist's questionnaire, 1968, Addison Gallery Archives.
6. Lader, p. 16.

CHARLES SHEELER, SUN, ROCKS, TREES

1. Charles Sheeler to William Lane, 25 October [1956], The Lane Collection files.
2. Carol Troyen and Erica Hirschler, *Charles Sheeler: Paintings and Drawings* (Boston: Little, Brown, 1987), pp. 216–17.
3. For a more complete discussion of these working methods, see Troyen and Hirschler, pp. 35–36; and Karen E. Haas, "'Opening the Other Eye': Charles Sheeler and the Uses of Photography," in Theodore E. Stebbins, Jr., Gilles Mora, and Karen E. Haas, *The Photography of Charles Sheeler: American Modernist* (Boston: Bulfinch Press, 2002), pp. 134–36.

NORMAN BLUHM, Untitled

1. "26 Things At Once: An Interview with Norman Bluhm by John Yau and Jon Gams," [1999/2000,] <www.culturereport.com/culturereport/artists/bluhm/index.html> (21 May 2003), p. 3.
2. See John Yau, "Drawing in Color: A Portrait of Norman Bluhm, 1921–1999," in *Norman Bluhm: Opere su carta, 1948–1999* (Milan: Gabriele Mazzotta, 2000), pp. 13–28.
3. See James Harithas, "Norman Bluhm Works on Paper," in ibid., pp. 11–12.

BARNETT NEWMAN, Untitled

1. Brenda Richardson, *Barnett Newman: The Complete Drawings, 1944–1969* (Baltimore: The Baltimore Museum of Art, 1979), p. 14. This entry is greatly indebted to Richardson's investigations.
2. Ibid., p. 158.
3. Ibid.

JOSEPH CORNELL, HOMAGE TO BRANCUSI

1. Deborah Solomon, *Utopia Parkway: The Life and Work of Joseph Cornell* (New York: Farrar, Straus, Giroux, 1997), pp. 101, 113, 316, 340; Cornell created homages inspired by such famous persons as Greta Garbo, Marilyn Monroe, Marie Taglioni, and Susan Sontag.
2. Ibid., pp. 261, 273–75.
3. See Victor Manta, "Constantin Brancusi: The Early Work," 2002, <www.marci-postale.com/Romania/romania-en.htm> (28 May 2003). The stamp, one of seven issued, pictures a bronze head entitled *Vanity (Orgoliu)*, c. 1905–6 (Craiova Art Museum).
4. Lynda Roscoe Hartigan, "Joseph Cornell: A Biography," in *Joseph Cornell*, ed. Kynaston McShine (New York: The Museum of Modern Art, 1990), p. 101: Cornell first saw Marcel Duchamp at the Brummer Gallery during the Brancusi exhibition he organized in the fall of 1933, and their formal introduction probably occurred at the screening of Cornell's film *Rose Hobart* at the Julien Levy Gallery in December 1936. The men's friendship flourished from 1942 until Duchamp's death in 1968.

BRUCE CONNER, WATER

1. Walter Hopps, "Artists on Artists: Bruce Conner," *Bomb* (Summer 2002), p. 10.
2. Peter Boswell, "Bruce Conner: Theater of Light and Shadow," in *2000 BC: The Bruce Conner Story Part II* (Minneapolis: Walker Art Center, 1999), p. 42.

BEVERLY HALLAM, ARABESQUE

1. Edward Betts, introduction to *Beverly Hallam: Paintings, Drawings, and Monotypes, 1956–1971* (Andover: Addison Gallery of American Art, 1971), n.p.
2. Carl Little, *Beverly Hallam: An Odyssey in Art* (Washington, D.C.: Whalesback Books, 1998), p. 57.
3. Beverly Hallam to Susan C. Faxon, 2 February 1998, Addison Gallery Archives.

CARROLL DUNHAM, UNTITLED

1. This text is excerpted from the entry written by Klaus Kertess for Susan C. Faxon et al., *Addison Gallery of American Art, 65 Years: A Selective Catalogue* (Andover: Addison Gallery of American Art, 1996), p. 360.

JOHN NEWMAN, UNTITLED

1. John Newman to Heather Leavell, 31 January 2002, Addison Gallery Archives, explains that the similarly rendered figure in *Jaw Breaker*, 1992 (a color lithograph in the collection), "is directly related to the large drawing."
2. "Jawbreaker," *American Heritage Dictionary*, 2d ed. (Boston: Houghton Mifflin, 1985).
3. Angela Fritz, "*Character Armor, 1983*," in *John Newman: Sculpture and Works on Paper* (Fort Wayne, Ind.: Fort Wayne Museum of Art, 1993), p. 12.
4. Konrad Oberhuber, *John Newman: Drawings* (New York: David Nolan Gallery, 1991), pp. 5–6.

JANE HAMMOND, PLAYERS

1. All quotes from a telephone interview with the artist by the author, 23 April 2003.

JOSÉ BEDIA, ISLOTE INACCESIBLE, LEJANO, SOLO

1. Interview with Carla Hanzal, 7 December 2000, in *Rodeado de Mar: An Interview with José Bedia* (Virginia Beach: Contemporary Art Center of Virginia, 2001), p. 7.
2. Kerin Gould, "Amate Paper," 6 December 2001, <home.earthlink.net/~kering/amate.html> (31 January 2003).

TERRY WINTERS, SCATTERING CONDITIONS, 5

1. Marvin Heiferman and Carole Kismaric, eds., *To the Rescue: Eight Artists in an Archive* (New York: Lookout, 2000), pp. 84–85.
2. Ibid., p. 85.

JASON MIDDLEBROOK, SITE LINES

1. Quoted in Chloe Kinsman, "In Contemplation of a Quiet Catastrophe," in *Jason Middlebrook* (Siena: Palazzo delle Papesse Centro Arte Contemporanea, 2003), p. 22.

257

The work as a **concept** NEW ATTITUDES TO WORKING ON PAPER IN THE LATE TWENTIETH CENTURY TREVOR FAIRBROTHER

D uring the 1960s a burgeoning spirit of experiment spawned Pop art,
Minimalism, Conceptual art, Earth art, and Body art. Performance art
became an umbrella term covering rambunctious fast-action Happenings
and the conceptually rigorous approaches inspired by John Cage and
the Fluxus group. While many artists eschewed painting as an exhausted tradition,
some hoped that innovative futures for the medium existed in such styles as Color
Field, Hard Edge, and Op art. By 1970 the most advanced position was to circumvent
the taken-for-granted status of art as a precious saleable object (i.e., painting and
sculpture) in favor of art as a broad field of investigation that framed propositions
and presented information. This situation fostered new attitudes to working on paper
and gave particular significance to documents, texts, and photo-based information.[1]
This unprecedented artistic ferment reflected the fact that American society had
entered a phase of reform spurred by political activism and the new "counterculture."
There were moves to ban nuclear weapons, to end racial discrimination, to liberalize
education, to empower women, and to liberate sexual mores. Numerous indicators—
economic prosperity, leisure time, interstate highways, plastic products, jet travel,
television, satellites, computers, a vibrant new epoch in popular music—suggested
in their different ways that a massive cultural makeover was underway. But anger
and skepticism soon added sour notes to the hedonism, for the war on Communism
was escalating in Vietnam, dividing American opinion, and radicalizing many young
artists inspired by the sixties.

This complicated and often confusing decade of experimentation and soul searching
seemed to alter everything, including the ways in which a work of art on paper might

be produced, categorized, and valued. One need only read the intriguingly tendentious title of an exhibition organized by Mel Bochner late in 1966—*Working Drawings and Other Visible Things on Paper Not Necessarily Meant To Be Viewed as Art*—for an indication of the changes afoot. Intending to draw attention to the preparation and planning that precede the production of a work of art, Bochner gathered a diverse group of paper documents: quick sketches, diagrams, notes, and such "anonymous" items as a cash register receipt, a baseball score card, and numerous scientific diagrams and formulations. The participants included Jo Baer, John Cage, Eva Hesse, Sol LeWitt, Robert Smithson, and Karlheinz Stockhausen. When the host institution (Visual Arts Gallery, New York City) insisted that many of these items were not worthy of framing, Bochner took additional radical steps. He photocopied the individual sheets, compiled four sets of the reproductions in loose-leaf binders, and pointedly displayed each notebook on a pedestal, as if it were a sculpture.[2] This episode embodied several new thoughts concerning the making and display of art: any kind of information relevant to the conception of a work is worthy of attention; in some circumstances a reproduction serves just as well as "the real thing"; and books or manuals compiled by an artist can constitute an exhibition. In June 1967, just months after Bochner's exhibition, Sol LeWitt outlined the concerns that he and his colleagues were exploring in his essay "Paragraphs on Conceptual Art." Particularly relevant to our consideration of the shifting attitude towards works on paper are these words by LeWitt:

> If the artist carries through his idea and makes it into visible form, then all the steps in the process are of importance. The idea itself, even if not made visual, is as much a work of art as any finished product. All intervening steps—scribbles, sketches, drawings, failed works, models, studies, thoughts, conversations—are of interest. Those that show the thought process of the artist are sometimes more interesting than the final product.[3]

What follows is a consideration of some of the transformations that occurred to works on paper during this period. My headings take inspiration from the specific examples that the Addison Gallery's curatorial team chose to feature in this publication.

Putting Ideas First

According to Sol LeWitt's now-famous observation about Conceptual art, "The idea becomes a machine that makes the art."[4] LeWitt's innovative role in the movement is evident in the ten everyday picture postcards that were the raw materials for *Ten Postcards* (1971). His notion was to devise a language-mediated work that involved the participation of others away from his studio. He wrote a specific task on the back of every postcard and mailed each in succession to Lucy Lippard, a curator, art historian, and close friend. All of the postcards have an identical eight-cent stamp, which reproduces an American urban realist painting that was progressive in its day (John Sloan, *Wake of the Ferry*, 1907; Phillips Collection, Washington, D.C.). The mail system's handling procedure canceled the stamp and added postmarks, and Lippard usually made her own marks to fulfill the artist's instructions. For example, on one card LeWitt had written "PLEASE DELETE THIS BLOCK OF PRINTING" and Lippard drew a large green cross through his rectangular grouping of words. At first glance this work is spare, unemotional, and repetitive, but knowledge of its origins combined with close looking reveals it to be a rich mixture of found objects, words, marks, and chance effects.

Frederick Barthelme's Substitution project captured the interrogative and anti-art currents that were an aspect of Conceptual art. His devotion to activities which evaded established notions of "Art" mirrored the stance of the multifaceted sixties counterculture. Barthelme devised an official-looking form for reporting on things he had decided to do instead of making traditional objects. In an increasingly bureaucratized society and during a time of draft registration and resistance, it may have been cathartic defiance that prompted Barthelme's thought, "Instead of making art I filled out this form."

Process and Procedure

An early and notorious instance of a new emphasis on process was Rauschenberg's concept of the "all-eraser drawing." His *Erased de Kooning Drawing* (1953; San Francisco Museum of Modern Art) presents a verbal and visual paradox that we now honor as a landmark on the path from Duchamp and Dada to the idea-driven art of the 1960s. De Kooning went along with Rauschenberg's edgy proposal and pointedly gave him a drawing that he knew would be difficult to erase![5] By the late sixties the young sculptor Richard Serra would pronounce: "I do not make art, I am engaged in an activity; if someone else wants to call it art, that's his business."[6] Rather than convey a subject or theme, Serra's process-oriented objects were uncompromising embodiments of specific physical activities: lead that had been folded or rolled, lead that had been melted and splashed, and so on.

Between 1966 and 1968 Lawrence Weiner produced drawings on graph paper that related to his sculptural involvement with the configuration of materials in a particular space. For an untitled work of 1967 he outlined a large rectangular site on the paper and then proceeded to fill individual squares with m-shaped marks (his code for "mass"). The production of the drawing was an exercise to generate irregular forms that disrupted the rigid order of the graph paper. The finished drawing has a stark appearance, but it would be a mistake to see it solely in negativistic terms: it exists as a rather complicated record of time-based mental and physical activities.

The quiet Minimalist appearance of Michelle Stuart's *Little Turtle Pond, Kingston, N.Y.*, is deceptive because the processes used to create it derive from the artist's great passion for the natural world. Stuart placed the surface of a heavy sheet of paper against a geological sample (perhaps a small area of the earth or a pulverized sample that she collected from a particular site). The imprinting of paper against this "earth" created indentations and punctures. She then covered the sheet with an even layer of fine graphite, and the gray graphite field created an enormously complicated spatial infinity. Stuart's drawing is a straightforward record of a set of activities, and yet has the metaphoric potential to suggest skin, planet, and cosmos.

A recent work on paper by a veteran of this field, Mel Bochner, attests to the fact that an intellectually stringent concept for a work of art can be translated into a visually ravishing end product. As his title suggests, Bochner followed an orderly procedure

261

when he made *Counting: 4 Rotations (Continuous)*. Careful scrutiny allows one to realize that the artist superimposed four layers of numbers when making this work, rotating the sheet between each application. He began by covering the paper with a deep blue ground, and seems to have lightened the color of each layer of numbers. This sheet demonstrates Bochner's awareness that an orderly procedure can foster lyricism and abstraction.

Plans and Diagrams

In 1959 Jasper Johns told a reporter for *Time* magazine: "Looking at a painting should not require a special kind of focus like going to church. A picture ought to be looked at the same way you look at a radiator."[7] His attitude exemplifies the move to demystify art that was crucial to much work created in the 1960s. Furthermore, a burgeoning disdain for galleries and museums, and a concomitant infatuation with cheap nontraditional materials, helped some artists reach the conclusion that the realization of their works was secondary to the conception. Lawrence Weiner, for example, decided in 1968 that the descriptive phrases he prepared in advance of his sculptures were in fact the primary form of his art. Since then he has always affirmed that "the piece need not be built."[8]

Many drawings produced during this period have the appearance of diagrams or working descriptions, and they may indeed be surrogates for works that were not taken to a further state of realization. Barry Le Va's *Tangle Distribution* diagrams a kind of "Anti-Form" sculpture that was devoted to the random distribution of ephemeral scraps. The artist's use of graph paper hints at the workaday practices of a drafting office and provides the matrix for an aerial view of the work. Le Va's annotations indicate that a variety of pieces of felt (from three-quarter-inch "particles" to twenty-four-foot "strips") are laid out as a "tangle distribution." They also indicate the overall dimensions to be approximately thirty-five by fifty-five feet. A variety of ink markings, from little dots to long straight lines, generate a schematic picture of a field of felt elements that moves chaotically from areas of lesser to greater visual density. Another of Le Va's drawings uses ink lines and sprayed white paint to evoke a sculpture or installation in which chalk lines seem to be veiled by areas of wiped chalk. Both of these works on paper are related to installations that Le Va made in 1968.[9]

Although Robert Mangold's untitled graphite drawing of 1973 did not immediately inspire a larger work, its composition anticipates his X-shaped paintings of the early 1980s. Mangold prepared a delicate grid of pencil lines on his sheet and elaborated his composition against that framework. The main image is set down in clear dark lines that readily recall the restrained demarcation of area and of linear motif that he has explored since the sixties. What makes this drawing especially pleasing is the ghostlike grid that allows one to see the geometry that underpins his visual decisions. Along similar lines, Carl Andre's *Working Map: India Triennale Piece* (1973) demonstrates the way in which a drawing can telescope a large sculpture into a small but precise informational package.

Imagining in New Languages

During the period under consideration representational images abounded in various guises, from painting to photography, film, and video. Their prevalence and vitality reflected the supposed failure of abstraction as well as the pervasive boom in popular culture. Carl Andre was twenty-five and not yet acclaimed as a sculptor when he completed *Passport* in 1960. This book of collages and other works on paper mirrors the freewheeling climate of its day with extraordinary wit, intelligence, and precision. Its zany mixture of images includes: maps and technical diagrams; printed ephemera; recurring references to Byron, Napoleon, and Sir Walter Raleigh; souvenirs of Andre's close friendship with his contemporary, the painter Frank Stella; references to Andre's recent marriage; and reproductions of works by famous painters and sculptors (including Botticelli, Holbein, Rembrandt, Clodion, Goya, Ingres, Manet, and Brancusi). As a choreographed sequence of visual occurrences, it is more overtly "personal" than Andre's reductive sculpture. There are, nonetheless, several inclusions that distill Andre's mature aesthetic: a tall thin monochromatic rectangle of intense red contained by a tessellated border; a black and white photograph of a sexy male portrait by Bronzino overlaid by a grid of hundreds of tiny red dots; and the word "green" typed repeatedly to create a dense, even visual field (these are pages 13, 18, and 14 respectively). Voluble and at times playfully absurd, *Passport* is a valuable reminder of the complicated imagination that was essential to the emergence of reductive sculpture in this period.

There may be no easier way to sense the liberation from inhibitions that took place in the late 1950s and 1960s than to look at the art of Claes Oldenburg. In a famous statement first published in 1961 he wrote: "I am for an art that is political-erotical-mystical, that does something other than sit on its ass in a museum.... I am for the art that a kid licks, after peeling away the wrapper.... I am for art that sheds hair.... I am for the art of cock-and-ball trees and flying cows and the noise of rectangles and squares."[10] Oldenburg's blithe rejection of museumlike Depression-era prudery led directly to a world in which every object has multiple sensory overtones. He frequently used drawing to dream up monuments that were for the most part too amazing and outrageous to be built. His *Design for a Tunnel Entrance in the Form of a Nose* shows a colossal nose slumped in the "bosom" of two grand hills. Oldenburg's rapid execution produced an image that remains memorably real, even if it only exists on paper.

Seeing Old Art from New Perspectives

One benefit of all artistic innovations is the opportunity to see one's surroundings and the art of the past with altered eyes. Thus, in conclusion, I would suggest that the new approaches to making works on paper discussed in this essay enlarge our capacity to marvel at a variety of historical works. Mark Tobey's *Lines of the City* (1945) seems to presage the process-oriented drawings of later decades. His abstracted, schematic representation of urban forms and energies feels like an exercise in making lines, and his intuitive balancing of order and chaos has much in common with the efforts of LeWitt and Le Va discussed earlier. Blanche Lazzell's series of

Cubist compositions have the rigor of theme, variation, and serial development that was often explored by artists in the 1960s. Even Victorian calligraphy takes on a new dimension after contemplating the rhythmic repetitions of Minimal and Conceptual art. The pen-and-ink exercises by Matilda Elizabeth Schmahl were created in a scholastic setting and served, in part, to instill exemplary values. It is easy to pigeon-hole them as charming but meaningless ephemera from a bygone time. But in light of the late-twentieth-century works on paper discussed in this essay, we may be more inclined to experience them as ideas, plans, and working processes. Such a perspective makes it easier to imagine the social conditions and cultural framework that prompted Schmahl to explore the art of drawing: education, discipline, propriety, class, gender stereotyping, boredom, mental escape, and the pleasure of accomplishment.

Notes

1. Three exhibitions and catalogues that presented these ideas in New York in 1970 were: Donald Karshan, comp., *Conceptual Art and Conceptual Aspects* (New York Cultural Center); Kynaston L. McShine, ed., *Information* (Museum of Modern Art); and Jack Burnham, ed., *Software; Information Technology: Its Meaning for Art* (Jewish Museum).

2. Bochner's manual of photocopies for *Working Drawings and Other Visible Things on Paper...* has since been published in facsimile (Geneva: Cabinet des estampes du Museé d'art et d'histoire; Cologne: Verlag der Buchhandlung Walther König; Paris: Picaron Editions, 1997).

3. Reprinted in *Sol LeWitt: Critical Texts*, ed. Adachiara Zevi (Rome: I Libri di AEIUO, 1995), p. 80. The text was first published by *Artforum*.

4. Ibid., p. 78.

5. Rauschenberg in Emile de Antonio and Mitch Tuchman, *Painters Painting* (New York: Abbeville Press, 1984), pp. 91–92.

6. Quoted in Karshan, *Conceptual Art*, p. 6.

7. Quoted in *Jasper Johns: Writings, Sketchbook Notes, Interviews*, ed. Kirk Varnedoe (New York: Museum of Modern Art, 1996), p. 8.

8. The sentence is one of the three givens in a statement that has accompanied presentations of Weiner's work since 1969. See Ann Goldstein and Anne Rorimer, *Reconsidering the Object of Art: 1965–1975* (Los Angeles: Museum of Contemporary Art; Cambridge, Mass.: MIT Press, 1995), p. 222.

9. For images of the two installations see *The New Sculpture, 1965–1975: Between Geometry and Gesture*, ed. Richard Armstrong and Richard Marshall (New York: Whitney Museum of American Art, 1990), p. 121.

10. Claes Oldenburg, "Statement," reprinted in *Pop Art: A Critical History*, ed. Steven Henry Madoff (Berkeley and Los Angeles: University of California Press, 1997), pp. 213–15. The text first appeared in the catalogue for the exhibition *Environments, Situations, Spaces* at the Martha Jackson Gallery, New York, 1961.

The work as a **concept** PORTFOLIO

This mid-nineteenth-century drawing of a lion is part of the calligraphic folk-art tradition in America. While animal drawings often appeared in conjunction with writing samples, they also were made independently as displays of an artist's virtuosity. The most commonly illustrated animals were lions, birds, leaping deer, fish, and horses, and the majority of calligraphic drawings, including this one, were done with a steel pen.[1]

Students of penmanship learned writing and drawing through rigorous practice from a writing master, a copybook, or a combination of both.[2] Solitary calligraphic animals, as well as decorative flourishes and figural embellishments adorning text, were created with strokes similar to those used for letterforms but served as diversions from strict penmanship and as opportunities for design and creativity.[3] In this drawing, the artist outlined the contours of the lion's body and constructed a decorated platform for it to stand on. Calligraphic strokes shape the lion's three-dimensional form, defining its haunches, torso, and face and even filling in its ears and tail. Light strokes of the pen form the lion's fluffy mane and delicate whiskers, while heavy applications of ink create his nose, mouth, eyes, and claws.

Mary P. Foster was probably a schoolgirl practicing forms with her pen, pleased enough with the result to place her signature on the verso of the drawing. Such works are representative of a period of American history in which beautiful writing was a valued and practical skill. While the widespread use of computers in today's world is displacing fine penwork, it also increases our appreciation of calligraphy as an art form.

GGS

266 ## Mary P. Foster

LION, mid-19th century

Iron gall ink on beige (2), moderately thick (2), smooth wove paper

12 7/8 x 16 1/2

Signed in iron gall ink on verso u.l.: Mary P. Foster; u.c.: Mary P. Foster; in ink on verso c.r.: Mary P. Foster / West Salisbury / New Hampshire

Museum purchase

1959.48

THE NOTES FOR THIS SECTION BEGIN ON PAGE 322

267

BORN
19 May 1837
New Jersey

DIED
1906

Matilda Elizabeth Schmahl proudly presented these two calligraphic works as her own, integrating her name into the formal design of *Select Sentences* (p. 271) and including it on a ribbon in the beak of a bird in *Friendship*. The works date to the early 1850s, when the artist was a schoolgirl, practicing the art of penmanship at New York City's Public School Number 4, where she would later teach. In the mid-nineteenth century, penmanship was considered an integral part of the education of most young people in the United States.[1]

In *Friendship*, Schmahl displayed her penmanship as if on the pages of an open book, supported by musical instruments and flora and crowned by a simple bird. The objects and the writing were likely created with the same instrument, the steel pen, which came into widespread use in the second quarter of the nineteenth century.[2] The calligraphy is a form of Copperplate, or Roundhead, script, a simple legible script promoted in one of the first American calligraphy treatises, *The Art of Writing*, published by John Jenkins of Boston in 1791.[3]

In *Select Sentences*, Schmahl practiced two distinctly different scripts. The proverbs that fill the center of the work are written in Copperplate and are decorated by flourishes that, drawn after the completion of the text and free from the letterforms, serve as ornamentation. The larger script encircling the central text is similar to Fraktur writing, a style popularized by the Pennsylvania German.[4] Through these works, Matilda Schmahl demonstrated her talent and her education, fulfilling one of the proverbs in *Select Sentences* that "a fair piece of writing is a speaking picture."

GGS

268 Matilda Elizabeth
Schmahl

FRIENDSHIP, c. 1852

Ink and iron gall ink on beige (1), medium weight (1), smooth wove paper

6 5/16 x 8 3/16

Signed in ink in design u.r.: M.E. Schmahl

Gift of William B. Miller (PA 1935) in recognition of the 25th anniversary of the Addison Gallery of American Art

1957.19.1

270 Matilda Elizabeth Schmahl

SELECT SENTENCES, c.1852

Ink and iron gall ink on beige (1),
medium weight (1), slightly textured (1)
wove ledger paper

6 3/8 x 8

Signed in ink in design l.c.: Matilda E.
Schmahl.

Gift of William B. Miller (PA 1935) in
recognition of the 25th anniversary of the
Addison Gallery of American Art

1957.19.2

Select Sentences.

Folly commonly punishes itself. Youth should re-
spect seniority. Innocence is a never failing beauty. Vanity and presumption ruin many a promising youth. Be slow in choosing friends, yet slower
in changing them. Learning is the ornament of youth and the comfort of age. Prefer
sound argument to vain wit. A fair piece of writing is a speaking picture. Make pro-
vision for want in time of plenty. Flattery tends more to amuse than to instruct us.
Man has much to learn and but a short time to live. Laziness is commonly pun-
ished with want. Sincerity is the bond of friendship. Contented not for honors
of which you are undeserving. Cultivate nothing of thy absent or
speak as a friend. Hope is the anchor of the soul.

Matilda L. Schmidt.

271

BORN
10 October 1878
Maidsville, West Virginia

DIED
1956
Morgantown, West Virginia

After a year of study in Paris with the Cubist masters Fernand Léger and Albert Gleizes, Blanche Lazzell returned to the United States in 1924 and entered the mature phase of her work: a continuous exploration of balance and rhythm in form and space through serial compositions.[1] Produced at the very start of this period, the four drawings shown here illustrate Lazzell's rigorous experimentation with the Golden Section.[2] Taught by Gleizes as a foundation for Cubist structure in his sessions with students like Lazzell, this formula is best known for its influence in the architecture of ancient Egyptian, Greek, and Renaissance traditions.[3]

The simplicity of the formula, in which all sections of a whole increase or decrease in size by the same harmonious proportion, provided Lazzell with a rigid enough organizing principle to which she could add her own twists. Her effort to adhere to the harmony of proportional shifts can be seen in the erased and corrected lengths of the rectangles that anchor the four drawings. To this consistent format, Lazzell introduced a rotation of planes and variation in pattern (a spectrum of hatches, dots, grids, lines, and fill) to define a layered space of distinct surfaces. The reverberation between the stable mathematical structure, the winding planes, and the broken patterns of surface give Lazzell's works of this era a formal strength from which she went on to produce series in other media. Through her later oils, batiks, rug designs, monotypes, and most notably woodblock prints, she continued to explore variations in color, as well as pattern, to define the planes of her compositions.[4]

JM

Blanche Lazzell

Untitled, c. 1924

Graphite on cream (2), thin (2), smooth wove paper

10 9/16 x 8 5/16

Unsigned

Gift of Martin and Harriette Diamond

1995.58

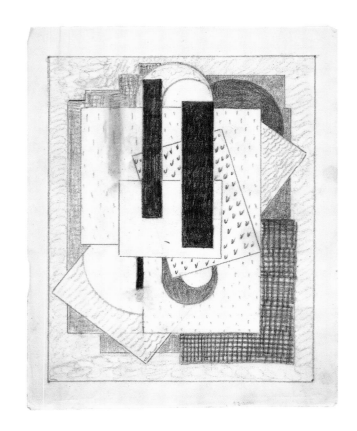

274   Blanche Lazzell
Untitled, c. 1924

Graphite on cream (2), thin (2), smooth
wove paper
10 9/16 x 8 3/8
Unsigned
Gift of Martin and Harriette Diamond
1995.59

Untitled, c. 1924

Graphite on cream (2), thin (2), smooth
wove paper
10 1/2 x 8 5/16
Unsigned
Gift of Martin and Harriette Diamond
1995.60

Untitled, c. 1924

Graphite on cream (2), thin (2), smooth
wove paper

10 9/16 x 8 5/16

Unsigned

Gift of Martin and Harriette Diamond

1995.61

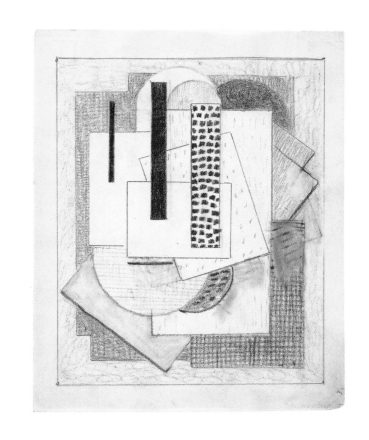

BORN
11 December 1890
Centerville, Wisconsin

DIED
24 April 1976
Basel, Switzerland

This flickering white maze of verticals, horizontals, sharp angles, and layered planes captures the soft electric grid of a system. The title, *Lines of a City*, is a cue for understanding Mark Tobey's abstraction of what he called "the frenetic rhythms of the modern city"[1]: a map of pulsing traffic, a network of neon lights, a layered cityscape of skyscrapers, the constant buzz of urban energy.

While they suggest such multiple connotations, Tobey's lines also reflect some systems that influenced his artistic impulses and distinguished him from his New York contemporaries: traditional calligraphy and the Baha'i religion.[2] His study of East Asian medieval scripts and ornament evolved into his own "white writing," which the artist Lyonel Feininger described as a unique "handwriting," attuned to the dynamism of the modern West.[3] Weaving both spontaneous and controlled strokes into an interconnected linear network, he developed a surface rhythm of tension and immediacy: soft and sharp, in and out, expanding and contracting.[4] Tobey characterized this sense of his compositions as a unified and continuous breathing mesh as a consequence of his Baha'i faith:

> I've been influenced by the Baha'i religion which...is based on the theory that man will gradually come to understand the unity of the world and the oneness of mankind. It teaches...that science and religion are the two great powers which must be balanced....
> I feel my work has been influenced by these beliefs. I've tried to decentralize and interpenetrate so that all parts of a painting are of related value.[5]

Guided both by his belief in a leveling, universal interconnectedness and by traditions of symbolic mark-making, Tobey applied these systems of expression to his reflections of the American city.

JM

276

Mark Tobey

LINES OF THE CITY, 1945

Opaque watercolor on brown, very thick smooth paper board

17 7/8 x 21 3/4

Signed in opaque watercolor l.r.: Tobey / 45

Inscribed in graphite on verso c.:
Lines of the City

Bequest of Edward Wales Root

1957.36

BORN
15 June 1914
Ramnicul-Sarat, Romania

DIED
12 May 1999
New York, New York

Style for Saul Steinberg is a language, a disguise to be used at will. It is an interrogation of appearances, a search for reality, which, like nesting Russian dolls, may not exist. As Steinberg said, "The tradition of an artist is to become someone else."[1] He changed styles as one might change clothes, creating appearances to suit the occasion. Instead of being imprisoned by a signature style, style for him was freedom, freedom to create in a multiplicity of genres simultaneously.

In 1954 Steinberg published his book *The Passport*, a work which had been in development since 1948. As critic Harold Rosenberg wrote, "*Passport* [was] a book about: FALSE DOCUMENTS, PASSPORTS, DIPLOMAS, CERTIFICATES, FALSE PHOTOGRAPHS, (WITH FALSE AUTOGRAPHS), FALSE ETCHINGS, FALSE WINE LABELS...."[2] The Addison's *Diploma* (1955) is of the sort published in this volume and is among the finest of the genre.[3] This impressive and authoritative-looking document confers all the rights and privileges recorded therein—none. The seals, emblem, signatures (with their calligraphic flourishes) appear to be real. Upon close observation one sees that they are devoid of content. Not surprisingly, *Diploma* suggests connections to many styles. The marks on this paper are abstractions disguised as information. As such they establish a link with abstract calligraphic works of the period. Like any good forger, Steinberg's technique is by necessity consummate. His *trompe l'oeil* effects are worthy descendents of nineteenth-century artists such as William Harnett. Its ironic quality heralds the critique of Pop and the disdain for authority of Fluxus.

In *Diploma* individuality is in fact hidden—both the person receiving and bestowing it. The signatures conceal; they do not reveal or validate. The *Diploma* shows that fact (or the semblance thereof) can be fiction. And that our culture increasingly prizes style over substance.

ADW

278 Saul Steinberg

DIPLOMA, 1955

Ink, foil stamp, paper stamp, postal stamp, and stamp impression on cream (3), moderately thick, smooth wove paper

21 15/16 x 34

Unsigned

Museum purchase

1959.58

BORN
16 September 1935
Quincy, Massachusetts

As Carl Andre explained, *Passport* is a memento of passage through his early history and a record of evolution toward his mature conceptual and creative practice:

> For some unconscious reason I gathered together these excerpts which reflect my state of mind at the time and things which I was interested in then…because I had reached the point when I left wood carving behind and had started using separate elements and it was a time when I was going onto some new things and leaving some old things behind. So *Passport* is I suppose my own visa stamp on my own progress as an artist.[1]

Completed when Andre was just twenty-five years old, the bound volume catalogues his personal influences and betrays his innate attraction to materials, and his proclivity for sequencing them. Each unique page preserves a sample of symbol and texture: a foil cigarette wrapper saved from Andre's eye-opening Europe tour in 1954 precedes a swatch of embroidered fabric used by his new wife in their just-made wedding bedspread; a manipulated postcard of an old master painting collected while visiting the Frick Collection with fellow artist Frank Stella leads to a photograph of Andre's own wood sculpture by his close friend, Hollis Frampton; samples of his concrete poetry, built-up patterns of words like "green" or "rain," echo his designs with stamped ornaments in repeating units.[2]

Collectively, *Passport* avoids dilution into a narrative progression. Instead, each page maintains a distinctive character, most accurately reflecting the appreciation for and sensitivity to "the specific" that would characterize Andre's forthcoming sculpture. Antecedent to his seminal horizontal configurations of sequenced units that resulted in his one-man exhibition at the Solomon R. Guggenheim Museum in 1970,[3] *Passport* granted Andre license to pursue those landmark explorations.

J M

280

Carl Andre

PASSPORT, 1960

Collage, graphite, and ink on 95 bound sheets of cream (2), medium weight (2), slightly textured (1) wove paper; unbound cover sheet: ink on cream (3), medium weight (2), smooth graph paper

11 x 8 1/2 x 7/8

Signed and inscribed in ink on cover page u.c.: PASSPORT / CARL ANDRE / 1960; COLLECTION: VIRGINIA DWAN; l.c.: DWAN GALLERY / SETH SIEGELAUB / NEW YORK / 1969; inscribed in ink on verso u.c.: PASSPORT IS ONE OF A SET OF / SEVEN BOOKS IN A UNIFORM / MANUSCRIPT EDITION OF 36 / SIGNED AND NUMBERED SETS / SET NUMBER ___ OF 36 SETS; l.c.: © CARL ANDRE 1969

Gift of the artist (PA 1953)

1983.35.1-96

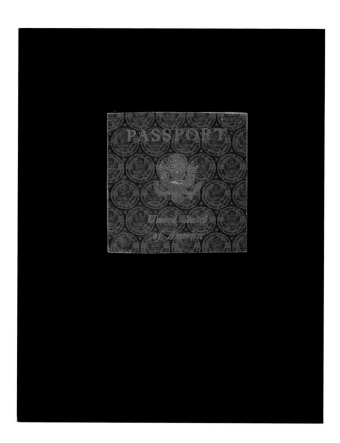

FAR LEFT
Cover
Embossed paper on linen and paper
on linen and board
1983.35

RIGHT, TOP TO BOTTOM
Page 12 [Hollis Frampton photograph
of Carl Andre with sculptures]
Gelatin silver print mounted on paper
1983.35.12

Page 13 [Red column with border]
Collage and ink on paper
1983.35.13

greengreengreengreengreengreengreengreengreengreengreengreengreengreengreen...

[Page 14: The word "green" typed 784 times in columns of 14 x 56]

282 Carl Andre
Page 14 [The word "green" typed 784 times
in columns of 14 x 56]
Typewriter ink on paper
1983.35.14

Page 18 [Reproduction of Bronzino's
Lodovico Capponi with red dots]
Ink on collage on paper
1983.35.18

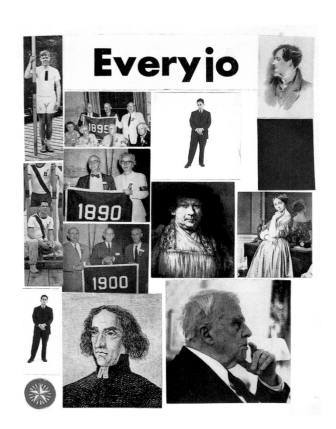

Page 22 [Everyjo, assorted portraits]
Collage on paper
1983.35.22

Page 37 [Sculptures]
Gelatin silver print mounted on paper
1983.35.37

BORN
22 March 1912
Maklin, Saskatchewan, Canada

Since the production of her first mature work in the late 1950s, line and drawing have been essential to the art of Agnes Martin. Line has typically manifested in quiet, humble grids. The grid came from an experience of hiking in the mountains of New Mexico and suddenly coming upon a plain, when she had a revelation about the expansiveness of the horizon and the line it created.

Untitled (1960) was made when she had first realized the grid. The square format (in her drawings typically eight by eight inches) is commonly considered by modern artists to be a nonhierarchical structure. She wrote, "My formats are square but the grids never are absolutely square; they are rectangular, a little bit off the square, making a sort of contradiction, a dissonance.... When I cover the square surface with rectangles, it lightens the weight of the square, destroys its power."[1] In *Untitled* the grid itself is softened further by the way it is drawn. The spare lines are ever so slightly tremulous. The delicate wash of white pigment submerges the fragile grid. Her use of an overall pattern gives the work a oneness, as if the grid had been hiding within, waiting for the artist to discover it, springing from the very material of the paper itself. The drawing exists as a simple fact of life, like the markings of a stone or the veins of a leaf. It is not from nature but of nature. It is discovery as much as creation.

Untitled is an affirmation, but also self-effacement; individuality is seemingly subsumed by the grid. She wrote: "I can see my ego and see its intentions...it is the same as all nature, impotent in the process of dissolution of ego, of itself."[2]

ADW

284 Agnes B. Martin

UNTITLED, 1960

Ink, watercolor, and graphite on cream (3), thin (2), smooth wove paper

11 3/4 x 11 15/16

Unsigned

Inscribed in graphite l.l.: 12

Gift of Frank Stella (PA 1954), Addison Art Drive

1991.46

BORN
10 February 1942
Bronx, New York

Since 1967, Lawrence Weiner's interest in sculpture's potential effect on space has resulted in installations not of objects, but of poetically curt wall texts that describe sculptural gestures. These descriptions stand alone, without the need for a physical manifestation or concrete action.[1] Through stenciled phrases, such as A WALL CRATERED BY A SINGLE SHOTGUN BLAST or A CUP OF SEA WATER POURED UPON THE FLOOR,[2] he evokes explicit yet indeterminate images of how space could be affected or displaced by matter over time (with permanent scars of scattershot holes or a slick pool of evaporating liquid, for example).

Before Weiner devoted himself to these language-defined projects, he explored the nature of sculpture through paintings and drawings of an equally terse and ordered aesthetic. His series of "grid time drawings" marks the moment in his career where he began to map the terrain between physical, abstract, and conceptual definitions of sculptured space.[3] In this untitled piece of 1967 Weiner delineated a rectangular plane on a sheet of commercial graph paper, and filled the area with a slanting cascade of forms that fall in loose rows of seven, as if days on a calendar slipping askew. Each of these slightly chipped forms is made up of units with proportions of 9 to 5. The m-shaped marks that build up these units Weiner has defined as "mass as represented by an arbitrary marking of time."[4] Without necessarily being a literal abstraction of familiar monthly and daily representations of time, Weiner's drawing can expand our conceptual understanding of the time that fills our days into marks that represent concrete form. Such works would eventually lead the artist to ask the question: if time can be the medium for a sculpture, why not "language and the materials referred to"?[5]

JM

Lawrence Weiner

286

Untitled, 1967

Ink on cream (3), thin (2), smooth wove graph paper

10 15/16 x 8 1/2

Signed in graphite l.l.: L. Weiner–1967–New York

Gift of Lucy Lippard (AA 1954), Addison Art Drive

1991.129

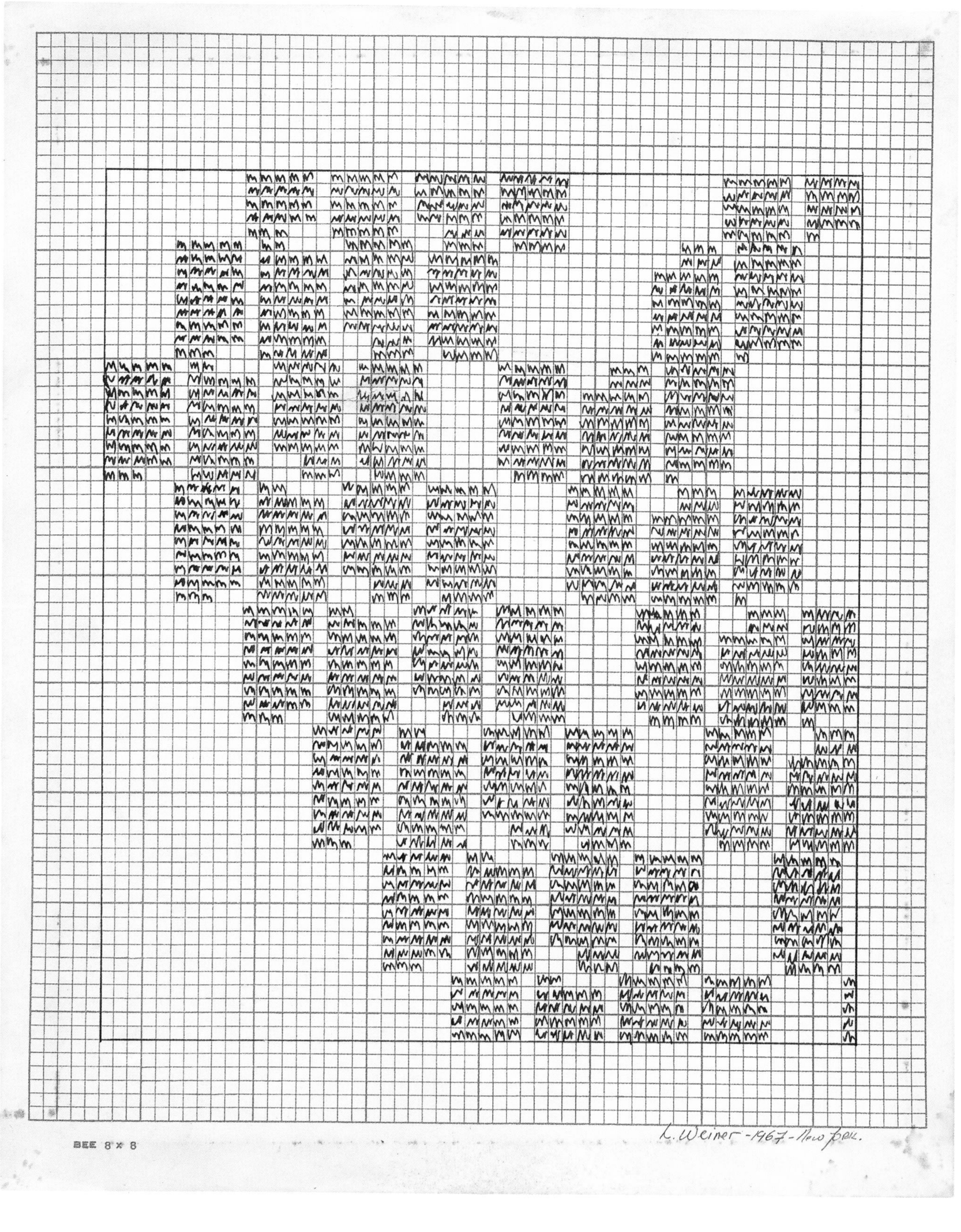
BEE 8 x 8
L. Weiner -1967- New York

BORN
28 December 1941
Long Beach, California

"I became intrigued by the idea of visual clues...the way Sherlock Holmes managed to reconstruct a plot from obscure visual evidence."

—Barry Le Va[1]

Sprawled across these graph paper grids are tangled, scattered clues to Barry Le Va's earliest sculptural investigations of location in space and action over time. Like floorplans of a crime scene—where trip wires have been tugged and threads snarled, or where white powder has been spilled and lines blurred—the drawings mark the coordinates of chaotic twists imposed on a space of order. Directly related to Le Va's seminal installations of strewn felt strips and spilled chalk dust, they serve as lasting blueprints of his ever-evolving spatial concepts, what he describes as "plan views."[2]

Initially trained in mathematics and architecture, Le Va earned an MFA in Los Angeles in 1967 and then spent two years teaching art courses in Minneapolis before going to New York in 1970. During this period of aesthetic shifts and personal self-discovery, he sought to incorporate the expansive scale of Abstract Expressionism, the theoretical structure and material directness of Minimalism, and the intellectual rigor of Conceptualist questioning into his own form of sculpture-as-evidence. He asked, "How could one deal with what sculpture does to the physical body of the viewer, without making an object?"[3] Le Va sought answers not in precious materials or perfect form, but in evocative configurations of raw ingredients. The resulting floorscapes (felt, dusted flour, broken glass, spilled oil, unraveled paper towels, aligned ball bearings) were essentially two-dimensional patterns of activity—delicate sifting, explosive violence, geometric dispersion, organic accumulation—whose physical presence prompted viewer's bloodhound perception, detection, and deduction about the motivation, sequence, and timing of their making. As accomplices to his sculptural conundrums, Le Va's drawings chart patterns but defy solution.

JM

288

Barry Le Va

TANGLE DISTRIBUTION, 1967

Ink and graphite on cream (1), medium weight (2), smooth graph paper

17 1/8 x 22 1/8

Signed in ink l.l.: B. Le Va 1967

Inscribed in ink l.r.: tangle distribution / approx 35'x55' / strips to particles –; c.r.: grey felt / 3/4" x 24'

Gift of Mel Bochner

1983.62

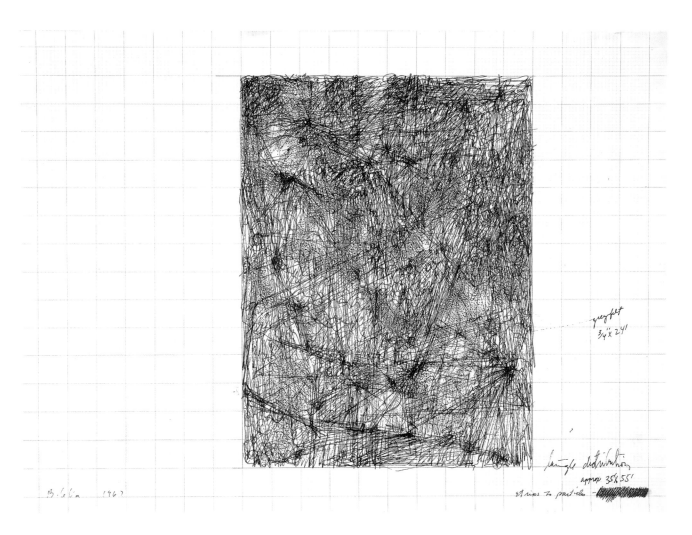

grayfelt
3/4" x 24'

triangle distribution
approx 35' x 55'

strips to particles — ▨▨▨▨▨

B. LaVa   1967

290 Barry Le Va
25 CHALK LINES, 25 CHALK WIPINGS,
1968

Ink and acrylic on cream (1), medium weight
(1), smooth graph paper

17 x 22 1/16

Signed in ink l.l.: B. Le Va 1968

Inscribed in ink l.r.: 25 chalk lines / 25 chalk
wipings

Gift of Klaus Kertess (PA 1958),
Addison Art Drive

1992.5

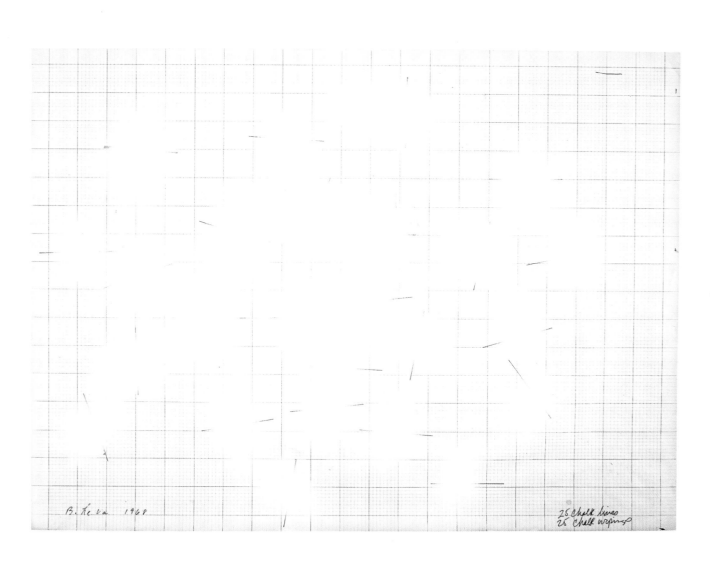

B. Leka 1968

25 Chalk lines
25 Chalk wipings

291

BORN
28 January 1929
Stockholm, Sweden

I am for an art that takes its form from the lines of life itself, that twists and extends and accumulates and spits and rips...I am for art you can sit on. I am for art you can pick your nose with or stub your toes on.

—Claes Oldenburg, 1961[1]

Here is the secret ingredient of Oldenburg's work: the ability to pair and praise life's twisted contradictions—the literal and exaggerated, the charming and disgusting. His works reflect a world of conceptual "what-ifs," where small can be huge, holes become thruways, and a giant nose becomes a tunnel inset in tree-topped, rolling cheek-hills.

Seldom without a notebook, for more than fifty years Oldenburg—who nearly abandoned art for journalism—has incessantly drawn what he calls "the *complete* landscape,....(some of which I imagine)," explaining "I am unable to leave things out, so I compress and superimpose to get a subject I can handle."[2] Curious about why we think bigger is better, he began a series of "proposed monument" drawings in 1965, overlaying images of small-scale objects (including electric fans, ice cream bars, and baked potatoes) onto wide-angled views of New York's cityscape. He eventually went on to fabricate and install sculptural blow-ups of everyday objects (clothespins, buttons, badminton birdies) on public plazas, campuses, and city blocks the world over. Although better known for these colossal monuments, he has affirmed: "Drawing is my basic method. I think of drawing as a form of writing. My concrete images are drawings realized—'monumentalizations.'"[3]

Clearly, this nose need not be "realized" as an actual tunnel; however, the fact that the impossible proposal eventually took form as a handkerchief design is an ironic testament to the witty convergence of impractical and practical in Oldenburg's Pop art explorations.[4]

JM

292

Claes Oldenburg

DESIGN FOR A TUNNEL ENTRANCE
IN THE FORM OF A NOSE, 1968

Crayon on cream (1), thick, smooth wove paper

22 7/8 x 28 15/16

Signed in crayon l.r.: CO 68

Inscribed in crayon l.c.: Nose

Gift of Donnelley Erdman (PA 1956)

1977.185

Nose

CD 68

BORN
31 March 1937
New York, New York

In the late 1960s, the sculptor Robert Grosvenor explored the sensations of gravitational force and weightlessness in ceiling installations: massive beams of wood and steel suspended above the floor from a single brace point. In the presence of these large-scale hanging sculptures (some forty feet long) one might experience the contradictory perceptions of buoyant levitation and a deadly heavy mass—a physical paradox, irreconcilable with our comfortably familiar understanding of spatial relationships. As described by Robert Smithson in 1966, Grosvenor's "suspended structural surfaces cancel out the notion of weight" and, as if frozen in air, "reverse the orientation of matter within the solid-state of inorganic time."[1]

Grosvenor often recorded his investigations of a sculpture's gravitational presence through drawings: cross-sectioned views that implied the space between ceiling and floor in which a suspended mass might float or sit. Within an area bound by two parallel horizontal lines, he would insert a form (often made out of layers of cleanly cut black tape or masking tape)[2] to define the mass of the hanging piece on the paper's surface.

In this untitled drawing of 1969, Grosvenor's signature focus is poetically inverted: instead of presenting us with the massive presence of a solid structure with applied tape, he left us with the absence, or "negative presence," of this form within the space it occupies. Removing the tape that had masked a surface softly rubbed with graphite, Grosvenor created a floating phantom out of the paper's whiteness in a space defined by the haze of drawing material. Here, he captures an image that hovers between the representation of a solid in a void and a void in a solid—of suspended gravity in both senses of the phrase.

JM

294 Robert Grosvenor

Untitled, 1969

Graphite and ink on cream (2),
medium weight (1), very smooth, Navajo
Ledger Mohawk wove paper

14 x 16 7/8

Signed in graphite l.r.: R. Grosvenor '69

Gift of Lucy Lippard (AA 1954),
Addison Art Drive

1991.135

295

BORN
10 October 1943
Houston, Texas

Fill-in-the-blank forms. Much more than neutral information-gathering tools, they are charged with potential connotations: Innocent records of the truth? Invasive devices of bureaucratic control? Blank slates for "mad-lib" subversion? In his mock documents, Frederick Barthelme exploited the form's function, using it as a potent means to question, undercut, and (ironically) affirm the validity of "making art."

While the choice of typewriter ink on cheap photo-offset sheets gives each work an intentional institutional blandness, their essential content is derived from the sarcastic candor of Barthelme's typed texts. As literal substitutions for art-making, Barthelme's works embody the search for an alternative to the precious object that spurred Conceptual art's rise by the late 1960s. At the time, art magazines were the arena for heated debates about the shifting nature and function of art, from a commodity to be bought and owned to an idea to be understood and distributed

freely.[1] Barthelme credits their influence: "Magazines became my teachers, the writers [including Lucy Lippard], the artists making art then [including Joseph Kosuth]."[2] Between the lines of his aversion to "art" is an attraction to its power to communicate. Instead of making art products, language-based conceptualists executed theory through "statements." By 1967, Barthelme was working in New York with such artists as Kosuth, Lawrence Weiner, and Robert Barry, and by 1969–70, his Substitution works were shown in landmark conceptual exhibitions.[3]

After activist Seth Siegelaub's 1968 "published exhibition" *Untitled (Xerox Book)* paved the way for the distribution of Conceptual art in book form, Barthelme experimented with books as "art objects." However, his proclivity for language-based expression eventually drew him toward purely literary interests, and soon after leaving New York, he "decided to think of books as literary objects rather than art containers."[4] Instead of making visual art, Barthelme now writes widely acclaimed fiction.

J M

Frederick Barthelme

INSTEAD OF MAKING ART I,
SUBSTITUTION: 9, DATE: OCTOBER
26, 1969, 1969

Typewriter ink and collage on photo-offset
printed cream (1), medium weight (1)
smooth paper

11 x 8 1/2

Unsigned

Gift of Lucy Lippard (AA 1954),
Addison Art Drive

1991.133

DATE: October 26, 1969

SUBSTITUTION: 9

INSTEAD OF MAKING ART I cut this
picture out of a magazine (Science Journal,

October 1969, Volume 5A, Number 4, p. 95).

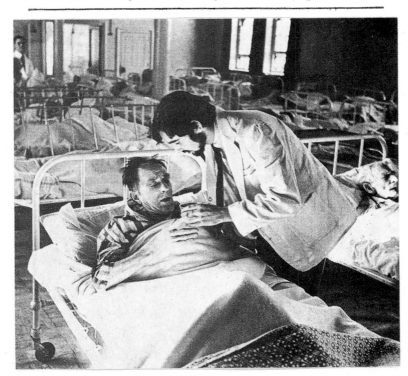

Frederick Barthelme

INSTEAD OF MAKING ART I,
SUBSTITUTION: 27, DATE: MARCH 12,
1970, 1970

Typewriter ink on photo-offset printed cream
(3), medium weight (1), smooth paper

11 x 8 1/2

Unsigned

Gift of Lucy Lippard (AA 1954),
Addison Art Drive

1991.134

DATE: March 12, 1970
SUBSTITUTION: 27

INSTEAD OF MAKING ART I ____filled____
out this form.

_____

_____

_____

299

Although as humble and straightforward in its composition as many of his trademark modular floor sculptures, Carl Andre's *Working Map: India Triennale Piece* is an anomaly and represents an unusual synthesis within his mature work. As a "map" of his only documented piece of non-repeating color units, the drawing is one of a kind. Using abbreviated words as two-dimensional building blocks for a three-dimensional visual idea, the drawing is also significant in that it unites Andre's two creative interests—constructing concrete poetry on paper and sculpture in space—as never before.

True to the artist's inscription, *Working Map* charts the piece he made in New Delhi for the second India Triennial in 1971: *The Life and Revival of Art Painting in North America*. The piece is catalogued as thirty bars of modeling clay in various colors (each 1 x 1 x 6 inches) set end-to-end to create a floor piece approximately 180 inches long; only the drawing reveals *how* and *which* colors were aligned, beginning ReD, ORange, BRown, YEllow, PInk.[1] Though raw, unmolded clay rods may be as full of "potential" as the metal plates, wood beams, stone slabs, and other manufactured yet culturally unshaped materials that Andre preferred for his sculpture,[2] their bold, suggestive color, pliable nature, and free-form sequence are as incongruous with his work of the period as they are congruous with his poetic compositions of the late 1950s through 1960s.

Just as he had laced letters through grids on graph paper, or repeatedly typed color words into textured shapes in his word poems (see page 14 of *Passport* on p. 282),[3] in *Working Map* Andre strung together what could be read as an American melting-pot lineup of skin tones, but what he might argue to be simply the physical fact of color juxtaposed.[4]

J M

300 Carl Andre

WORKING MAP: INDIA TRIENNALE
PIECE, 1971

Marker ink on cream (3), medium weight (2), smooth graph paper

5 3/8 x 8 1/2

Unsigned

Inscribed in ink l.c.: WORKING MAP / INDIA TRIENNALE PIECE / @ 1971

Gift of Lucy Lippard (AA 1954), Addison Art Drive

1991.132

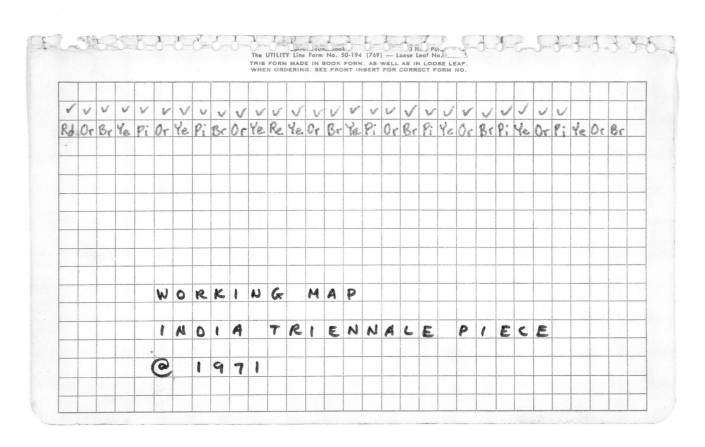

| | ✓ | ✓ | ✓ | ✓ | ✓ | ✓ | ✓ | ✓ | ✓ | ✓ | ✓ | ✓ | ✓ | ✓ | ✓ | ✓ | ✓ | ✓ | ✓ | ✓ | ✓ | ✓ | ✓ | ✓ | ✓ | ✓ | ✓ | ✓ | ✓ | | |
| | Rd | Or | Br | Ye | Pi | Or | Ye | Pi | Br | Or | Ye | Re | Ye | Or | Br | Ye | Pi | Or | Br | Pi | Ye | Or | Br | Pi | Ye | Or | Pi | Ye | Or | Br | | |

WORKING MAP

INDIA TRIENNALE PIECE

© 1971

BORN
9 September 1928
Hartford, Connecticut

This work could arguably be defined as a record of a collaborative exchange between the artist Sol LeWitt, countless United States postal workers, and the recipient and agent of his written instructions, Lucy Lippard.[1] LeWitt defined the format, schedule, and set of conceptual terms to begin this cycle of transactions, yet he depended entirely on the faithful hands of others to fully realize the work. Testing his trust in the mail service in New York, he sent Lippard ten serial-numbered postcards during the month of October 1971.

Although the printed captions on the cards indicate that LeWitt chose wide-ranging images (from the Yale Bowl in New Haven, Conn., to the birthplace of Lyndon B. Johnson in Stonewall, Tex., to horseback riding in Tennessee, to the skyline of New York City) perhaps indiscriminately, he also set up visual consistencies within the series. All ten cards are marked with the same stamp in the upper right, the same address in the lower right, his initials and series number on the bottom, and "editing" instructions in the message section below each caption. Choosing control over certain terms, while relishing the lack of control in others, LeWitt could not have known exactly where (or if) his cards would be postmarked or smeared in transit, if they would reach his intended recipient, or how Lippard would follow his directives (in colored or black ink?) if at all. The final mounting of the complete series, with much of the text, and all of the postcards' images obscured, is a testament to the paradoxical relationship of what can and cannot be seen, as well as to what can be produced within systems both certain and uncertain.

JM

302 Sol LeWitt

TEN POSTCARDS, 1971

Ink, marker ink, printed stamp, and postal stamps on postcards mounted on board

19 x 11 13/16

Signed in ink on each card l.c.: SL

Inscribed in ink on each card l.r.:
LUCY LIPPARD / 138 PRINCE / NYC [or]
NEW YORK 10013

Gift of Lucy Lippard (AA 1954),
Addison Art Drive

1991.79

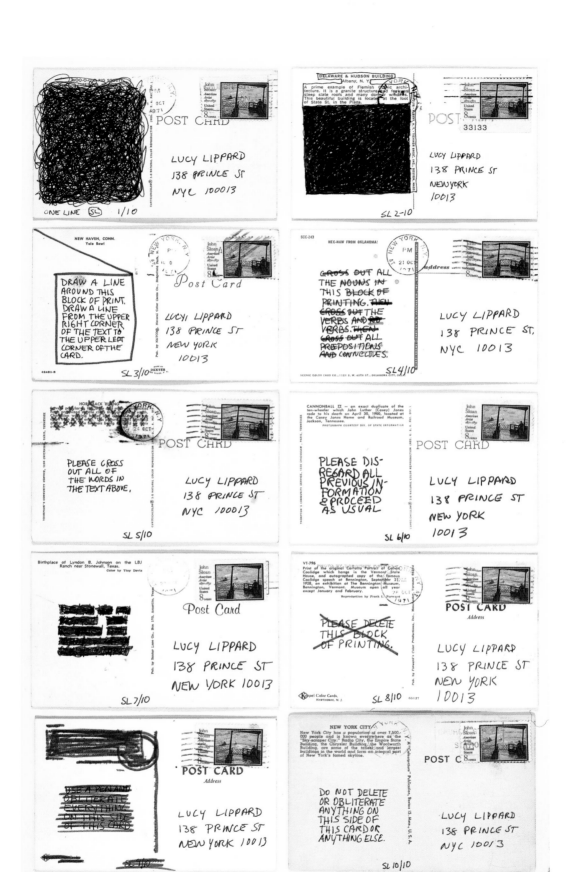

303

BORN
9 September 1928
Hartford, Connecticut

LeWitt's serial mailing *Fifteen Postcards* of 1976 employs the same system of exchange but a different level of control than those he had sent to Lucy Lippard five years earlier.[1] Instead of an interactive invitation to "edit out," this series is a poetic illustration of accumulation. Not only were the fifteen cards numbered sequentially by LeWitt, postmarked daily by the Postal Service, and progressively collected by Lippard, but the drawings themselves are accruals of vertical strokes in color combinations built up on each previously sent iteration.[2] (A close look at the cards reveals LeWitt's text pencil notations under each drawing: "1 yellow vertical," "2 black," "3 red," "4 blue," "1 yellow/2 black," "1 yellow/3 red," "1 yellow/4 blue," and so on.)

While more systematic than LeWitt's earlier postcard series, this work is also more self-reflective and personal in reference both to his own aesthetic explorations and Lippard's, and to a mutual connection with their close friend, the sculptor Eva Hesse, who had died in 1970. Although LeWitt's drawings evidence his emergent signature use of line and primary colors in serial systems, his choice of "not straight" lines was inspired by Hesse, whose quirky organic serial and linear sculptures he encouraged and admired.[3] The cards on which he drew this work and his chosen time to send them would have held a particular resonance for Lippard: all fifteen are announcement cards for an earlier exhibition of drawings by Hesse,[4] on whom Lippard was writing a monograph at the time.[5]

JM

304

Sol LeWitt

FIFTEEN POSTCARDS, 1976

Ink, marker ink, printed stamp, and postal stamps on postcards mounted on board

Unsigned

Inscribed in ink on each card l.r.:
LUCY LIPPARD / 138 PRINCE / NYC 10012

26 1/2 x 13 3/4

Gift of Lucy Lippard (AA 1954),
Addison Art Drive

1991.80

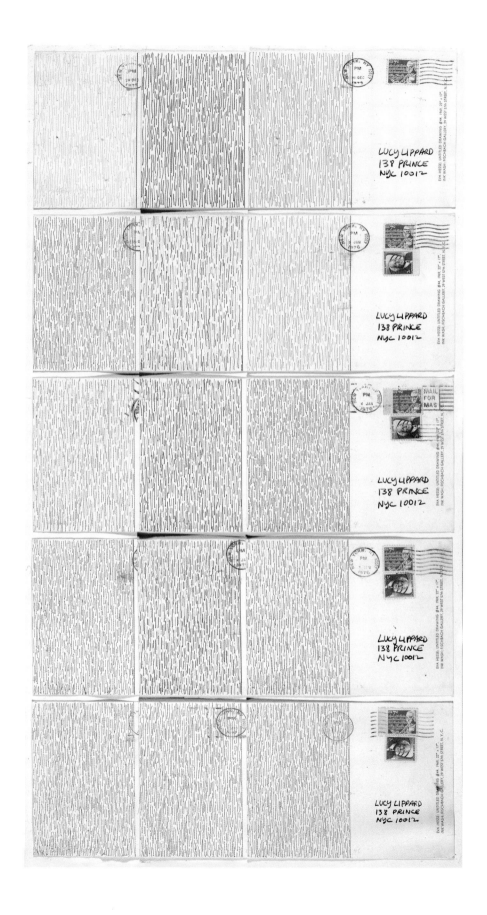

BORN
9 September 1928
Hartford, Connecticut

Since the late 1950s, drawing has been at the heart of Sol LeWitt's creative enterprise, from his earliest pencil and ink studies and the drawings based on the works of old masters such as Piero della Francesca, to his abstract "working drawings" of the early 1960s, to his wall drawings (which had their inception in 1968). LeWitt's drawings on paper represent a touchstone for this process, the carrier of his intuitions, and the playing out of his conceptual project.

For two decades LeWitt's drawings, typically in square format, consisted primarily of lines drawn in ink and pencil in black and the three primary colors. In the 1960s, the lines were straight though variously horizontal, vertical, diagonal, or superimposed. In the early 1970s, he introduced to his vocabulary arcs, circles, and lines that were not straight, were random, or were broken, and he sometimes experimented as well with darker and lighter lines.

The title of this drawing, *Parallel Straight Lines from a Diagonal*, like all of LeWitt's titles, is a description of the work itself. This subtle, evanescent drawing produced in ink and pencil on a sixteen and one-quarter inch square sheet of paper reveals a diagonal from the lower left corner to the upper right corner formed by the juncture of lightly drawn parallel pencil lines on the left and slightly stronger parallel ink lines on the right. What is rather mysterious and paradoxical in this work is the strong presence of the diagonal even though no diagonal line is actually drawn. The work is a visual contradiction about line and shape, substance and dematerialization, presence and absence.

ADW

306 Sol LeWitt

PARALLEL STRAIGHT LINES
FROM A DIAGONAL, 1973

Ink and graphite on white, moderately thick, very smooth wove paper

16 1/4 x 16 1/4

Signed in graphite on verso c.: Sol LeWitt / Jan 18 1973

Inscribed in graphite on verso c.: Parallel lines from a diagonal (Straight) / Left: Pencil Right: Ink (Black)

Partial gift of the artist and partial museum purchase with funds from Mimi Won and anonymous donor

2002.45

307

BORN
12 October 1937
North Tonawanda, New York

From the time of his earliest "area paintings" of the 1960s Robert Mangold was concerned with flatness—the notion that paintings are a surface seen all at once, from one point of view, and as such are distinct from three-dimensional art.[1] His works minimized gesture and largely eliminated references to nature. He created uninflected surfaces and the application of paint was to be "matter of fact."

In 1968 and '69 Mangold produced a series of paintings referred to as the "circle paintings" or the W, V, X series, which considered the relation of fragment to whole. These irregular-shape acrylic paintings consist of sections of joined Masonite panels whose internal divisions create linear W's, V's, and X's and which anticipate this untitled drawing. It reflects the artist's preoccupation with fragment and whole—the spaces of the shapes themselves and the spaces created by the

shapes. The X creates a single quasi-emblematic form—"combination surface shape rather than an object." The work's sparseness reflects the essentials of his ideas. The drawings of this time "were done to work out ideas more quickly than would have been possible in a painting…the problems being dealt with were more about structure than color and surface." Hence, it is no surprise that "this is a unique image that was never developed into a painting."[2]

This drawing relates to a group of paintings of linear graphite squares on geometric canvases, in particular *Four Squares in and out of a Circle (Tan)* (1975). Significantly, it anticipates some of his most celebrated works "that came much later—the +, X, and frame paintings, 1980–84."[3] The X paintings are made from three joined canvases positioned on the wall in a manner suggesting an X. This drawing may be the artist's earliest conception of their radical structure.

ADW

308 Robert Mangold

Untitled, 1973

Graphite on cream (2), moderately thick, smooth wove paper

14 x 11

Signed in graphite l.l.: R. Mangold 1973

Gift of the artist

2000.55

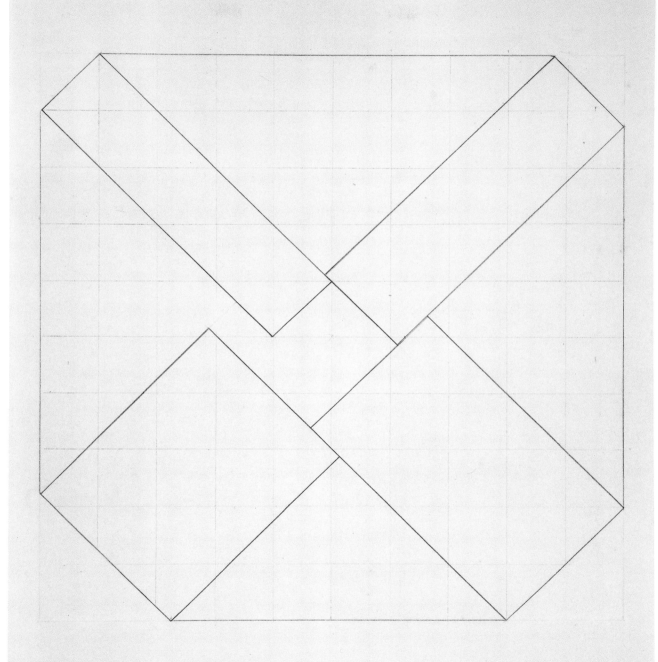

R. Mangold 1973

BORN
10 February 1940
Borrego Springs, California

To record a true impression of place on paper, one might limn a detailed image. However, as accurate and identifiable as the resulting picture may be, it is a translation to the realm of two-dimensional illusion. Michelle Stuart's records of place approach this traditional drawing practice with a conceptual twist. Instead of drawing an image, Stuart opts for making a concrete physical connection: site-specific rubbings. Her works are literally re-collected impressions, integrating into paper the textures and tones of the raw earth, replete with the histories of nature and culture it has rooted and sifted through.

Stuart recently explained, "It isn't to prove anything that one collects and/or re-collects from [a] place. It is to commit to memory. Memory is a beginning, a form of natural history."[1] Stuart recalled that *Little Turtle Pond,* *Kingston, N.Y.,* was part of a series of much larger works titled *Turtle Pond, Kingston, New York,* from a site she "found particularly enchanting."[2] In her early practice (before she started adding information through photographs or aligning grids), Stuart simply oriented works through location names.[3] Stuart clarified the process: "The paper was pounded with gravel and earth from that site,....and then rubbed (with my hands) so that the residue permeated the paper and became part of it, then I put a layer of micro-fine graphite over all to bring out the indentations. [It is] possible the veil of graphite was superimposed because there was a veil of foggy air over the pond at the time that I was there."[4] Produced both aggressively and gently, her inflected surfaces are at once scintillating and serene, and suggest magnitudes of allusions, from the night sky to the universe of the cellular.

JM

Michelle Stuart

310

LITTLE TURTLE POND, KINGSTON, N.Y., 1974

Graphite and soil on white, moderately thick, rough (1) wove paper

14 x 11

Signed in graphite on verso u.l.: Michelle / Stuart / 1974

Gift of Lucy Lippard (AA 1954), Addison Art Drive

1991.126

BORN
23 August 1940
Pittsburgh, Pennsylvania

As this elegant drawing illustrates, Mel Bochner is a master of tangency and balance who explores points of connection at their most pivotal and provocative. Since the 1960s, he has investigated the space where thinking and seeing—the conceptual and perceptual—meet and merge through visual executions of geometric relationships, numeric sequences, serial progressions, and systems of measurement in the form of installations, sculptures, paintings, and drawings. Approaching all media with rigor and sensitivity, Bochner especially appreciates how only drawing "couples a directness of means with an ease of revision," creating a space of uninhibited freedom that can absorb and record "the results of an investigation into the nature of relationships."[1]

Via Santo Spirito is one of Bochner's several "color-shape" drawings inspired by the rich influences of Italy. A visit to a Pythagorean temple prompted his sculptural and drawn investigations of the great mathematician's universal theorem, which dictates a triangle's shape through the area of three tangent squares.[2] Bochner's initial interest in paradoxical discrepancies in the theory's illustration soon gave way to a visual captivation with the relationships between color, shape, and space.[3] In Italy's art-saturated atmosphere, Bochner observed that the sanguine and black in the region's architecture and painting seeped into his palette, and that the irregular, non-orthogonal layout of cities like Siena encouraged his own break from the grid toward more dynamic radial compositions.[4] The sharp edges between his geometries gave way to streaks and smears, open revelations of process and decision-making that echo the pentimenti, or revised marks, in old master drawings or frescoes.[5] Bochner titled *Via Santo Spirito* for the location of its making, his studio's street in Florence, itself named after a nearby church designed by renowned architect Brunelleschi,[6] an early Renaissance master of tangency and balance.

JM

312

Mel Bochner

VIA SANTO SPIRITO, 1975

Crayon, graphite, and charcoal on cream (2), moderately thick, rough (1) wove paper

24 5/8 x 18

Signed in graphite l.r.: BOCHNER 1975

Inscribed in graphite on verso u.l.: TITLE; VIA SANTO SPIRITO / DATE; 1975 (FLORENCE) / SIZE: 24 5/8 x 18″ / MEDIUM: CHARCOAL, PENCIL, CONTÉ CRAYON / ON PAPER / PROVENANCE: ARTIST TO BARRY LEVA

Gift of Barry Le Va

1983.63

BOCHNER 1975

BORN
2 December 1930
New Bremen, Ohio

Since the 1960s, Jim Melchert's career has encompassed the roles of artist, educator (as professor of ceramics at the San Francisco Art Institute and sculpture at U.C. Berkeley), and administrator (as director of the Visual Arts Program of the National Endowment for the Arts and the American Academy at Rome). An early student of renowned ceramist Peter Voulkos, Melchert first engaged in unprecedented conceptual explorations in clay that helped redefine this traditional medium. However, during Conceptual art's height in the Bay Area through the 1970s, he turned from clay to slide projections, performance, and drawings, making a clean break from the physical to the experiential.[1]

In this period, fascinated by the "notion of circular communication" whereby "a message goes to the viewer and the viewer projects back into it," Melchert created a series of drawings that leave room for such dialogue.[2]

Convinced that "commonplace [things] have a magic of their own once we find a way of getting to it," in the Addison's two drawings Melchert paired ghostly silhouettes of evocative objects—snapshots and letters found in flea markets—with his own notations about their significance or mystery.[3] (The combination of trace and text creates potential readings far more elusive and less obvious than the rubbings of ancient Japanese stele that originally inspired the project.) While intrigued by the idea of an object's poetic aura, his ceramist's "feel" for material presence also influenced the making of these drawings: "I always discovered something about the object when I did the rubbing. I'd thought I'd understood an object, but its physicality always had something more to say." As if delicate X-ray "filters," the graphite impressions in these works prompt inspection and introspection, like overturned cards in the childhood game of Concentration that test our sense of memory and association.

JM

314

Jim Melchert

SNAPSHOTS OF BRONCO RIDERS
AT A RODEO ARRANGED SO
THAT THE HORIZON LINE IN EACH PAIR
IS CONTINUOUS AND PARALLEL
WITH THE OTHER., 1976

Graphite on cream (1), thin (2), smooth wove paper

23 15/16 x 20

Signed in graphite l.r.: J. Melchert 4–76

Inscribed in graphite as image: Snapshots of bronco riders at a rodeo / arranged so that the horizon line in each / pair is continuous and parallel with / the other.

Museum purchase

1991.97.3

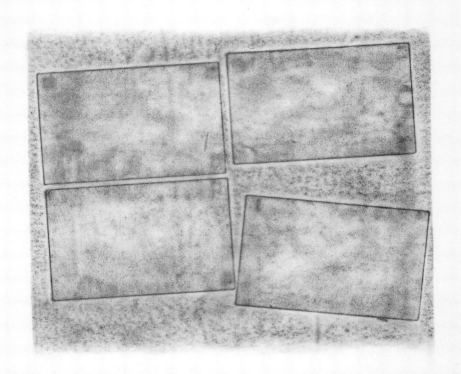

Snapshots of bronco riders at a rodeo
arranged so that the horizon line in each
pair is continuous and parallel with
the other.

J. Meehan 4-76

316   Jim Melchert
AN EMPTY ENVELOPE THAT ARRIVED
IN THE MAIL WITH A FEW LINES
ABOUT SILENCE TYPED ON IT., 1977

Graphite on cream (1), thin (2), smooth
wove paper

23 15/16 x 20

Signed in graphite l.r.: J. Melchert 3–77

Inscribed in graphite as image: An empty
envelope that arrived / in the mail with a few
lines / about silence typed on it.

Museum purchase

1991.97.6

An empty envelope that arrived
in the mail with a few lines
about silence typed on it.

BORN
9 September 1928
Hartford, Connecticut

In his drawings of the early 1980s, Sol LeWitt's previously spare pencil and ink lines became bands, and flat geometric shapes were sometimes superimposed on others. Simultaneously, as *Cube* reveals, the artist moved toward painterliness through his use of opaque watercolor. The application of this water-based pigment varied from opaque to transparent with the colors often having a mottled effect, as in *Cube*. LeWitt still used his basic primary palette, but the primary colors were not quite primary: yellow is more like ochre, red is more like crimson, and blue is more like cobalt.

In the 1980s LeWitt also transformed two-dimensional geometric forms into volumetric shapes. He had been interested in the cube early on because its "most interesting characteristic…is that it is relatively uninteresting…. The cube lacks aggressive force, implies no motion; and is least emotive. It is also immediately understood that the cube represents the cube, a geometric figure that is uncontestably itself."[1] This cube is indeed itself. However, it does have an incidental emotiveness. The edges are anything but crisp, the application of the paint anything but uniform, and the way in which it is positioned a bit off center within a black field and a gray border lends it a vulnerability. This twenty-two by twenty-two inch square was produced as one of a number of related works at a time when LeWitt was moving towards more complex forms. It was exhibited (and published in an accompanying catalogue) in the celebrated *Sol LeWitt Drawings 1942–1958* exhibition organized by Rudi Fuchs at the Haags Gemeentemuseum.[2] Other contemporaneous drawings reveal "forms derived from cubes" in which LeWitt removed portions of the volume to create both symmetrical and asymmetrical variations.

ADW

318 Sol LeWitt

CUBE, 1984–88

Opaque watercolor and graphite on cream (1), thick, moderately textured (3), Fabriano wove paper

22 x 21 7/8

Signed in graphite l.r.: LeWitt 1984/88

Inscribed in graphite on verso l.l.: #208

Partial gift of the artist and partial museum purchase with funds from Mimi Won and anonymous donor

2002.55

BORN
23 August 1940
Pittsburgh, Pennsylvania

Woven into *Counting: 4 Rotations (Continuous)* is Mel Bochner's enduring concern with the systematic and the sensory. Provoked by the assumption that "systematic thinking has generally been considered the antithesis of artistic thinking,"[1] Bochner has spent his career exploring the tensions between neutral order and crafted control through works that marry logical operations with artful execution.

Initially inspired by Pop artist Jasper Johns's stenciled-number works of the 1950s and '60s, Bochner's interest focused on Johns's use, not of the numbers as image, but of the stencil as a tool to delimit the parameters of his work. Bochner recognized "numbers as numbers, universal tools upon which to build and show a process of mental progression," and differentiated his works from Johns's pictures explaining that he "was interested in the relationships numbers had to themselves, and not in using them as a device to make a painting."[2] In drawings exhibited at the Museum of Modern Art in 1971, Bochner distinguished himself by making abstract counting operations into facts of art through observable *use*.[3] These early works invited viewers to reconstruct the drawing by re-counting the numerals—a mental experience that merged artistic and systematic thinking into one.

The Addison's 1997 drawing revisits Bochner's original interest in sober system-based art, but reflects a ripened romance with the visual. Maintaining the serial operation defined by its title, Bochner stretches his earlier definition of serial work, where "order takes precedence over the execution."[4] Here, delicate mark-making confirms he is as conscious of sensory rhythms between the numbers' scale and shape and the saturated flow of white paint on rich blue as he is of the perfectly defined count that structures the drawing. Ultimately, the numbers become dually "abstract" gestures, both conceptual signifiers of amount and sequence *and* expressive brushstrokes in lush color.

JM

320 ## Mel Bochner

COUNTING: 4 ROTATIONS
(CONTINUOUS), 1997

Oil on white, thick, rough (1), Aquarelle Arches wove paper

30 1/4 x 22 1/2

Signed in graphite on verso l.r.: MEL BOCHNER 1997

Inscribed in graphite on verso l.r.: COUNTING: 4 ROTATIONS (CONTINUOUS)/OIL ON PREPARED PAPER

Gift in honor of David Underwood (PA 1954), on the occasion of his 45th reunion, for a number of reasons....

1999.18

MARY P. FOSTER, LION

1. John Ebert and Katherine Ebert, *American Folk Painters* (New York: Charles Scribner's Sons, 1975), p. 173.
2. Ibid., pp. 167–68.
3. *Calligraphy: "Why Not Learn to Write?"* (New York: Museum of American Folk Art, 1975), p. 3.

MATILDA ELIZABETH SCHMAHL, FRIENDSHIP and SELECT SENTENCES

1. *Calligraphy: "Why Not Learn to Write?"* (New York: Museum of American Folk Art, 1975), p. 3.
2. John Ebert and Katherine Ebert, *American Folk Painters* (New York: Charles Scribner's Sons, 1975), p. 173.
3. Ross Green, Introduction in William E. Henning, *An Elegant Hand*, ed. Paul Melzer (New Castle, Del.: Oak Knoll Press, 2002), p. 1.
4. Jean Lipman and Alice Winchester, *The Flowering of American Folk Art: 1776–1876* (New York: Viking Press and Whitney Museum of American Art, 1974), p. 104.

BLANCHE LAZZELL, Untitled Drawings

1. See Nancy Malloy, "The Provincetown Years," in *Blanche Lazzell: A Modernist Rediscovered* (New York: Archives of American Art/Smithsonian Institution, 1991), n.p.
2. For other works of c. 1924, see *Blanche Lazzell: American Modernist* (New York: Michael Rosenfeld Gallery, 2000), pp. 12–15.
3. See Nic Madormo, "The Early Years," in *Blanche Lazzell: A Modernist Rediscovered*.
4. See Malloy.

MARK TOBEY, LINES OF THE CITY

1. Elizabeth E. Rathbone, *Mark Tobey: City Paintings* (Washington, D.C.: National Gallery of Art, 1984), p. 20.
2. Ibid., p. 18.
3. Julia and Lyonel Feininger, "Comments by a Fellow Artist," in exhibition program *Mark Tobey*, 31 November–8 December 1945, Willard Gallery Papers, Archives of American Art, Smithsonian Institution, Washington, D.C., microfilm reel N 69-118, frames 22–23.
4. Fred Hoffman, "Mark Tobey's Paintings of New York," *Artforum* 17, no. 8 (April 1979): 25.
5. Rathbone, p. 20.

SAUL STEINBERG, DIPLOMA

1. Quoted in Harold Rosenberg, *Saul Steinberg* (New York: Alfred A. Knopf, 1978), p. 10.
2. Ibid. p. 240.
3. Sheila Schwartz, director, Saul Steinberg Foundation, to Adam Weinberg, 25 February 2003: "The Addison Diploma is marvelous. Saul did a lot of them and they vary in quality, but yours is one of the best."

CARL ANDRE, PASSPORT

1. Quoted in Lynda Morris, "Carl Andre Poems: 1958–1974," *Studio International* 190, no. 977 (Sept.-Oct. 1975): 160–61.
2. For a more detailed analysis of *Passport*, see James Meyer, "Carl Andre," in Susan C. Faxon et al., *Addison Gallery of American Art, 65 Years: A Selective Catalogue* (Andover: Addison Gallery of American Art, 1996), pp. 313–14.
3. See Diane Waldman, *Carl Andre* (New York: Solomon R. Guggenheim Museum, 1970), pp. 6–21.

AGNES B. MARTIN, UNTITLED

1. Agnes Martin, "Answer to an Inquiry," in *Writings* (Ostfildern, Germany: Cantz, 1992), p. 29.
2. Agnes Martin, "The Untroubled Mind," in ibid., p. 41.

LAWRENCE WEINER, UNTITLED

1. "1. An artist may construct a work / 2. A work may be fabricated / 3. a work need not to be built." Lawrence Weiner, *Works & Reconstructions* (Bern: Kunsthalle Bern, 1983), p. 8.
2. Ibid., pp. 10, 16.
3. Ibid.
4. Ibid.
5. Gary Garrels, *Lawrence Weiner: Displacement* (New York: Dia Center for the Arts, 1991), n.p.

BARRY LE VA, TANGLE DISTRIBUTION

1. Barry Le Va on influences on his work during his years in Minneapolis, quoted in Elaine A. King, "Logical Interferences," in *Barry Le Va: 1966–1988* (Pittsburgh: Carnegie Mellon University Press, 1988), p. 9.
2. Ibid., for sculptural installations related to the drawings in the Addison collection; see pp. 42–4 for works in gray felt, and p. 48 for works in powdered chalk.
3. Quoted in ibid., p. 10.

CLAES OLDENBURG, DESIGN FOR A TUNNEL ENTRANCE

1. Claes Oldenburg, "I Am for an Art…" (1961), reprinted in Kristine Stiles and Peter Selz, *Theories and Documents of Contemporary Art: A Sourcebook of Artists' Writings* (Berkeley and Los Angeles: University of California Press, 1996), p. 335.
2. In an untitled 1969 text republished in *Claes Oldenburg* (London: Arts Council of Great Britain, 1970), p. 13.
3. "Items toward an Introduction," ibid., p. 7.
4. See Constance W. Glenn, *The Great American Pop Art Store* (Santa Monica, Calif.: Smart Art Press in association with the University Art Museum, California State University, Long Beach, 1997), p. 67.

ROBERT GROSVENOR, Untitled

1. Robert Smithson, "Entropy and the New Monuments," in *The Writings of Robert Smithson*, ed. Nancy Holt (New York: New York University Press, 1979), p. 10.
2. For examples and explanation, see Christine Mehring, "Robert Grosvenor," in Pamela Lee et al., *"Drawing is another kind of language": Recent American Drawings from a New York Private Collection* (Cambridge: Harvard University Art Museums, 1997), pp. 56–59; and for later works, see Cornelia H. Butler, *Afterimage: Drawing through Process* (Los Angeles: Museum of Contemporary Art; Cambridge: MIT Press, 1999), pp. 45, 126, 138.

FREDERICK BARTHELME, INSTEAD OF MAKING ART

1. See Kristine Stiles, "Language and Concepts," in Kristine Stiles and Peter Selz, *Theories and Documents of Contemporary Art: A Sourcebook of Artists' Writings* (Berkeley and Los Angeles: University of California Press, 1996), pp. 806, 808, 909 (notes): in February 1968, *Art International* published Lucy Lippard's infamous assertion about Conceptual art's "dematerialization of the art object," which in turn provoked more ink: manifesto-like "statements" by conceptual artists and theorists, including Joseph Kosuth, proselytizer of "Art as Idea as Idea," who was expounding on "Art after Philosophy" in *Studio International* by October 1969.

322 Notes

2. Frederick Barthelme to Jen Mergel, 28 July 2003, Addison Gallery Archives.

3. Barthelme was included in Lucy Lippard's index card project, *557,087*, at the Seattle Art Museum in 1969 (see review by Peter Plagens, "557,087: Seattle," in *Artforum* 8, no. 3 [November 1969]: 64–67) and Kynaston McShine's *Information* exhibition at New York's Museum of Modern Art in 1970.

4. Barthelme to Mergel.

CARL ANDRE, WORKING MAP: INDIA TRIENNALE PIECE

1. Carl Andre, Johannes Gachnang, and Angela Westwater, *Carl Andre: Sculpture 1958–1974* (Bern: Kunsthalle Bern, 1975), p. 57, no. 1971-1.

2. Sandy Ballatore, "Carl Andre on Work and Politics" (1976), quoted in David Bourdon, "A Redefinition of Sculpture," in *Carl Andre: Sculpture, 1959–1977* (New York: Jaap Rietman, 1978), p. 27: "The materials I use have been processed by manufacture," [Andre] said, "but have not been given the final shape of their destiny in the manufacturing culture…. I wouldn't ever be interested in laying a brick wall with mortar." Andre believes that by leaving his units unjoined, he leaves their potential free: "If my work has any subject matter at all, it is the immense potentiality of the things around us."

3. On Andre's concrete poetry, see Thom Betterton, "Carl Andre," in *Minimalism and Post-Minimalism: Drawing Distinctions* (Hanover, N.H.: Hood Museum of Art, Dartmouth College, 1990), p. 52; and Diane Waldman, *Carl Andre* (New York: Solomon R. Guggenheim Museum, 1970), pp. 57–72.

4. Carl Andre, "Quotations from the Artist," in *Carl Andre: 1969* (Brussels: Daled Brussels, 1975), p. 5: "There is no symbolic content in my work. It is not like a chemical formula but like a chemical reaction. A good work of art, once it is offered in display and shown to other people, is a social fact."

SOL LEWITT, TEN POSTCARDS

1. Lucy Lippard (AA 1954), an art critic and historian, had been a strong supporter and close friend of LeWitt since writing reviews of his work as early as 1965. See Susanna Singer, "Selected Bibliography," in *Sol LeWitt: Critical Texts*, ed. Adachiara Zevi (Rome: I Libri di AEIUO, 1994), p. 461.

SOL LEWITT, FIFTEEN POSTCARDS

1. See previous entry.

2. Each card is postmarked sequentially from 26 December 1975 to 10 January 1976. The introduction of a new stamp partway through the series reflects the postage increase by two cents at the turn of the new year.

3. See Sol LeWitt, "Excerpts from a Correspondence, 1981–83," interview with Andrea Miller-Keller, in *Sol LeWitt: Critical Texts*, ed. Adachiara Zevi (Rome: I Libri di AEIUO, 1994), pp. 108–09: "AMK: Was your introduction of the not straight line, in part, a quiet homage to Eva Hesse and her unique sensibility? SL: Yes. I wanted to do something at the time of her death that would be a bond between us, in our work. So I took something of hers and mine and they worked together well. You may say it was her influence on me."

4. Each card has a caption for the unseen illustration, recto, from an exhibition that opened 3 April 1970, which closely preceded Hesse's death: Eva Hesse: *Untitled Drawing #44*, 1969, 22" x 17" / Ink wash: Fischbach Gallery 29 West 57th Street NYC.

5. Lucy Lippard, *Eva Hesse* (New York: New York University Press, 1976).

ROBERT MANGOLD, Untitled

1. See Nancy Princenthal, "A Survey of the Paintings," in *Robert Mangold* (London: Phaidon, 2000).

2. Robert Mangold, artist's questionnaire, 17 October 2000, Addison Gallery Archives.

3. Ibid.

MICHELLE STUART, LITTLE TURTLE POND

1. Michelle Stuart, *Michelle Stuart: Natural Histories* (Santa Fe: Bellas Artes, 1996), p. 4.

2. Michelle Stuart to Jen Mergel, email, 19 December 2002.

3. Lawrence Alloway, "Michelle Stuart," in *Michelle Stuart: Voyages* (Syracuse: Everson Museum of Art, 1985), p. 51.

4. Stuart to Mergel.

MEL BOCHNER, VIA SANTO SPIRITO

1. Mel Bochner, *Mel Bochner: Twenty-Five Drawings 1973–1980* (n.p., 1981), p. 5.

2. Richard S. Field, *Mel Bochner: Thought Made Visible 1966–1973* (New Haven: Yale University Art Gallery, 1995), pp. 54–55: "I was in Bari, Italy in 1972, staying with some friends. They told me that in a town called Metaponte, there was a Pythagorean temple. Pythagoras was a forerunner of Plato, possibly his teacher. He believed that all reality was based on numbers and their relationships…. So I went to visit this site which was a ruined Doric temple…. It was a really haunting place. I thought I'd like to do something there, a little homage to Pythagoras. To his 'spirit.' I thought the obvious thing was to do the Theorem of Pythagoras…$c^2=a^2+b^2$…$5^2=4^2+3^2$ or 25=16+9. So I picked up 50 pebbles and laid them down and had three left over…. Suddenly it dawned on me what was happening. On the one hand you have theoretical space where points are defined as having no dimensions. And on the other hand you have a real space where the three corner points overlap. So, of course, it only took 47 stones. It was a kind of epiphany for me…. Because it was my realization that sculpture exists in the space where the mental and physical overlap."

3. Ibid., p. 56; and Brenda Richardson, *Mel Bochner: Number and Shape* (Baltimore: The Baltimore Museum of Art, 1976), p. 37.

4. Richardson, p. 48.

5. Ibid., p. 43.

6. Mel Bochner, artist's questionnaire, 11 December 1990, Addison Gallery Archives.

JIM MELCHERT, SNAPSHOTS OF BRONCO RIDERS and AN EMPTY ENVELOPE

1. Suzanne Foley, *Jim Melchert Points of View: Slide Projection Pieces* (San Francisco: San Francisco Museum of Art, 1975).

2. This and otherwise unattributed quotations are from a conversation between the artist and author, 8 August 2003.

3. Quoted in Joe Bolster et al., "Class of 1952 Distinguished Classmate Award for Excellence in Career: James Frederick Melchert," 1 June 2002, <alumni.princeton.edu/~cl1952/melchert.htm> (22 July 2003).

SOL LEWITT, CUBE

1. Sol LeWitt, "Paragraphs on Conceptual Art" (1967), in *Sol LeWitt Critical Texts*, ed. Adachiara Zevi (Rome: Libri de AEIUO, 1995), p. 81.

2. *Sol LeWitt Drawings 1942–1958* (The Hague: Haags Gemeentemuseum, 1992), no. 208.

MEL BOCHNER, COUNTING: 4 ROTATIONS (CONTINUOUS)

1. Mel Bochner, "Serial Art, Systems, Solipsism" (1967), reprinted in Gregory Battcock, ed., *Minimal Art: A Critical Anthology* (Berkeley and Los Angeles: University of California Press, 1995), p. 94.

2. Bochner as documented in Eric Spenser, "Mel Bochner," in *Minimalism and Post-Minimalism: Drawing Distinctions* (Hanover, N.H.: Hood Museum of Art, Dartmouth College, 1990), p. 26.

3. Robert Pincus-Witten, "Bochner at MoMA: Three Ideas and Seven Procedures" (1971), reprinted in Richard S. Field, *Mel Bochner: Thought Made Visible 1966–1973* (New Haven: Yale University Art Gallery, 1995), pp. 233–35. Bochner's exhibition at New York's Museum of Modern Art was the first major introduction to these "counting" works.

4. Mel Bochner, "The Serial Attitude," *Artforum* 6, no. 4 (December 1967): 28.

323

acrylic – a water-miscible paint in which the pigment is suspended in a thermoplastic polymer or copolymer of acrylic acid.

adhesive bandage – strip of material used to protect or cover wounds to the skin, attached through the means of a gummed or sticky substance.

chalk – a soft, compact form of calcium carbonate or fine-grained limestone, used as a pigment or in crayons, paint, rubber products, linoleum, and putty.

charcoal – a porous, organic, carbon-based material, often used in stick or pencil form. Stick or vine charcoal is created by heating thin twigs of wood until only dry carbon remains. Compressed charcoal is created by grinding charcoal and mixing it with a binder, and can be formed into pencils with different levels of hardness.

collage – the process of creating compositions by arranging and adhering various media. For the purposes of this publication, collage is low-relief and primarily two-dimensional, with media attached to a paper-based support.

color pencil – a narrow, generally cylindrical drawing instrument commonly of wood containing compact colored pigments.

crayon – a drawing instrument of any material (i.e., charcoal, chalk, colored wax) in stick form.

egg tempera – a water-based paint in which ground pigments are suspended in egg, either just the yolk, or the whole egg.

foil stamp – a thin, flexible sheet of metal cut into a shape and affixed with adhesive.

graphite – a hexagonally crystallized form of carbon; soft, opaque, ranging in color from steel-gray to black. Drawing and writing pencils are commonly made of graphite in combination with varying amounts of clay, which affects the degree of hardness.

grease pencil – black or colored crayons, usually in pencil or stick form with peel-off paper casing. Commonly used to write on surfaces such as glass or china, they are also known as china markers.

ink – a fluid, opaque drawing medium created by mixing pigment with water, usually applied with a pen or writing implement.

ink wash – a thin film of diluted ink, usually applied with a brush.

iron gall ink – a drawing medium formed by suspending iron salt particles in gall extract. Gall is a liquid produced within small swellings formed on oak trees owing to injury or disease. Although the ink is nearly black when first applied, it turns brown over time.

linoleum block print – a printing process in which the image is carved into the surface of linoleum mounted on wood blocks, which is then inked and printed. Also known as linocut.

lithograph – a print made by the lithographic process, in which the image is drawn on a flat surface, generally stone, sheet zinc, or aluminum, and chemically treated so that the printing ink adheres only to the greasy areas of the design. The printed image is a reverse of the original.

lithographic crayon – oil-based crayon in pencil or stick form made of wax, soap, and lampblack to which can be added spermaceti, shellac, or tallow (or these in combination). It is used to create an image for lithographic printing, in which the printing ink adheres to the marks made by the crayon.

marker ink – black or colored inks contained within the shaft of a cylindrical drawing instrument and applied via a variety of blunt or pointed felt, nylon, or fiber tips.

metalpoint – a process in which the image is made by a stylus, rod, or wire of metal which, as it is drawn over a sheet of specially prepared paper, leaves minute particles of metal. Also known as silverpoint, copperpoint, etc.

monotype – a unique print created by painting on a sheet of glass or a polished metal plate, then transferring the wet image to a sheet of paper by hand-pressing. If a metal plate is used, the image can also be transferred in an etching press.

oil – a paint formed by binding pigments in a water-insoluble oil, such as linseed oil or a vegetable drying oil.

pastel – ground pigment mixed with chalk, water, and gum tragacanth, usually used in soft, stick form.

photocopy – a mechanical reproduction created by a machine employing a light-sensitive process. Since the mid-twentieth century, photocopies have been created by the Xerographic process, in which the image of the original is reproduced by using the attractive forces of electrical charges and heat-set toner powder. The final product is a positive reproduction of the original image.

photo offset – a lithographic printing process in which the image is photographically transferred onto a plate, then transferred to an intermediary surface such as a rubber blanket, which is then printed. This offset, double-printing process results in a re-reversal of the image, so that the final product is a positive reproduction of the original design.

Note

Sources useful in formulating the glossary definitions were: *Art & Architecture Thesaurus On Line*, 2000, <www.getty.edu/research/conducting_research/ vocabularies/aat> (November 2002); Ralph Mayer, *The Artist's Handbook of Materials and Techniques* (4th rev. ed; New York: Viking Press, 1985); and *The American Heritage Dictionary of the English Language* (Boston: Houghton Mifflin, 1989).

pressure-sensitive tape – a continuous, narrow, flexible strip of plastic, paper, or cloth coated on one side with adhesive that holds with application of pressure (i.e., cellophane [Scotch] tape, masking tape, drafting tape).

stain – a penetrating liquid dye or tint, made with an oil, alcohol, or water base.

stamp impression – impressed, printed, perforated, or embossed marks made by a hard object on a soft surface.

string – a long, flexible cord made of fibrous material that is thinner than rope and thicker than thread.

twine – a strong cord or string composed of two or more fibrous strands twisted together.

watercolor – a paint created by suspending pigments in water and gum arabic, often applied with a brush on special watercolor paper. Watercolor can be transparent or opaque.

transparent watercolor – a water-based paint which, when applied, transmits light.

opaque watercolor – a water-based paint that contains an additional binder that renders the paint surface opaque to light. Used here instead of such terms as tempera, casein, and gouache.

wood engraving – the process of creating a print by using a sharp instrument such as a graver to cut a relief image in the end grain of a wood block. When applied, the ink sits on the raised surfaces remaining after the non-printing areas were cut away. The image is then transferred onto paper by hand pressure or in a press.

GLOSSARY OF SUPPORTS

amate paper – a support made of bark that is boiled and soaked overnight until soft enough for the fibers to pull apart. It is then pounded until the pulp is evenly spread out in the shape wanted and dried in the sun. The color and grain of the paper depends on the bark used to make it; sizes and thicknesses vary.

bond paper – a strong, durable, superior-grade white paper used for documents, letterhead, and stationery. Bond paper has a variety of quality levels; commonly, it is made of the long fibers of spruce, but that of the highest quality is made from rag pulp and has a smooth finish.

coated paper – paper treated with a substance that creates a surface layer especially suited for drawing in metalpoint.

graph paper – paper with printed lines in a grid pattern of small squares of equal size.

illustration board – paper board that has paper layers glued on one or both sides, and is commonly used as a temporary support.

kraft paper – a tough paper, usually light brown in color, originally made from rope but now produced from unbleached sulfate wood pulp.

laid paper – paper formed on wire molds that create in the final sheet a characteristic appearance of close, thick and thin lines intersecting at right angles.

ledger paper – paper found most often bound as pages in books that are used for account-keeping purposes.

paper – a thin sheet material made of a felted or weblike mass of interlaced cellulose fibers derived from wood or rag pulp and processed by deposit from an aqueous solution.

paper board – thick, strong rag or pulp paper, usually used in constructing boxes (i.e., pasteboard and cardboard).

particle board – board made from wood chips bonded with a synthetic resin. Masonite is a trademarked name for particle board.

Plexiglas – a trademarked name for a light, permanently transparent, weather-resistant synthetic resin made by polymerization of acrylic acid esters.

rice paper – soft, tissue-thin paper made from the pith of the rice-paper tree, a small tree grown in eastern Asia.

tracing paper – a thin, translucent paper through which an underlying image or design can be traced.

wax paper – flexible paper coated with a thin layer of wax to create a moisture-proof surface.

wood pulp paper – paper made from various cellulose fibers ground from wood and chemically processed.

wove paper – paper formed on closely meshed wire molds that create in the final sheet an even, unlined appearance in transmitted light.

CAROL CLARK, the William R. Kenan, Jr., Professor of Fine Arts and American Studies at Amherst College, was co-author of the catalogue raisonné of Maurice Prendergast and Charles Prendergast (1990). Among her other publications are the monographs *Thomas Moran: Watercolors of the American West* (1981) and *Charles M. Russell* (1983), as well as catalogues of American works in the William Marshall Fuller Collection (1978) and in the Robert Lehman Collection at the Metropolitan Museum (1992).

TREVOR FAIRBROTHER is an independent scholar who has curated and written on a wide range of art topics. His publications include *The Bostonians: Painters of an Elegant Age, 1870–1930* (1986), *Robert Wilson's Vision* (1991), and *Family Ties: A Contemporary Perspective* (2003). He has written often about Andy Warhol and John Singer Sargent, including *Sargent: The Sensualist* (2000). He has served as a curator of American painting and of contemporary art at the Museum of Fine Arts, Boston, and as Deputy Director for Art at the Seattle Art Museum.

SUSAN C. FAXON, Associate Director and Curator of Art before 1950 at the Addison Gallery of American Art, organized and co-wrote a history of the Phillips Academy campus (2003), was co-author of *Addison Gallery of American Art, 65 Years: A Selective Catalogue* (1996), and contributed to *Frank W. Benson: A Retrospective* (1989). Her curatorial projects have included *Point of View: Landscapes from the Addison Collection* (1992), and *Circle of Friends: Art Colonies of Cornish and Dublin* (1985). She was director of the University Art Galleries at the University of New Hampshire, Durham, from 1975 to 1986.

FAYE HIRSCH is an authority on contemporary drawings and prints and was editor of *Art on Paper*, an international periodical on prints, drawings, books, and photography from 1996 to 2002. She has written numerous articles and reviews, most recently for *Art in America*; her publications include *Part Fantasy: The Sexual Imagination of Seven Lesbian Artists Explored through the Medium of Drawings* (1992), *Roland Flexner: Figures and Vanitas* (1996), *Nicole Eisenman, Mural Project: Underwater Film Shoot* (1998), and *Thomas Chimes: Faustroll Landscape* (2003).

LINDA KONHEIM KRAMER, director of the Nancy Graves Foundation in New York, has written extensively on prints and drawings, including *French Nineteenth-Century Drawings and Watercolors at the Brooklyn Museum* (1993); *Milton Avery in Black and White: Drawings, 1929–59* (1990); *The Graphic Works of Philip Pearlstein: 1978–1994* (1995); and *The Prints of Janet Fish: A Catalogue Raisonné* (1997). She has served as curator of prints and drawings at the Brooklyn Museum of Art.

All photographs of works in the Addison Gallery of American Art collection not specified otherwise below are by Frank E. Graham or Greg Heins. Photographs for works in other collections are courtesy of the owner unless indicated otherwise.

Michael Agee, WACC *45, 60, 119, 143, 267/flap, 295*

Michael Agee, © Estate of David Smith/Licensed by VAGA, New York, NY *135*

Michael Agee, © Tom Wesselmann/Licensed by VAGA, New York, NY *145*

Michael Agee, Heritage Gallery, Los Angeles *199*

Michael Agee, © Adolph and Esther Gottlieb Foundation/Licensed by VAGA, New York *213/flap*

Michael Agee, © 2004 Lawrence Weiner/Artists Rights Society (ARS), New York *287*

Art © Carl Andre/Licensed by VAGA, New York, NY *301*

© 2004 Milton Avery Trust/Artist Rights Society (ARS), New York *227*

José Bedia and George Adams Gallery, New York *249*

Charles E. Burchfield Foundation/Kennedy Galleries, NY *201*

Art © The Joseph and Robert Cornell Memorial Foundation /Licensed by VAGA, New York, NY *237*

Estate of Stuart Davis/Courtesy VAGA *129/jacket, 131*

D. James Dee *134*

Frank E. Graham *76/flap, 137/flap, 149/flap, 159/flap, 181/flap, 303/flap, 321/flap*

Frank E. Graham, Art © Carl Andre/Licensed by VAGA, New York, NY *280, 281, 282/flap, 283*

Greg Heins *27, 41, 53, 79, 97, 99/jacket, 101/jacket, 102/flap, 109, 113/jacket, 115, 125, 127/flap, 139/flap, 167, 169, 171, 175, 185, 187/jacket, 191/flap, 197, 231/flap, 243, 277, 285, 313/jacket*

Greg Heins, Isamu Noguchi Foundation, Inc., New York *193*

Greg Heins, © 2002 by Kate Rothko Pizel and Christopher Rothko *209*

Michael Kohn Gallery, Los Angeles *239*

Koplin Gallery, Los Angeles *81, 141*

The Estate of Norman Lewis, Iandor Fine Arts, Newark, New Jersey *221*

© 2004 Estate of Reginald Marsh/Art Students League, New York/Artists Rights Society (ARS), New York *218, 219*

Photograph © 1998 The Metropolitan Museum of Art *92*

© 2002 Museum of Fine Arts, Boston *98, 118*

© Charles Seliger, Michael Rosenfeld Gallery, New York, NY *229*

James Sheldon *163/flap, 173/flap, 177, 215, 303*

© The Saul Steinberg Foundation/Artists Rights Society (ARS), New York *279*

© Tom Wesselmann/Licensed by VAGA, New York, NY *144*

328   INDEX OF ARTISTS REPRESENTED